Our Puppet Government

by
John R. Krismer, MHA, LFACHE

Health Systems Institute, Inc.

Second Edition

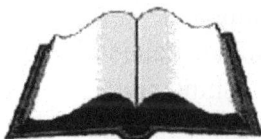

CCB Publishing
British Columbia, Canada

Our Puppet Government

Copyright ©2008, 2013 by John R. Krismer
ISBN-13   978-1-77143-067-8
Second Edition

Library and Archives Canada Cataloguing in Publication
Krismer, John R., 1927-
Our Puppet Government / written by John R. Krismer – 2nd ed.
Includes bibliographical references.
ISBN 978-1-77143-067-8
Also available in electronic format.
Additional cataloguing data available from Library and Archives Canada

Publisher: CCB Publishing
             British Columbia, Canada
             www.ccbpublishing.com

My wonderful wife Betty passed away on February 11, 2011, following my long and tedious days of research and writing, and I could not have completed this work without her unrelenting support and critique to this book's successful completion. Thanks so much Betty, for I could never have accomplished this without you.

Contents

Appendix

Postscript

Bibliography

Preface

Section I

I trusted my country before researching the material for *Our Puppet Government* — a country I'd previously taken an oath to protect by volunteering to fight in its behalf. Then after seriously scrutinizing all the things that were going on in this great nation, I decided to thoroughly investigate what I'd found regarding a shadow like "New World Order" (NWO) that was weakening the sovereignty of our nation by unfairly profiting from this country's workforce — the backbone of this nation. And as you read *Our Puppet Government,* it's important you not let your reactions drift into denial, for our democracy is definitely at stake, and it's time that everyone who lives in this great nation fully understands the intent of this subtle and subversive attack against our freedoms. Yes, it's time for every American to wake up to the fact that our country is now in greater peril than ever before, and we need every citizen to speak out strongly and knowledgeably to protect this once hallowed Republic. Currently over two-thirds of our population is already thinking something isn't quite right about this horrible situation our nation finds itself in — or why this nation has taken such an aggressive and unjust unilateral path toward perpetual war — while our Congress ignores the people they are appointed to represent. Perhaps you've even been wondering why the news media never fully explains what's really going on in Washington, or why our Congress has become so submissive to this NWO's corrupt and powerful lobbyists. Haven't we all begun to wonder why we're intentionally kept so confused and fearful so much of the time, or why we remain entrapped in an insane state of apathy? Well let me assure you that this subversive invisible NWO actually exists, and has a plan of accomplishment that inevitably forfeits the very freedoms we all sought when we created this great nation some two hundred and thirty-seven years ago. And more recently they've now imposed a *"slight-of hand trick"* that intends to successfully enforce their unilateral monopoly over the entire world economy as they destroy this nation's sovereignty and the world's open market — once again, forcing this great nation into bondage.

So let's look at the big picture and follow the money trail, the real mega bucks of these *"Invisible Money Barons"* that have been keeping our duly appointed representatives in Washington under their thumb since the beginning of the twentieth-century. But to accomplish this, we must first study the actual bloodline of this monopolistic hierarchy that has so ruthlessly suppressed our working class.

In looking back at our history, the powerful *"Rothschild Empire"* that originated in Germany and the Rockefeller *"Robber Barons"* of Colorado are where these monopolistic concepts first got their start. And yes, these same monopolistic concepts assured John D. Rockefeller Sr., that his financial oil supremacy was protected under his powerful oil monopoly. More recently however, Rockefeller's great grandson David Rockefeller Senior, the now 94-year-old creator and undisputed *"Overlord"* of the many Rockefeller foundations and the former Chairman of the Chase Manhattan Bank — along with his closely knit inner circle of multinational investment bankers all band together to support John's subversive *"Shadow Government"* tactics. And yes, this has been at the cost of the working class of this country, who inadvertently and unknowingly forfeited their treasure and national sovereignty to these powerful and invisible organizations by becoming too comfortable with their freedoms. Traditionally, a Democracy inherently promotes equality and freedom to their workforce because they are the productive element within any sovereign nation; however, this country's democracy, equality, and freedom has now clearly fallen by the wayside at the bequest of this informal power that does not hold these same principles as their primary goal or objective. In fact, even some of our past President's legacies can be identified with this obvious lack of democratic principle, which has inadvertently forced this secretive *"Money Baron"* scam out into the open, causing almost everyone to pause and think a bit about the *"con-job"* we've all been experiencing. And now, after recently suffering the largest budget breaking period in our history, we're all beginning to wonder if we'll ever be able to protect the financial and moral benefits to our working class — thereby keeping our future job related benefits and employment from being forced into today's outrageous world-wide profit seeking arena. I think we all now realize that if we're ever going to be able to salvage our employment benefits, it will require a knowledgeable and just leadership that is capable of differentiating between an *"Open Market"* and a *"Noncompetitive Market,"* which is essential in maintaining a healthy and productive workforce. By allowing our human services to be placed in the open market arena, we've allowed these *"Invisible Money Barons"* to actually steal directly from our public treasury; thereby seriously challenging the working classes' equality. And yes, we've allowed these invisible industrial and banking aristocracies to do exactly that, as they now openly and blatantly buy off our dysfunctional Congress and our puppet like leaders with their many gifts and benefits. So let's study this stealing aristocracy that wants to profit from our working class by stealing our Social Security, our healthcare from our sick and disabled, and our many God given natural resource — such as oil. Isn't it strange that we promote universal oil ownership with the Shiites, the Sunni, and the Kurds in Iraq, when *"We the People"* no longer own our own natural resources in the United States? We propose a Democracy in Iraq and other countries, when we're losing our freedoms in the United States. We propose standards and regulations for China when we can no longer maintain standards for our own products, services and tax to humankind, or even protect our borders because this NWO seeks to someday profit from and control the entire planet. In fact, hasn't this wealthy aristocracy's insatiable appetite for profit from our human services totally overshadowed our freedom and equality — forcing *"We the People,"* back into the same bondage of the 1929 depression? Could this be why these closely knit *Money Barons* continually keep us in such a high state of fear and denial with all their unjust wars, lies, and deceit — all designed to intentionally divert our awareness from their corrupt *"slight-of hand tactics,"* which make them tons of money while they degrade this nation's once unblemished and respected reputation throughout the world?

Therefore it's my hope that *Our Puppet Government* will help to expose this NWO's plan of destruction regarding these human services to humankind, as it identifies the many dangerous informal powers that have bought off our Congress and our Administration.

Our Puppet Government also proposes potential solutions to this dilemma, since this time Americans have no place to run. Yes, this nation was originally started by those who wanted to escape from bondage, showing their faith and courage as they sought liberty and freedom from previous controlling aristocracies. And yes, by coming to America, all these immigrants either intentionally or unintentionally created a nation that was successful and abundant in both equality and freedom. But here again, for a second time, we've become the complacent and apathetic victim, dependent on these corrupt informal plutocrats that neither represent the working class or their duly appointed representatives. In World War II, the Japanese quickly recognized they'd awakened a sleeping giant when they bombed Pearl Harbor — a giant that fought desperately to protect this country's freedom and equality. And perhaps it's time for this apathetic giant, *"We the People,"* to once again claim our freedom from these self serving international power brokers that seek to replace our sovereign nation's constitution with their NWO — a new world government that's designed to level this great nation to that of others, while predictably making these modern day *"Money Barons"* very wealthy.

Here are but a few of the many self appointed organizations that are discussed in this book, all trying to replace our government which was previously appointed by this country's working class:

> The Council on Foreign Relations (CFR)
> The Trilateral Commission (TC)
> The American Legislative Exchange Council (ALEC)
> The American Israel Public Affairs Committee (AIPAC's)
> The World Constitution and Parliament Association (WCPA)
> The North American Free Trade Agreement (NAFTA)
> The Bilderbergers
> The Federal Reserve
> The International Investment Banks and Corporations
> The United Nations (UN)

And there are many other less prominent fringe groups that all remain suspects. David Rockefeller, the undisputed *"Overlord"* of his family's corporate monopoly, was one of the founders of the TC, which was his brainchild. And in addition to this, he also served as the Director Emeritus (Honorary Chairman) of the CFR, which the Rockefellers have heavily funded from its inception. This powerful family has also been heavily involved in funding the Bilderbergers organization, where David first proposed the shadow like Trilateral Commission. All suggesting that the infamous Rockefeller *"Robber Barons"* still rule this country's working class — but this time under a powerful NWO that has been taken over by the invisible multinational investment banks and industrial corporations destined to become our *Shadow Government*. History clearly states that John D. Rockefeller Sr. was a monopolist who hated competition. And although these monopolistic *"Money Barons"* have yet to realize they are doomed to failure in their current venture towards world dominance, they are currently intentionally moving this nation toward a second Great Depression as they selfishly seek more profit and control through their plutocratic invisible government. Is it possible that these monopolistic tendencies are having a far greater influence over this sovereign nation and its working class than we'd really like to admit? With the current President and our duly elected Congress rendered so dysfunctional, perhaps it's time to pause and evaluate if we really want to replace our constitution and its representatives with such an organization — supporting a dysfunctional UN constitution that was designed and crafted by the Rockefeller TC to level this great country to the same level as other countries. Shouldn't we at least conduct an unbiased investigation, or vote, if we feel there is a conflict of interest regarding our sovereignty? Shouldn't we determine what *"We the People"* actually desire before we let some *Kleptocratic Aristocracy* take over our noncompetitive market under some powerful *Multinational Shadow Government?*

THE DECLARATION OF INDEPENDENCE

Action of Second Continental Congress, July 4, 1776: Using the Freedom of Speech, WHEN in the Course of human Events, it becomes necessary for one People to dissolve the Political Bands which have connected them with another, and to assume among the Powers of the Earth, the separate and equal Station to which the Laws of Nature and of Nature's God entitle them, a decent Respect to the Opinions of Mankind requires that they should declare the causes which impel them to the Separation. We hold these Truths to be self-evident, that all Men are created equal, that they are endowed by their Creator with certain unalienable Rights, that among these are Life, Liberty and the Pursuit of Happiness -- That to secure these Rights, Governments are instituted among Men, deriving their just Powers from the Consent of the Governed, that whenever any Form of Government becomes destructive of these Ends, it is the Right of the People to alter or to abolish it, and to institute new Government, laying its Foundation on such Principles, and organizing its Powers in such Form, as to them shall seem most likely to effect their Safety and Happiness.

Section II

Now that this ridiculous and costly 2012 election is finally over, and we know for a fact that *"We the People"* still have a voice, isn't it time we increase the pressure on the Washington Plutocrats and the one-percent of International Investment Banks and corporate monopolies that comprise today's NWO? And if this nation truly wishes to prevent such a take-over, we can no longer inadvertently confuse our vitally important globalization efforts with this new Fascistic world order — which clearly intends to subjugate ninety-percent of this country's working class, the elderly, the sick and the disabled, and the unemployed that constitutes this country's middleclass, the backbone of this nation. We must also realize our enemy within includes far too many Senators and members of the House of Representatives that are led by this incredibly wealthy International Billionaire's Club that has over the last century slowly and methodically gained almost total political and financial control over our dysfunctional Congress. But most importantly, we need to follow a well thought out plan of accomplishment before we even attempt to successfully recover our once respected Democracy that so many of us love and fought for. In fact, we are already well on the way to becoming our own worst enemy if we do not universally, as a nation, demand today's plutocrats adopt and prepare policies that deal with solutions to the following problems which are discussed in greater detail in Section II:

- Donations to politicians

- Changing the tax systems

- Protecting the working class entitlements and benefits

- Repealing the Federal Reserve Act

- Controlling all expenditures

- Enforcing ear-mark transparency

- Balancing foreign trade

- Controlling no-bid contracts

- Stop policing other countries

- Stop exporting jobs

- Coordinating elections

- Abiding by the Geneva Convention

1

The Bondage
Of The 30's

Globalization prospers when the working class benefits, and when they do not, powerful business monopolies historically and predictably gain in power as their profits soar. Placing the working class's human services and benefits on the competitive global market inevitably drives the workforce back into bondage. To better understand why this great Democracy is once again revisiting the 1929 economic tragedy, one needs to analyze what took place before, during, and after the depression of the 1930's. Prior to the 1907 panic, the United States had no central bank, which forced Congress to create a National Monetary Commission. This was accomplished under the leadership of Senator Nelson Aldrich, who was the father-in-law of John D. Rockefeller, Jr. Although Article I, Section 8, of the U.S. Constitution, granted the Congress the power to coin money and regulate its value, this Commission suddenly recommended the creation of a privately owned Central Bank, in 1913.

Senator Charles Lindbergh, Sr., said:

> *"This act establishes the most gigantic trust on earth...the invisible government by the money power, proven to exist by the Money Trust investigation ... The new law will create inflation whenever the trusts want inflation ... they can unload the stocks on the people at high prices during the excitement and then bring on a panic and buy them back at low prices...the day of reckoning is only a few years removed." (1)*

1

The House Committee on Banking and Currency Chairman, Congressman Louis McFadden, said:

> *"When the Federal Reserve Act was passed, the people of these United States did not perceive that a world banking system was being set up here. A super-state controlled by international bankers and industrialists...acting together to enslave the world...Every effort has been made by the Fed to conceal its powers but the truth is--the Fed has usurped the government." (2)*

Even today, the working class really does not fully understand that the Federal Reserve banking system is privately owned and is not subject to oversight by either the Congress or the President. Lending money and investing the public's investments are how these powerful privately owned international investment banks make their huge profits, and since these banks establish their own policies and own the majority of stock in the Federal Reserve, the working class has essentially relinquished their tax dollars and their interest income to these privately held Federal and international investment banks. The wealthy controlling stockholders of these international banks and the Federal Reserve include the powerful J.P. Morgan; Carnegie; Rothschild; Lazard; Seiff; Loeb; and Sachs families; as well as the always present and powerful "Overlord," the Rockefellers — All listed in greater detail by Peter Kershaw, in "Economic Solutions."

According to Devvy Kidd, in "Why A Bankrupt America?"

> *"The Federal Reserve pays the Bureau of Engraving and Printing approximately $23 for each 1,000 notes printed. 10,000 $100 notes (one million dollars) would thus cost the Federal Reserve $230. They then secure a pledge of collateral equal to the face value from the U.S. government. The collateral is our land, labor, and assets... collected by their agents, the IRS. By authorizing the Fed to regulate and create money (and thus inflation), Congress gave private banks power to create profits at will." (3)*

And that day came in 1929, with the stock market crash and the Great Depression.

Bernard Baruch, one of these wealthy bankers, was assigned to indoctrinate Woodrow Wilson at the Democratic Party headquarters in 1912, advising him before he became President on the importance of supporting the proposed Federal Reserve Act and this country's first income tax, which occurred just after the Supreme Court of the United States held that Standard Oil was an illegal monopoly in the year 1911. This is also when John D. Rockefeller, Sr. left the management of Standard Oil to set up and manage his foundations. The total number of tax-evasion foundations owned by the Rockefeller's has been estimated to exceed more than 200.

In 1913, Wilson was elected President after beating the former incumbent William Howard Taft, who was vehemently opposed to any privately owned central bank. Wilson's guardian of the Federal Reserve Act was Colonel Edward M. House, who helped guide this Act through Congress. At the same time, House had said the constitution was a product of:

> *"... eighteenth-century minds...was thoroughly outdated; that the country would be better off if the Constitution could be scrapped and rewritten..."(4)*

Coincidentally, World War I began in 1914, and as with all wars, it produced a large national debt and huge profits for these closely knit *Money Barons.* Baruch, the head of the War Industries Board; the Rockefellers; Cleveland Dodge, who sold munitions to the allies, the Rothschild's, and J.P. Morgan who loaned hundreds of millions, all benefited enormously with the U.S. entry into World War I. And just as planned by these current multinational banks, the national debt suddenly went from $1 billion to $25 billion. Both Baruch and Rockefeller were reported to have earned more than $200 million in interest alone during World War I.

William Hoar reveals in *Architects of Conspiracy* that during the 1950s government investigators examining the early records of the "Carnegie Endowment for International Peace" and found that the Carnegie trustees had actually planned to involve the U.S. in World War I, to set the stage for world government under a global international banking system.

Their main obstacle to war was the working class did not want war at that time, so they needed to create some type of provocation. This occurred when the Lusitania, carrying 128 Americans was sunk, resulting in considerable anti-German sentiment. What was not revealed at the time, however, was that the Lusitania was transporting war munitions to England, making it a legitimate target for the German subs. A last-minute add in a New York newspaper had actually discouraged passengers from buying tickets for that trip. In fact, the majority of evidence suggested a deliberate plan to have the ship sunk. German naval codes had been broken by the British, who knew approximately where the German U boats were located, and according to Colin Simpson, in his book *The Lusitania*, Commander Joseph Kenworthy, of British Naval Intelligence, said:

> *"The Lusitania was deliberately sent at considerably reduced speed into an area where a U-boat was known to be waiting...escorts withdrawn." (5)*

As a result of this sinking, America suddenly found itself involved in a European war. In fact, Colonel House had committed the U.S. to this conflict much earlier, and the working class actually had very little to say in the matter.

Point fourteen of Wilson's famous "fourteen point document," described the general association of nations, while even back then proposing a *One World Government*, which was the League of Nations. However, the League of Nations failed because the U.S. Senate did not ratify the Versailles Treaty. Pat Robertson, in *The New World Order*, states that Colonel House, along with other internationalists, finally realized that the people would not support any scheme for a one world government at that time — however, following World War I, it was secretly decided that a privately owned "Institute of International Affairs," with two branches would be formed, one in the United States and one in England. As a result, The Council on Foreign Relations (CFR) was incorporated as the American branch in New York on July 29, 1921. According to Gary Allen, in the October 1972 issue of *"AMERICAN OPINION."* The privately selected founding members included Colonel House, and ...

> *"such potentates of international banking as J.P. Morgan, John D. Rockefeller, Paul Warburg, Otto Kahn, and Jacob Schiff...the same clique that had engineered the establishment of the Federal Reserve System," (6)*

The CFR founding president was John W. Davis, J.P. Morgan's personal attorney, while the vice-president was J.P. Cravath, who also represented the Morgan interests.

Professor Carroll Quigley characterized the CFR as ...

> *"a front group for J.P. Morgan and Company in association with the very small American Round Table Group." (7)*

Later, the Morgan influence was transferred to the Rockefeller's monopoly, who found that a one world government better fit Rockefeller's stated business philosophy of *"Competition is Sin."*
Antony Sutton, a research fellow for the Hoover Institution for War, Revolution, and Peace at Stanford University, wrote of this philosophy:

> *"While monopoly control of industries was once the objective of J.P. Morgan and J.D. Rockefeller ... the most efficient way to gain an unchallenged monopoly was to 'go political' and make society go to work for the monopolists-- under the name of the public good and the public interest." (8)*

As large corporations eventually went international, they also found they needed a one world system of government controlled by them from behind the scenes to remain in command. And this had been the plan since the time of Colonel House — but first they had to weaken the U.S. politically and economically if they were to eventually gain total control. When the stock market crashed in 1929, many small investors were ruined, but not the *Money Barons* — they got out of the market, according to Allen and Abraham's book, *None Dare Call It Conspiracy,* with their fortunes intact, and the *Money Barons* next bought companies for a fraction of their worth, while once again their wealth increased by dimensions.

Louis McFadden, Chairman of the House Banking Committee declared:

"It was not accidental. It was a carefully contrived occurrence...The international bankers sought to bring about a condition of despair here so that they might emerge as rulers of us all." (9)

There is much more to say about these opportunists and their plans to take over our federal government, but after having forced the working class back into bondage during the Great Depression, they now had to deal with a total collapse of this country's government. Fortunately, in November 1932, in the midst of the depression, this nation elected what was later determined to be a legitimate leader named Franklin Delano Roosevelt (FDR), who was appointed to the Presidency for four consecutive terms. FDR was an honest man who helped the working class to regain their faith in themselves. He was also a leader that was capable of demonstrating indomitable courage because he had previously been stricken with crippling poliomyelitis in the summer of 1921 at the age of 39, never regaining the use of his legs. Having fought endlessly and hopelessly to try and walk, he was certainly qualified to extend compassion to others, a characteristic that perhaps overshadowed the wealthy banking aristocracy he was raised in. In treating his affliction he frequently traveled to Warm Springs, Georgia, where he swam in the natural therapeutic hot springs and visited with others that were being treated for similar disabilities. In fact, few people even realized FDR was disabled, because he seldom appeared in public in a wheel chair. Prior to his Presidency, he'd dramatically stood with crutches at the 1924 Democratic Convention to nominate Alfred E. Smith, because he didn't want the public to see he was disabled. Later, when he became President, FDR brought hope in his first Inaugural Address when he famously asserted:

". . . the only thing we have to fear is fear itself." (10)

He also promised prompt and vigorous action to correct the problems of the depression — and then proceeded to do just that. In his first term, he implemented several federal and state programs, and because the banks had suddenly been shut down, people urgently needed financial help. Almost everyone had lost their savings and it was estimated that some thirteen million people were unemployed. This prompted him to implement programs for businesses and agriculture and relief to the unemployed, along with financial assistance for those in danger of losing their farms or homes to these powerful bankers that were opportunistically waiting in the wings. He also created the badly needed Tennessee Valley Authority where the people were hurting the most, and then responded with the Social Security program, heavier taxes on the wealthy, new standards, regulations and controls over banks and public utilities, as well as a major relief program for the unemployed. During those hard times, the people were much less cynical about the societal risk of community and government programs, because of the numerous crises that existed. In a letter FDR wrote to an associate dated November 21st 1933, he said:

> *"The real truth of the matter is, as you and I know, that a financial element in the large centers has owned the government ever since the days of Andrew Jackson. (11)"*

Then later in a speech in Philadelphia on June 27, 1936, he said:

> *"Out of this modern civilization, economic royalists carved new dynasties. New kingdoms were built upon concentration of control over material things. Through new uses of corporations, banks and securities, new machinery of industry and agriculture, of labor and capital - all undreamed of by the Fathers - the whole structure of modern life was impressed into this royal service.... . These economic royalists complain that we seek to overthrow the institutions of America. What they really complain of is that we seek to take away their power. Our allegiance to American institutions requires the overthrow of this kind of power. In vain they seek to hide behind the flag and the Constitution. In their blindness they forget what the flag and the Constitution stand for."(12)*

A total overthrow of the United States Democracy was actually attempted during FDR's first term, when these very same powerful bankers and corporations attempted to unseat him in a plot that was publicly exposed by retired Marine Corps Major General Smedley Butler, at the 1934 McCormack- Dickstein Congressional Committee meeting. In Butler's testimony, he told the committee that on July 17, 1932, he was approached by several wealthy businessmen who had asked him to help overthrow this nation's democracy in a military coup. In the Congressional Committee's report, Butler's allegations were validated, but no prosecutions or further investigations ever followed, which is usually what happens when it involves any member of the exclusive upper crust. In retrospect, the devastation of the Great Depression had caused many of these very rich families to actually question the foundation of our Democracy, considering Fascism, Socialism, or even Communism as an alternative that would give them greater control over their wealth. By 1935, most of these bankers and large corporations openly opposed FDR's "New Deal," and because FDR was forced to abandon the gold standard, it was also becoming far more possible for these privately owned banking systems to extend unlimited credit. In fact, without the gold standard, there was no way to protect one's savings should any type of inflation occur. Other countries were also forced to float their unregulated currencies, since our global currency was no longer backed up by a gold standard. This meant the dollar would be regulated by the unstable market forces, which were totally owned and manipulated by these very powerful bankers. Gold had previously served as one's protector of property rights, but now this uncontrolled deficit spending had inadvertently opened the door to a much larger banker's scheme of confiscating and acquiring the world's wealth.

In the late thirties, FDR was also seeking neutrality legislation that would keep the United States out of war during this nation's recovery from the Great Depression. To accomplish this he pledged the United States to a "Good Neighbor" policy by modifying the Munroe Doctrine into a plan that promised mutual cooperation against any foreign aggression. Then when France fell to Hitler, and England was under siege in 1940, FDR fulfilled his pledge by first sending England all possible aid, without any military involvement — however; after the Japanese attacked Pearl Harbor on December 7, 1941, FDR was forced to enter the global war. During World War II, sixteen million men and women served in this nation's armed forces, with more than four hundred and fifty thousand American soldiers giving up their lives to protect our freedom. Victory over Europe Day (VE-Day) occurred May 8, 1945, and three months later, on August 6, 1945, a nuclear bomb called "Little Boy" was dropped on Hiroshima,

Japan. On August 9, 1945 a second nuclear bomb called "Fat Man" was dropped on Nagasaki, both at the direction of then President Harry S. Truman. As a result of these nuclear bombs, the surrender of Japan finally occurred on August 15, 1945, ending World War II. However, the formal Japanese signing of the surrender terms took place on board the battleship *USS Missouri* in Tokyo Bay on September 2, 1945, with President Truman declaring September 2 to be VJ-Day. By November 20, 1945, the remaining leaders of *Hitler's Third Reich* were placed on trial in Nuremberg, Germany. The Nuremberg Trial was conducted by a joint United States-British-French-Soviet military tribunal, with each nation supplying two judges.

The four counts in the indictment were:

Count 1 – Conspiracy to commit crimes.
Count 2 – Crimes against peace, including planning, preparing, starting, or waging aggressive war.
Count 3 – War crimes, including violations of laws or customs of war.
Count 4 – Crimes against Humanity, including murder, extermination, enslavement, persecution on political or racial grounds, involuntary deportment, and inhumane acts against the civilian population.

These policies still exist under the Geneva Convention, and ironically, the United States violated all four of these same counts as it relates to the unjust Iraq war. So is there any wonder why Americans have reached this stage of complacency and apathy in today's market driven society? By placing international corporate earnings above consumer security pits corporate goals against social justice for our middle class. Yes, the working class clearly understands that an open and competitive market contributes to a healthy global economy, but when powerful international monopolies control both the government and the noncompetitive products and services that were established to benefit the workforce they inevitably find themselves in direct conflict with these powerful monopolies. This buy off of our politicians and the NWO's efforts to monopolize the entire world economy has already resulted in an enormous amount of fear and hatred as these ruthless power brokers now skillfully buy off other countries outside our porous borders — just as they have the United States, by placing each country's duly appointed leaders in direct conflict with the people these leaders are supposed to represent. Perhaps it's time to ask ourselves if this is why our dysfunctional leaders lie to us when they promise to place our Social Security in a lock box, exclusive of race, disability or creed; when they promise that our tax dollars will protect the borders and that they will improve our education system, which is under-funded in this country by almost $30 billion. Perhaps this is why they fail to provide alternative energy, improve the environment, stop global warming, protect our forests and water, and stop air pollution or the threat of poison, germ and nuclear wastes. Yes, they lie because they've become a shadow government of the *Money Barons* — and therefore they actually have little concern over the management of this once sovereign nation. On top of all this, we've now deregulated and decentralized our healthcare system, while under funding so many other human services that involve our infrastructure, our education, our transportation industry, our energy and utility services, our highways, bridges and dams, and our police and fire services. Is there any wonder, why Americans are currently stuck between this strange state of *Complacency* and *Apathy?* And isn't it ironic how all our human services are following this same destructive path, with healthcare and the depletion of our natural oil resource leading the way? Isn't it time for us to understand that a profit oriented monopoly over the entire world market will never be successful in distributing social justice? Yet, these same powerful international czars continue to selfishly and intentionally flatten the United States by outsourcing this nation's technology and jobs so they can continue to garner these huge profits, which can only have an alarming impact on our economy and its workforce. Yes, the United States is clearly confusing its role in protecting human service freedoms and jobs from profit incentive freedoms. And yet if we would only look over our shoulder, we'd soon find that this nation is the only nation, let alone democracy, commercializing all of its vitally important human services solely for the benefit of their making profit. By briefly reviewing what actually happened with our natural resource of oil over the last one hundred years, (See Chapter 7 p. 100) and healthcare since 1965 (See Chapter 8 p. 112) — perhaps we could all better understand why these human services eventually became unaffordable. It should also be noted that as other countries submit to this monopolistic control and destruction of competitive globalization, they will eventually find themselves in direct conflict with their own businesses, just as we have in the United States. Perhaps our history of free markets; free enterprise; and as little government control and regulation as possible has blinded our legislators as to what is really going on. But eventually this country will need to decide if a human service can ever be placed on the competitive open market and remain capable of distributing social justice equally to the working class. If we are to submit to globalization without a free and open economy, we will all be doomed to an industrial dictatorship, a revolution, a monopoly, and the greatest contrived depression this world has ever seen. Numerous books speak to the threat of such an aristocracy taking over our Democracy, and a few that you may find interesting are:

The Ascendancy of the Scientific Dictatorship: An Examination of Epistemic Autocracy, From the 19th to the 21st Century, by Paul & Phillip Collins

The Syndicate: The Story of the Coming World Government, by Nicholas Hagger

World revolution: The plot against civilization, by Nesta Helen Webster

America's Secret Establishment: An Introduction to the Order of Skull & Bones, by Antony C. Sutton

Secret Societies and Subversive Movements, by Nesta H. Webster

---

1 Blase, William. *"The Council on Foreign Relations (CFR) and the New World Order."* The Courier. 1995. page 2-3
http://www.conspiracyarchive.com/NWO/Council_Foreign_Relations.htm

2 Ibid page 3

3 Ibid page 3

4 Ibid page 4

5 Ibid page 5

6 Ibid page 5

7 Ibid page 5

8 Ibid page 6

9 Ibid page 6

10 www.whitehouse.gov /history/presidents/fr32.html.

11 Alexander James, "The Hidden History of Money," page 46
http://portland.indymedia.org/en/2004/03/282679.shtml

12 Ibid page 46

2

The Invisible
Money Barons

The invisible Money Barons, now firmly established as the New World Order (NWO), have totally bought off our dysfunctional puppet like Congress, who have proven themselves to be everything but conservative. By controlling those that should be representing us, these power brokers are in point of fact now pilfering directly from our public treasury, while they are intentionally forcing this country's working class back into bondage and another depression that will inevitably upset the entire world economy. And as one studies this selfish and demeaning suppression of the United State's workforce, we find that this upper crust has for more than 100 years been secretly planning to create and control this country before they eventually monopolize the entire global economy.

James Alexander, the author of, *The Hidden History of Money*, said it all very well:

> "The biggest problem facing all human beings today is the creeping slavery created by the monopoly on the issuance and creation of 'fiat' money (from nothing by the stroke of a pen or keyboard) that the Illuminati Bankers who own the central and local banks have managed to usurp from . . . the private US Federal Reserve Banks in 1913 and so on! These Illuminati Banking Dynasties lend this 'fiat' money to the people's Governments and corporations and charge interest on money they created from nothing; the debt and the associated interest payments are inherited and grow from generation to generation forever and have enslaved past, present and future

generations!! The only way to stop this pyramid scheme from collapsing is for governments to keep borrowing more and more!!! Whenever this pyramid collapses, the Illuminati Banksters go on a buying spree for bargains while others suffer!!!! Another way to keep the pyramid going is to create wars and terror in which all sides have to borrow money from the Banksters!!!!! Meanwhile, the number of enslaved peoples world-wide keeps growing begging for handouts at the mercy of the Illuminati Banksters whose wealth and power keeps skyrocketing!!!!! . . . (1)

Here are but a few examples of the many abusive forms of power these *Invisible Money Barons* have fashioned over the last century — just to satisfy their endless greed for money and control:

● The deregulation and decentralization of far too many human services for the working class by creating competitive units in a no longer affordable open market The services and benefits they have already stolen from include the following:

Healthcare
Prescription Drugs
Utility and Energy
Environment
Global Warming Programs
Postal Services
Education
Police and Fire Services
Transportation, Highways, Bridges and Dams
Drug and Narcotic Programs
Border Security and Illegal Immigration

All intentionally designed to secretly drain income and tax dollars directly from our public treasury, while all of these human services have now become unaffordable as they are ignored or systematically moved into the open and competitive market

● The illegal unilateral acts of aggression and wars that gain power over a country's economy, oil, or their natural resources, which are then protected by one or more of almost 800 U.S. military bases throughout the world. This not only humiliates the United States, but violates international law and markedly provokes the entire world over the many costly, unjust, and endless theocratic conflicts we become directly involved in.

• The torture, and detention tactics at Abu Ghraib and Guantanamo Bay, involving the labeling of prisoners as *"Enemy Combatants"* and the transfer of many of these victims to foreign countries for torture, which defies all rules of international and U.S. law, as well as due process of a fair and just trial — thereby eliminating trials and the writ of habeas corpus petitions under the "Military Commission Act of 2006."

• The violation and abuse of power involving our civil liberties under the Patriot Act; the unchecked telephone and drone surveillance, bombing and spying on innocent human beings; the repression of individual dissent and freedom of speech; and the creation of fear and anxiety by the open invasion of one's privacy.

• The skilful crafting of a budget deficit, which is far greater than this nation has ever seen in its entire history.

• The huge loans from private international banks, China, Japan, and our own Social Security, now estimated somewhere between $54 to $75 trillion dollars. We really don't know the actual amount for which we pay $409 billion dollars a year in interest, which equals close to two billion dollars a day.

• This NWO indirectly controls the world's most powerful military complex; the U.S Supreme Court and the Attorney General; the Intelligence and Homeland Security System; the International Banking System and the Federal Reserve; as well as the world's news media and propaganda networks — thereby maintaining a constant level of fear and terror, which causes the average citizen to become submissive and dependent when Americans should actually have nothing to fear but fear itself.

• They have intentionally corrupted corporations, politicians and lobbyists, and influenced CEO's involved in what has become known as "The Great Cover-up."

• They are indirectly responsible for the lack of adequate military training, equipment and the inadequate care plans for our veterans injured in their unilateral acts of aggression.

• They condone the *"no negotiation policy"* as demonstrated previously with Jerusalem, North Korea, Iran, Syria, Jordan, Pakistan, Afghanistan, Turkey, Venezuela, Cuba and others.

• The complete disregard for catastrophic events like the Katrina and Sandy hurricanes and some $854 million in pledges from other countries for the Katrina disaster of which approximately only $40 million was accepted; and more recently persuading our Congress to delay relief efforts for New Jersey for more than 90 days.

• The corrupt Federal Attorney crisis.

• The treasonous and intentional outing of CIA agents.

• The un-audited, no-bid, noncompetitive and fraudulent awarding of government contracts that favor only a few select international corporations, and the total lack of audit over the billions of working class tax dollars that were paid in the cash exchange scam with Iraq.

• The failure to properly investigate or correct documented voter fraud.

• The complete disregard to properly investigate numerous undisputable facts regarding the destruction of the Twin Tower's and building #7, as well as the Pentagon crime scenes.

● The two level tax reduction system, favoring the very wealthy top one-percent.

● The out of control campaign financing, which now occupies more of the politicians time than the work they do for the people they no longer represent.

● The out of control pork barrel favors and benefits that are extended to only a select inner circle of plutocrats.

● The complete disregard for President Ford's executive order banning assassinations by any US government agency, formerly known as *Murder Incorporated* and the secret and illegal drone bombing of innocent victims in non-warring countries.

● The intentional and persistent diversion and turmoil regarding racism, women's rights, stem cell research, and don't ask don't tell.

● The complete disregard for the international trade deficit reaching a high of more than $830 billion in 2007, and the growing off-shore tax fraud.

● The intentional leveling of this once great nation through the improperly administered North American Free Trade Agreement (NAFTA), the Central America Free Trade Agreement (CAFTA), and the Free Trade Areas of the Americas (FTAA) etc. And let's not forget the blatant exporting of jobs from America, as well as the overall reduction of average salaries across this nation.

In the mid sixties, these *Invisible Money Barons* secretly maneuvered themselves into a position where they could openly market our healthcare services to the working class by moving them into the competitive open market, where they could steal directly from the people's public treasury. Had we become so spoiled by our newfound freedom that we didn't think we needed to protect our workforce and their human benefits?

Didn't we realize that we needed a leadership that was capable of differentiating between the competitive unregulated **Open Market** and the **Noncompetitive Markets**, which are required to maintain a healthy and productive workforce?

> The ***Open Market*** involves the selling of competitive and unregulated products in a decentralized open market, where the consumer has a choice in what they receive for their dollar. And for any global economy to remain healthy, it needs to assure the public that the global market is not only open, but free — not a monopoly that is controlled by privately owned multinational banks, or some powerful multinational corporate monopoly.

> A ***Noncompetitive Market*** involves a benefit, a service, or even a product that is not intended to make a profit, which requires standards and regulations under a centralized system that is both efficient and cost effective. Because the consumer (the working class) has little or no choice in the benefit, service, or product they receive through their employer, these human services need to be protected.

For example: Healthcare is a human non-elective service, where the working class doesn't have much choice in what they receive for their money, and therefore the consumer needs policies and standards that protect them. Another example would involve a nation's God given natural resources, such as oil, which should benefit the citizens equally. Doesn't it seem strange that we ask Iraq to equally distribute its oil revenue to the Shiite's, the Sunni's, and the Kurd's, and then we turn around and let a select group of wealthy and powerful *Money Barons* control all our natural resources as well as the revenues. By placing these human services on the open market, we are actually allowing the *"have's"* to steal from the *"have-not's"* — thereby creating a two level system that challenges our working class's equality in what we still believe is a "Democracy." Alan Greenspan, the American economist who had earlier resigned as Chairman of the Board of Governors of this country's privately owned Federal Reserve, suggested that *"lowering salaries for the working class creates equality."* He said, *"Money doesn't provide happiness."* Yet he and these powerful international industrial aristocracies are making huge profits for those privileged few who are no longer afraid to openly and aggressively steal directly from our countries public treasury and the working class that represents the backbone of our nation.

Perhaps it's time for these *Money Barons* to be told they are awakening the very same sleeping giant that previously protected the United State's freedom during World War II. Perhaps it's time for our dysfunctional *Puppet Government* and this strange NWO to be told they will never be successful in marketing freedom or human services to the world by any other means than setting a creditable example.

So, let's more closely scrutinize these powerful and wealthy *Money Barons* that seek to return the working class back to bondage? Call it an *Aristocracy*; an *Empire*; a *Monarchy*; a *Kingdom*; a *Realm*; a *Domain*; a *Republic*; *the privately held Federal Reserve and its Multinational Banks; The Shrub Dynasty; The Trilateral Commission (TC); The Council on Foreign Relations (CFR); The Bilderbergers; The American Israel Public Affairs Committee (AIPAC's); The World Constitution and Parliament Association (WCPA); Profit Insurance; the Pharmaceutical Manufacturers;* or just the *Upper Crust* — it's still the very same bondage and oppression our families fled from when they escaped to America over two hundred years ago — when another *Kleptocratic Aristocracy* stole from that working class to increase their affluence and power. But this time it's important to remember — *The people have no place to run!*

Let's recall just one of the numerous and similar oppression when the Spanish, French and English all attempted to colonize the Caribbean. After the English finally drove the French and Spanish landowners off the islands in the 1650s — some two thousand white sugar plantation owners of the *Master-Mistress Aristocracy*, tried in 1733 to dictate to some seventy-nine thousand black slaves they'd placed under bondage — so they could flaunt their wealth and political and social power when they traveled back to their estates in England. But eventually this English upper class failed when the black slaves that had originally occupied those islands decided to revolt with overwhelming force, in what became known as the *Great Slave Rebellion*. The Maroons as they were called fought violently once they escaped into the mountains where thousands of them hid, some in holes in the ground, so they could eventually reclaim control of their own lives. England's "Eight New Rules of Torture" clearly described the type of public flogging, burning and dismem-berment tactics used to stop this rebellion, and although many of the revolutionary male slaves died violent deaths, the women were only burned with red hot irons as they poured scalding hot water down their throats, so they'd suffer a bit. Perhaps it's time for the United States to sharpen its understanding of such hypocrisies.

President Ford once said to this author:

> *"It's up to the President to maintain the delicate balance between the ends of a very heavy Iron Cross I carry. Each end of this cross represents a controlling power such as the politicians and the bureaucracy; the industrial complex and its lobbyists; the military; and the people. I've found that when a President allows too many gifts and benefits to flow in any one direction, things quickly get out of balance, like a loose string on a Stradivarius destroys the tone of a beautiful ballad."*

President Dwight Eisenhower also warned us as he left office in 1961, that our Industrial and Military Complex was becoming far too powerful. Yet, we've let the international industrial complex and the World Bank buy-off our administration, our politicians, and our military — breeding fear and stress amongst this world's many vulnerable and insecure human beings who are all becoming fatigued as they watch this nation's sovereignty, reputation, and financial well being self-destruct.

President Andrew Jackson, who believed that private multinational banks threatened the nation, wrote:

> *"The bold effort the present bank had made to control the government, the distress it had wantonly produced...are but premonitions of the fate that awaits the American people should they be deluded into a perpetuation of this institution or the establishment of another like it."* (2)

Thomas Jefferson wrote:

> *"The Central Bank is an institution of the most deadly hostility existing against the principles and form of our Constitution ... if the American people allow private banks to control the issuance of their currency, first by inflation and then by deflation, the banks and corporations that will grow up around them will deprive the people of all their property until their children will wake up homeless on the continent their fathers conquered." (3)*

In that these powerful *Money Barons* have direct access to government officials and policy makers as often as they wish — shouldn't we have standards that require these meetings be in open public forum, since they are speaking for us? Theodore Roosevelt, in a speech on April 19, 1906 said:

> *"Behind the ostensible government sits enthroned an invisible government owing no allegiance and acknowledging no responsibility to the people. To destroy this invisible government, to befoul the unholy alliance between corrupt business and corrupt politics is the first task of the statesmanship of the day." (4)*

And then again in 1919, speaking just before his death he said:

> *"These International Bankers and Rockefeller-Standard Oil interests control the majority of newspapers and the columns of these papers to club into submission or drive out of public office officials who refuse to do the bidding of the powerful corrupt cliques which compose the invisible government." (5)*

In 1922, John Hylan, Mayor of New York, said:

> *"The warning of Theodore Roosevelt has much timeliness today, for the real menace of our republic is this invisible government which like a giant octopus sprawls its slimy length over City, State, and nation... It seizes in its long and powerful tentacles our executive officers, our legislative bodies, our schools, our courts, our newspapers, and every agency created for the public protection... To depart from mere generalizations, let me say that at the head of this octopus are the Rockefeller-Standard Oil interest and a small group*

> *of powerful banking houses generally referred to as the international Bankers. The little coterie of powerful international Bankers virtually run the United States government for their own selfish purposes. They practically control both parties, write political platforms, make catspaws of party leaders, use the leading men of private organizations, and resort to every device to place in nomination for high public office only such candidates as will be amenable to the dictates of corrupt big business... These international Bankers and Rockefeller-Standard Oil interests control the majority of newspapers and magazines in this country."(6)*

In an effort to defuse the growing number of complaints over this type of government control in the early 1900's, these powerful *Money Barons* intentionally staged the prosperity of the "Roaring 20's" — only to later skillfully create the Great Depression of 1929, where they stole people's homes and property when they defaulted on their bank loans.

Note: This author's father, who was out of work because of the depression, was one day late with the last payment on his home mortgage because the banks had closed their doors, and they took his home from him.

Congressman Ron Paul at an event near Austin, Texas on August 30th, 2003 stated in an answer to a question from Eric Rainbolt, an audience member:

> *"Congressman Paul, ... If we can take a look at the big picture, could you tell us, the people in this room, any information that you may have of an international and deceptive conspiracy to overthrow the American Republic and its Constitution and Bill Of Rights in order to set up and usher in a totalitarian World Government likely espoused under the UN ?..."*

Congressman Paul responded:

> *"Yes". "I think there are 25,000 individuals that have used offices of powers, and they are in our Universities and they are in our Congresses, and they believe in One World Government. And if you believe in One World Government, then you are talking about undermining National Sovereignty and you are talking about setting up something that you could well call a*

Dictatorship - and those plans are there!..."(7)

Alexis de Tocqueville, sometimes referred to as Alexander Frazer Tytler, or Alexander Tyler, a Scottish history professor from the University of Edinburgh, and his controversial statement in, *The Fall of a Republic,* which is also referred to as *The Fall of a Democracy,* back in the early days of the industrial revolution said:

> *"A democracy is always temporary in nature. A democracy cannot exist as a permanent form of government. It can only exist until the voters discover that they can vote themselves money from the public treasure. From that moment on the majority always votes for the candidates who promise the most money from the public treasury, with the result that a democracy always collapses over loose fiscal policy followed by a dictatorship."* (8)

Tocqueville also explained how this democracy cycle moves from bondage to faith, to courage, to liberty, to abundance, to complacency, to apathy, and then dependence before returning all the way back to bondage; explaining how this whole cycle usually takes about two hundred years for a democracy to become a dictatorship. And yes, it's obvious that the United States is once again in the apathy stage, totally dependent on some powerful self serving aristocracy that will inevitably force the working class back into bondage by taking away their freedoms, while we foolishly languish in some sort of sustained state of apathy.

1 Alexander James, *"The Hidden History of Money, See*
http://portland.indymedia.org/en/2004/03/282679.shtml p.4

2 Blase, William. "The Council on Foreign Relations (CFR) and the New World Order." 1995. http://www.conspiracyarchive.com/NWO/Council_Foreign_Relations.htm

3 Ibid

4 The New World Order www.lagunajournal.com/new_world_order.htm - 61k - Cached

5 Alexander James, "The Hidden History of Money," page 45
http://portland.indymedia.org/en/2004/03/282679.shtml

6 Ibid page 45

7 *http://www.raven1.net/ronpaulowg.htm*

8 Alexander Tyler, *"The Fall of a Republic* http://www.mcsm.org/democracy1.html & Loren Collins, "The Truth About Tytler" http://lorencollins.net/tytler.html

3

The Tri-Lats

Let's review some of the many pervasive organizations called the *Tri-Lats* and discuss some of the ways they control our dysfunctional Congress and our President — causing our economy and *"We the People"* to grow weak, while the world becomes more fearful and unfriendly.

Note: A partnership among the ruling classes of North America, Western Europe and Japan — hence the term "Trilateral."

Here are but a few of the peripheral organizations, all seeking to replace our government which is still appointed by this country's working class:

The Trilateral Commission (TC)
The Bilderbergers
North Atlantic Treaty Organization (NATO)
The Council on Foreign Relations (CFR)
The American Legislative Exchange Council (ALEC)
The Federal Reserve
The International Investment Banks and Corporations
The Dysfunctional United Nations (UN)
The American Israel Public Affairs Committee (AIPAC's)
The World Constitution and Parliament Association (WCPA)
The North American Free Trade Agreement (NAFTA)

Perhaps with the current President and our duly elected Congress rendered so dysfunctional, these monopolistic organizations are having a far greater influence over our sovereign nation and its working class than we'd like to admit — and perhaps it's also time we pause and evaluate if

Americans really want to replace our constitution and our duly elected representatives with any of these *Tri-Lat* organizations. Shouldn't Americans at least conduct an unbiased investigation, or vote, if we feel there is a conflict of interest regarding our sovereignty? Shouldn't we determine what *"We the People"* actually desire before we let some *Kleptocratic Aristocracy*, like the NWO take over our noncompetitive market under a powerful *Multinational Shadow Government?*

The Trilateral Commission (TC) — The Bilderberg Group — and NATO

The UN constitution was intentionally designed and crafted by the Rockefeller TC members, to level this great country to the same level as other nations. David Rockefeller, the undisputed *"Overlord"* of his family's corporate monopoly was one of the founders of the TC, which was his brainchild. And in addition to this, he also served as the Director Emeritus (Honorary Chairman) of the CFR, which the Rockefellers funded from its inception. The Rockefellers have also been heavily involved in funding the Bilderberger's organization, where David first proposed his then secretive TC. History clearly states that John D. Rockefeller Sr. was a monopolist who hated competition, and he has funded their controlling dynasty's political aspirations for years. He first developed the idea of this politically powerful TC at one of their family meetings at the Rockefeller Pocantico Hills estate, located near New York City — while later presenting their plan for the TC at the annual 1972 meeting of their tightly knit and very secretive Bilderberg group in Knokke, Belgium. The Bilderbergers included international financiers, industrialists, media magnates, union bosses, academics and political figures whose countries were associated with the North Atlantic Treaty Organization (NATO), which had earlier been established on April 4, 1949 — and then later confirmed when Belgium, Canada, Denmark, France, Great Britain, Iceland, Italy, Luxembourg, the Netherlands, Norway, Portugal, and the United States all became members. Later, Greece and Turkey entered the alliance in 1952. West Germany (now Germany) entered in 1955, Spain in 1982, and the Czech Republic in 1999. Then Hungary, Poland, Bulgaria, Estonia, Latvia, Lithuania, Romania, Slovakia, and Slovenia all became members in 2004, bringing the total membership to twenty-six. NATO maintains headquarters in Brussels, Belgium and was one of the major Western countermeasures against any aggression by the Soviet Union during the Cold War, which we'd like to believe ended with the collapse of the Soviet Union in 1991. The name Bilderberg came from the name of the hotel where their founders first met in Holland in 1954. The Bilderbergers and the TC have somewhat different modes of operation, although they both hold an inordinate amount of influence over this country's duly appointed politicians. The Bildergerg group has dealt primarily with NATO, and constituted one of the very first *Shadow Governments* of the *Invisible Money Barons* that sought to influence their will over all these governments and their respective representatives of the working class. What is unique about the TC is that it also later brought the Japanese ruling elite into the inner circle of this power brokers association. However, the full TC control will never be assured until they've successfully flatten the United State's sovereign democracy to the same level as other nations, since in the past the U.S. has been far too powerful.

Grandson David Rockefeller was selected to spearhead the TC's secretive plan, probably because he'd served as CEO of the powerful Chase Manhattan Bank, now the retail and service arm of JP Morgan Chase. As the undisputed *Overlord* of his family's many tax evading foundations, and Founder and Honorary Chairman of the TC, he's been able to coerce other world-wide political leaders into his way of thinking, which promotes a major conflict of interest with any self governing democracy.

In 1973, following the successful 1945-1965 profit insurance take-over of this country's once successful single nonprofit healthcare system — David Rockefeller asked a young polish intellectual by the name of Zbigniew Brzezinski to serve as the Executive Director of what would become the TC, and put together an organization of top political and business leaders from around the World. What's even more frightening was that Brzezinski also served as co-chair of the Bush National Security Advisory Task Force, and served as National Security Adviser to both President Bush and Jimmy Carter. As Executive Director of the TC, he predictably recommended a membership that was made up of international bankers; foundations and Wall Street "think tank" executives; corporate lobbyist; lawyers; Pentagon military leaders; wealthy industrialists; media owners; international business executives; university presidents; as well as selected professors, Senators, Congressmen, U.S. Ambassadors, Secretaries of State, and prospective and past U.S. Presidents. More recently, the TC has now included a few selected representatives from Japan and the NATO organization. You might wish to look at the 2005 TC membership which can be found in Appendix I, page 218. After you study the TC membership, perhaps you'll better be able to connect the dots and understand why Congress refuses to abolish the *Money Barons* privately owned Federal Reserve, or why they continue to pass such devastating trade agreements. The TC headquarters is located at 345 East 46th Street, Suite 711, New York, NY 10017.

The TC provided the following description of their organization:

"The European Community, North America (US and Canada), and Japan - the three main democratic industrialized areas of the world - are the three sides of the Trilateral Commission. The Commission's members are about 325 distinguished citizens, [March 23, 1994] *with a variety of leadership responsibilities, from these three regions. When the first triennium of the Trilateral Commission was launched in 1973, the most immediate purpose was to draw together - at a time of considerable friction among governments - the highest level unofficial group possible to look together at the common problems facing our three areas. At a deeper level, there was a sense that the United States was no longer in such a singular leadership position as it had been in earlier post-World War II years, and that a more shared form of leadership - including Europe, and Japan in particular - would be needed for the international system to navigate successfully the major challenges of the coming years. These purposes continue to inform the Commission's work. The rise of Japan, and progress of the European Community over the past twenty years - particularly in the world economy - have validated the vision of the Commission's founders. At the same time, the end of the Cold War calls for a fresh vision of what this outward-looking partnership can accomplish in the coming years. The opportunities are remarkable, and yet, with the welcome end of the old Soviet threat, part of the 'glue' holding our regions together has dissolved. Helping meet that leadership challenge is at the heart of the Trilateral Commission effort." (1)*

The TC gathers behind closed doors every year to make decisions for our Democracy, deciding what our elected officials are told to do. However, many patriotic citizens disagree with this TC takeover and see it in a different light. Here are a just few of their opinions:

In *The New World Order*, Pat Robertson states:"

> *"Brzezinski idealized the theories of Karl Marx. In his book, 'Between Two Ages,' as in subsequent writings, he argued that balance-of-power politics was out, and world-order politics was in. The initial world order was to be a trilateral economic linkage between Japan, Europe, and the United States. David Rockefeller funded Brzezinski, and called together an organization, named the Trilateral Commission, with Brzezinski as its first executive secretary, and director . . . The stated goals of the Trilateral Commission are: 'Close Trilateral cooperation in keeping the peace, in managing the world economy, in fostering economic redevelopment, and alleviating world poverty will improve the chances of a smooth, and peaceful evolution of the global system.'"* (2)

In *The Shadows of Power*, James Perloff, states:

> *"How did the TC begin? 'The Trilateral Commission,' wrote Christopher Lydon in the July 1977 Atlantic, 'was David Rockefeller's brainchild.' George Franklin, North American secretary of the Trilateral Commission, stated that it 'was entirely David Rockefeller's idea originally.' Helping the CFR chairman develop the concept was Zbigniew Brzezinski, who laid the first stone in Foreign Affairs in 1970:*

> *'A new, and bolder approach is needed - creation of a community of the developed nations which can effectively address itself to the larger concerns confronting mankind. In addition to the United States, and Western Europe, Japan ought to be included ... A council representing the United States, Western Europe, and Japan, with regular meetings of the heads of governments as well as some small standing machinery, would be a good start.'"* (3)

Brzezinski elaborated on his thoughts in his book, *Between Two Ages*. It shows Brzezinski to be a classic Council on Foreign Relations (CFR) man and a global proponent more than lenient toward Communism. He declared that:

> *"National sovereignty is no longer a viable concept,' and that 'Marxism represents a further vital, and creative stage in the maturing of man's universal vision. Marxism is simultaneously a victory of the external, active man over the inner, passive man, and a victory of reason over belief..."'* (4)

But it was not all so innocent according to Jeremiah Novak who wrote in the *Atlantic* in July 1977:

> *"The 'Trilateralists' emphasis on international economics is not entirely disinterested, for the oil crisis forced many developing nations, with doubtful repayment abilities, to borrow excessively. All told, private multinational banks, particularly Rockefeller's Chase Manhattan, have loaned nearly $52 billion to developing countries. An overhauled IMF would provide another source of credit for these nations, and would take the big private banks off the hook. This proposal is the cornerstone of the trilateral plan."* (5)

Senator Barry Goldwater was less mercifully in his book, *With No Apologies*, when he termed the Commission:

> *"David Rockefeller's newest international cabal,' and said, 'It is intended to be the vehicle for multinational consolidation of the commercial, and banking interests by seizing control of the political government of the United States."'* (6)

In 1973, Jimmy Carter met with David Rockefeller at the Rockefeller Tarrytown, New York estate. Brzezinski, who was helping Rockefeller screen prospects for the Trilateral Commission, later told Peter Pringle of the London Sunday Times that . . . "we were impressed that Carter had opened up trade offices for the state of Georgia in Brussels, and Tokyo."

Barry Goldwater wrote about Jimmy Carter as follows:

> *"David Rockefeller and Zbigniew Brzezinski found Jimmy Carter to be their ideal candidate. They helped him win the nomination, and the presidency. To accomplish this purpose, they mobilized the money power of the Wall Street bankers, the intellectual influence of the academic community - which is subservient to the wealth of the great tax-free foundations - and the media controllers represented in the membership of the CFR , and the Trilateral"(7)*

The Gallup Poll had previously reported that less than four percent of Democrats favored Carter for President, but shortly after their meeting at the Rockefeller Tarrytown estate, Carter suddenly became the prime candidate.

Holly Sklar, who edited the book *Trilateralism* notes:

> *"Trilateralists are not only concerned with managing international events. They are determined to manage North American, West European, and Japanese democracy, fitting these societies ever more closely to the needs of global capitalism" (8)*

In other words, the public had no meaningful participation in these TC decisions that cross party lines and only include the elite and secretive money brokers.

Holly Sklar went on to say:

> *"It (TC) is intended to be the vehicle for multinational consolidation of the commercial and banking interests by seizing control of the political government of the United States." (9)*

A report presented at the plenary meeting of the TC in Japan in 1975 suggested the following goals:

- *The enlargement of central authority.*

- *A lack of confidence in democratically arrived-at public decisions.*

- *A program to lower the job expectations of those who received a college education.*

Paul Volcker, a former TC chairman, responded:

"The standard of the average American has to decline." (10)

In an article posted on June 24, 2005, entitled *Treasonous agenda of the Trilateral Commission,* Devvy Kidd made several frightening but profoundly accurate statements

". . . This treasonous operation is another one of the tentacles birthed by the elitists out to destroy our constitutional republic, turn us into a democracy and eventually merge all nations into a one world government."

"This is real — it is not a conspiracy theory, it is a heinous agenda that is all but complete except for the passage of <u>CAFTA</u> (Central American Free Trade Agreement), <u>FTAA</u> (Free Trade Area of the Americas) and nullification of the Second Amendment. If . . . CAFTA and FTAA are ratified, you will see another gigantic sucking sound of millions more jobs going south of the Hemisphere . . . Few Americans really understood back in 1993 what would happen under GATT (General Agreement on Tariffs and Trade 1947) *because few ever heard of it – too many simply bought the propaganda from politicians . . . Guess how many members of the entire Congress read GATT?" (11)* (It was only one member!)

She went on to say that a majority of the Senate ratified this insidious treaty without ever reading it. And sadly the American people continue electing these same sellouts back into office.

We have to rethink from top to bottom why we have elevated global free trade to the status of sacred cow, or moral dogma. It is a fatally flawed concept that will impoverish and destabilize the industrialized world while cruelly ravaging the Third World. (12)

Devvy also stated that our Republic is perilously close to being destroyed, and it's not a Republican vs. Democrat issue – it's an American issue. It's about remaining a free and sovereign nation and not falling into communist domination under a world government.

The late Sir James Goldsmith, a French financier, testified before the Ernest Hollings committee and was quoted in the *Washington Times*, Dec. 6, 1993 as saying:

> *Global free trade will force the poor of the rich countries to subsidize the rich in poor countries. (13)*

In trying to warn the American people about these Tri-lats, Barry Goldwater said it best:

> *The Trilateral Commission is international and is intended to be the vehicle for multinational consolidation of the commercial and banking interests by seizing control of the political government of the United States. The Trilateral Commission represents a skillful, coordinated effort to seize control and consolidate the four centers of power – political, monetary, intellectual and ecclesiastical . . . (14)*

In the *Trilateral Commission: World Shadow Government* — it stated the following:

> *"The Commission's purpose is to engineer an enduring partnership among the ruling classes of North America, Western Europe and Japan -- hence the term 'Trilateral' -- in order to safeguard the interests of Western capitalism in an explosive world. The private commission is attempting to mold public policy and construct a framework for international stability in the coming decades.*
>
> *To put it simply, Trilateralists are saying: The people, governments and economies of all nations must serve the needs of multinational banks and corporations.*

> *In short, Trilateralism is the current attempt by ruling elites to manage both dependence and democracy -- at home and abroad." (15)*

Yes, the purpose of these *Invisible Money Barons* is to mold public policy and construct a framework for the international ruling class. In actuality, they and George H. W. Bush's Shrub Dynasty actually have stated they intend to replace this sovereign nation with a *New World Government* (NWO) that serves the needs of multinational banks and corporations — controlling our duly appointed officials at home and abroad. Is there any need to ask why our Congress and President have become so dysfunctional? Do these dysfunctional representatives in Washington really believe we want to sell our country down the river? Do they really believe we want to destroy the sovereignty of this great nation and put the United States under global rule?

The former Sen. Barry Goldwater (R-Ariz.), summarized this Rockefeller family thing very well:

> *"The Trilateral organization created by David Rockefeller was a surrogate -- the members selected by Rockefeller, its purposes defined by Rockefeller, its funding supplied by Rockefeller. David Rockefeller screened and selected every individual who was invited to participate." (16)*

And to help accomplish this, David Rockefeller previously mobilized the Council on Foreign Relations (CFR), another Rockefeller-financed foreign policy pressure group similar to the Trilateralists and the Bilderbergers — all seeking to advance the enormous power of the Wall Street bankers and the intellectual influence of the academic community, which is totally dependent on the wealth of their huge tax-free foundations and the media. In other words, the international upper class has tightly band together to guarantee that political leaders who are brought to power will ensure their global financial interests.

This is no longer a two party issue — it's a survival issue. It's about our own freedom and sovereignty, and standing up to this wealthy aristocracy that wants to place the entire global economy under an industrially controlled NWO.

Devvy Kidd, in her article: *Treasonous agenda of the Trilateral Commission*, on June 24, 2005 referenced the late Sir James Goldsmith, who testified that GATT would gut the American textile market, outlined his quotes from the *Washington Times*, Dec. 6, 1993 article, which reflected Goldsmiths statements during the GATT hearings:

> *"What GATT means is that our national wealth, accumulated over centuries, will be transferred from a developed country like Britain to developing countries like Communist China, now building its first oceangoing navy in 500 years. China, with its 1.2 billion people, three Indochinese states with 900 million, the former Soviet republics with some 300 million, and many more can supply skilled labor for a fraction of Western costs ... It is quite amazing that GATT is sowing the seeds for global social upheaval and that it is not even the subject of debate in America ... If the masses understood the truth about GATT, there would be blood in the streets of many capitals. A healthy national economy has to produce a large part of its own needs. It cannot simply import what it needs and use its labor force to provide services for other countries." (17)*

On June 9, 2005, the House voted 338-86 to reject a motion to withdraw congressional approval of the 1994 agreement establishing the Geneva-based trading body (GATT-WTO).

The Council on Foreign Relations (CFR)

The Council on Foreign Relations (CFR) is an independent, nonpartisan foreign policy membership organization founded in 1921 by Colonel House and such high officials as JP Morgan, John D Rockefeller, Paul Warberg, Otto Kahn, and Jacob Schiff... the very same *Money Barons* that engineered the establishment of the current privately held Federal Reserve System.

The CFR has been called the most powerful agent of US foreign policy outside of the US State Department. It publishes the respected bi-monthly journal *Foreign Affairs*, and has an extensive website which features links to its "think tank" — "The David Rockefeller Studies Program." Its mission is to promote understanding of foreign policy and determine America's role in the world. It employs prominent scholars in international affairs and develops books and reports that propose policy and global economics on critical issues. Since its beginning, the CFR has supported globalization at the expense of U.S. sovereignty, proposing a *New World Order* that benefits its wealthy leaders far more than the working class of the United States. However, over the years the CFR has become much more than a "think tank," in that it invisibly influences U.S. foreign policy by totally controlling this country's duly appointed representatives of the people. In that the CFR is primarily owned and operated by powerful multinational banks and corporate monopolies, there is an inherent conflict of interest when you measure the benefits received by its owners. It is headquartered in New York, at The Harold Pratt House, 58 East 68th St., New York, N. Y. 10021, with an additional office in Washington, D.C.

> *"It bills itself as a research and educational institution 'that does not take any position on questions of foreign policy.' If you believe that you won't have any problem with believing Communist China is truly a 'People's Republic.' If the CFR takes no position, then one has to wonder why it has infiltrated the government from the presidency to all top official posts . . . Its members involved in the recent passage of China trade bill is a prime example of its establishment clout - Henry Kissinger, George Shultz, Brent Snowcroft, Donald Rumsfeld, Colin Powell, Presidents Clinton and Bush - all members of the CFR, plus Tri-lat Jimmy Carter, to name a few. Barry Goldwater wrote in With No Apologies that 'almost without exception the members of the CFR are united by a congeniality of birth, economic status, and educational background.' Goldwater quoted Rear Admiral Chester Ward, USN (Ret.), who was a CFR member for 16 years, as saying the most powerful CFR members have one objective in common. 'They want to bring about the surrender of the sovereignty and the national independence of the United States.' They want national boundaries and one-world government." (18)*

William Blasé wrote in his article "The Council on Foreign Relations (CFR) and The New World Order:"

"To understand how the most influential people in America came to be members of an organization working purposefully for the overthrow of the Constitution and American sovereignty, we have to go back at least to the early 1900's . . . That a ruling power elite does indeed control the U.S. government behind the scenes has been attested to by many Americans in a position to know. Felix Frankfurter, Justice of the Supreme Court (1939-1962), said: 'The real rulers in Washington are invisible and exercise power from behind the scenes.' In a letter to an associate dated November 21, 1933, President Franklin Roosevelt wrote, 'The real truth of the matter is, as you and I know, that a financial element in the large centers has owned the government ever since the days of Andrew Jackson.'"

February 23, 1954, Senator William Jenner warned in a speech:

"Outwardly we have a Constitutional government. We have operating within our government and political system, another body representing another form of government, a bureaucratic elite which believes our Constitution is outmoded."

Baron M.A. Rothschild wrote:

"Give me control over a nation's currency and I care not who makes its laws."

Georgetown professor Dr. Carroll Quigley (Bill Clinton's mentor while at Georgetown) wrote about the goals of the investment bankers who control central banks:

"... nothing less than to create a world system of financial control in private hands able to dominate the political system of each country and the economy of the world as a whole... controlled in a feudalist fashion by the central banks of the world acting in concert, by secret agreements arrived at in frequent private meetings and conferences." (19)

Congressman Louis McFadden, House Committee on Banking and Currency Chairman (1920-31), stated:

"When the Federal Reserve Act was passed, the people of these United States did not perceive that a world banking system was being set up here. A super-state controlled by international bankers and industrialists...acting together to enslave the world...Every effort has been made by the Fed to conceal its powers but the truth is--the Fed has usurped the government." (20)

As previously stated, few Americans understand the Federal Reserve is actually owned by the multinational banking system, and is not subject to oversight by either the Congress or the President. That means it makes its own policies, and they can buy government securities when they create low prices and sell when they create high prices. In 1913, these money barons intentionally created an income tax to protect the interest on their notes and they were then in a position to promote wars and open new markets whenever they desired to take their profits. With these multinational banks loaning money to the Federal Reserve, and our income tax providing a means to repay the debt, their wealthy nonprofit foundations found it a simple matter to escape tax — making it a *"Sweetheart Deal"* for these closely knit financial cliques. Now all they needed was a vehicle to control the government, and that was the CFR. The founding president of the CFR was John W. Davis, J.P. Morgan's personal attorney — however, over time, Morgan's influence was lost to the Rockefellers who found that one world government fit their philosophy of business best — giving Rockefeller the many creative government methods to allocate loans or promote wars and skirmishes, which made huge interest profits for all of them.

Peter Kershaw, in his *Economic Solutions* discusses how the working class is intentionally being bankrupt, as he provides proof that the Federal Reserve Bank is not federal at all, but a private corporation owned by some of the world's richest international banking families. In his book he quotes laws, court decisions, presidents and high-level government officials regarding this fraudulent Federal Reserve Banking system, which is essentially destroying the working class of this once great nation. He also exposes the IRS, which serves as the collection agency for these multinational bank czars, recommending we petition to repeal the Federal Reserve Act and the IRS code. He identifies the major shareholders of the Federal Reserve Bank System as:

> Rothschild (London and Berlin)
> Lazard Brothers (Paris)
> Israel Seiff (Italy)
> Kuhn - Loeb Company (Germany)
> Warburg (Hamburg and Amsterdam)
> Lehman Brothers (New York)
> Goldman and Sachs (New York)
> Rockefeller (New York)

Isn't it strange that he lists the Rockefeller *"Robber Barons"* last, when David served as the unquestionably powerful *"Overlord"* behind both the CFR and the TC? Doesn't this nation understand why the Rockefellers created tax-exempt foundations as repositories for their divested interests — making their assets non-taxable so they could avoid estate and gift taxes? Doesn't the public really care that the Rockefellers dump most of their income into more than 200 foundations and then turn around and deduct all their donations from their income tax?

Based on the *Invisible Money Barons* relentless corporate attack against this country's healthcare system over the last fifty years, it's important you also understand why the Rockefeller's oil companies and the drug manufacturers are in bed together — in that many drugs are made from coal tar derivatives that benefit both the oil companies and the drug manufacturers. Could this be one of the reasons they chose healthcare as number one on their hit parade in the mid 60's? — back when they first started this costly pharmaceutical monopoly and their intense drug advertising campaigns, all of which so heartlessly took advantage of the sick and disabled in the United States.

Frederick C. Howe clearly revealed their strategy of using government controlled monopolies in his 1906 book, *Confessions of a Monopolist*, saying:

> *"These are the rules of big business...Get a monopoly; let society work for you; and remember that the best of all business is politics..." (21)*

John D. Rockefeller senior always said he hated competition over monopoly, and to protect the multinational bank's monopolistic interests in the foreign market, David proposed this one world government from which his CFR could control the United States from behind the scenes, intentionally weakening the powerful U.S. politically and economically.

Louis McFadden, Chairman of the House Banking Committee spoke about the Great Depression saying:

> *"It was not accidental. It was a carefully contrived occurrence...The international bankers sought to bring about a condition of despair here so that they might emerge as rulers of us all." (22)*

Could this be why they promote terror and fear tactics, and the endless unilateral skirmishes that seem to go on forever — the loss of jobs to foreign countries, the out of control price gouging and the corporate monopolies — all at a time when we really should have nothing to fear but fear itself?

Curtis Dall, a son-in-law of FDR and a manager for Lehman Brothers, the investment firm, was on the N.Y. Stock Exchange floor the same day the market crashed in 1929. In his book, *FDR: My Exploited Father-In-Law*, he states:

> *"...it was the calculated 'shearing' of the public by the World-Money powers triggered by the planned sudden shortage of call money in the New York Market."(23)*

It should also be noted that FDR wasn't exactly Lily white — in fact, he had some very close ties to this multinational banking system, making huge sums of money for the *Invisible Money Barons* when he took America off the gold standard in 1934 — thereby opening this valueless and endless *"fiat"* money supply to them. In fact, the very same bankers that caused the depression — loaned America the money to recover from it under FDR's National Recovery Administration (NRA). George Swope, a CFR member worked directly with the NRA in helping to regulate wages, prices, and working conditions, which were all eventually ruled unconstitutional by the Supreme Court. And now, the same trends toward continuous wars and another depression is exactly what is happening again, all under the direct guidance of the CFR and the TC — but this time it was with the help of our totally dysfunctional Congress, and the *Shrub Dynasty's* strong support for establishing this NWO. And yes, the CFR plan for a one world government has once again been behind much of this sovereign nation's unjust skirmishes with other nations. In fact, since World War II, almost every Secretary of War, or Defense, was asked to become a member of the CFR, from Henry L. Stimson through Richard Cheney, as well as almost every United States Secretary of State. And yes, Vice-President Richard Cheney had a very serious conflict of interest in his dealings with both Halliburton and the CFR, and no one dared to face up to this glaring problem for fear of retaliation. Several published articles suggest that President John F. Kennedy, once a CFR member, was probably killed because he had the courage to disagree with the CFR, making the following statement in a speech at Colombia University just ten days before he was shot:

> *"The high office of President has been used to foment a plot to destroy the Americans' freedom, and before I leave office I must inform the citizens of this plight." (24)*

Yet no one, *"Conspirators"* as this Shadow Government refers to them, dare investigate such a suggestion, which prompts the question, should all public officials only be allowed to discuss public business and policy in a public forum?

In another Kennedy speech before the American Newspaper Publishers Association on April 27, 1961, he stated:

> *"The very word 'secrecy' is repugnant in a free and open society; and we are as a people inherently and historically opposed to secret societies, to secret oaths and to secret proceedings. We decided long ago that the dangers of excessive and unwarranted concealment of pertinent facts far outweighed the dangers which are cited to justify it."(25)*

As one studies the powerful names of the CFR members, you can readily identify the invisible power and the inherent conflict of interest between the people's interests and their membership. (See Appendix II page 249) For example: John Foster Dulles, the former Secretary of State, was a founding member of the CFR and an in-law of the Rockefellers, who also served as Chairman of the Board of the Rockefeller Foundation and the Carnegie Endowment for International Peace.

Here are just a few more of the current and past members of the CFR that should be of concern regarding a potential conflict of interest: Dick Cheney, Condoleezza Rice, Colin Powell, Donald Rumsfeld, Porter Goss, Alan Greenspan, John Bolton, Paul Wolfowitz, Richard Perl, Gen. Richard B. Myers, George Soros, Bill Frist, Newt Gingrich, Katherine Harris, Joseph Lieberman, John McCain, and Tony Snow, which just might give you some pause for thought. Worse yet, George H.W. Bush Sr. served as the Director of the CFR from 1977-1979. It's important to remember that the CFR and the CT are not just normal peripheral organizations, but two very powerful and well financed privately owned organizations that seek to create and control the American economic, social, political, and military policies as well as the administration, the CIA and the Federal Reserve of this nation through a world government. Other more cooperative CFR candidates for president have not only included George H.W. Bush, but Bill Clinton, George McGovern, Walter Mondale, Edmund Muskie, John Anderson, Lloyd Bentsen, along with Jimmy Carter, who were, or still are, members of the tightly knit Rockefeller TC and/or CFR — all supporting David Rockefeller's peaceful evolution to a global system under this NWO. They like to refer to their NWO as Globalization, since it does not have the dangerous connotation of a UN socialistic state or a communist dictatorship.

Isaiah Bowman, a founding member of the CFR, originated the idea of the United Nations in 1949, whose building is once again located on land donated by the Rockefeller family. Rockefeller sent almost fifty CFR members to the UN's San Francisco meeting in 1929 to control the drafting of the charter of the United Nations, which was specifically designed to replace this nation's sovereignty. Selected CFR members have also helped organize a mass media campaign that seeks to grant the

United Nations more authority as long as it remains under the power of the CFR's invisible government.

Rear Adm. Chester Ward, a former member of the CFR for 16 years, and an unsympathetic critic of the CFR, states in his book *Kissinger on the Couch:*

> *"The most powerful clique in these elitist groups have one objective in common — they want to bring about the surrender of the sovereignty of the national independence of the United States. A second clique of international members in the CFR comprises the Wall Street international bankers and their key agents. Primarily, they want the world-banking monopoly from whatever power ends up in the control of global government." (26)*

In the official publication of the CFR's 50th anniversary issue of *Foreign Affairs,* an article by Kingman Brewster, Jr. entitled "Reflections on Our National Purpose," suggests that the U.S. purpose should be:

> *"'To do away with our nationality,' to 'take some risks in order to invite others to pool their sovereignty with ours'... These 'risks' include disarming to the point where we would be helpless against the 'peace-keeping' forces of a global UN government. We should happily surrender our sovereignty to the world government in the interests of the 'world community.'" (27)*

And isn't this exactly what the CFR members like Rumsfeld, Cheney, and Powell have done in the past, by shorting our troops in Iraq, and thereby intentionally creating a perpetual and prolonged scuffle that eventually depletes our armed forces and our power as a world leader, while at the same time draining huge sums of money from our public treasury? The CFR explains that it is "host to many views, advocate of none," and "has no affiliation with the U.S. government," when it actually serves as the invisible U.S. government.

Richard N. Gardner, the former deputy assistant Secretary of State in *Foreign Affairs,* said on April 1974:

"In short, the 'house of world order' will have to be built from the bottom up rather than from the top down...An end run around national sovereignty, eroding it piece by piece, will accomplish much more than the old fashioned assault..." (28)

James Warburg, son of CFR founder Paul Warburg, testified before the Senate Foreign Relations Committee on February 17, 1950, saying:

"With the wealth of the world in their hands, what more could the MONEY-CHANGERS possibly want? Testifying before the Senate Foreign Relations Committee on Feb. 17, 1950, James Warburg (brother of Paul Warburg, the head of the Federal Reserve in 1913) confessed, 'We shall have world government whether or not you like it. The only question is whether World government will be achieved by conquest or consent.' Imagine a MONEY-CHANGER delivering such an ultimatum to the United States Senate and theoretically to the world. They want nothing less than a world-dictatorship commonly referred to as, 'New World Order.'"(29)

Devvy Kidd posted on her website on June 17, 2005 an article entitled "Treasonous agenda of the Council on Foreign Relations," which summarized the following important listing of quotes:

Arthur Schlesinger Jr., in the July/August 95 *Foreign Affairs*, CFR's flagship publication said:

"In Defense of the World Order ... U.S. Soldiers would have to kill and die"

Lou Dobbs, CNN Anchor on June 9, 2005 said:

". . . Tonight, an astonishing proposal to expand our borders to incorporate Mexico and Canada and simultaneously further diminish U.S. sovereignty ... Now, incredibly, a panel sponsored by the Council on Foreign Relations wants the United States to focus not on the defense of our own borders, but rather create what effectively would be a common border that includes Mexico and Canada."

Christine Romans, CNN Correspondent said:

> *"On Capitol Hill, testimony calling for Americans to start thinking like citizens of North America and treat the U.S., Mexico and Canada like one big country."*

Former Congressman John R. Rarick said:

> *"The CFR, dedicated to one-world government, financed by a number of the largest tax-exempt foundations, and wielding such power and influence over our lives in the areas of finance, business, labor, military, education and mass communication media, should be familiar to every American concerned with good government and with preserving and defending the U.S. Constitution and our free-enterprise system. Yet, the nation's right to know machinery – the news media – usually so aggressive in exposures to inform our people, remain conspicuously silent when it comes to the CFR, its members and their activities.*
>
> *The CFR is the establishment. Not only does it have influence and power in key decision-making positions at the highest levels of government to apply pressure from above, but it also finances and uses individuals and groups to bring pressure from below, to justify the high-level decisions for converting the United States from a sovereign constitutional republic into a servile member of a one-world dictatorship." (30)*

One has to ask if it is the mission of the Council on Foreign Relations, or the people of this nation to redefine American policy or move this democracy into a one-world government. Perhaps, that sleeping giant that lives in all of us just may have something to say about this CFR conquest, even though these powerful multinational bankers and corporate leaders believe their financial power and wealth will prevail — for it will take more than money now that this nation is finally experiencing and waking up to the political assassination of our sovereign nation. The effects of the CFR and the TC on the affairs of our nation are easy to recognize when we constantly see our own Government no longer acts in its own best interest, or ever win the wars we fight, while we constantly tie ourselves to some ridiculous international objective that only benefits the *Money Barons*. It's not the working class benefits or world peace these organizations are after, it's the wealth and control and satisfaction of their love of money and power that drives their desire to rule the world. And now that the working class is finally beginning to recognizing their greed, perchance they will demand these now *Invisible Money Barons* pay for their egregious crimes against humankind. And perhaps these *Robber Barons* do not fear this nation's working class — but those that have planned this take-over; and those who have taken an oath to defend and protect this nation and its constitution — may one day find that they have far more to fear than they ever realized.

American Legislative Exchange Council, (ALEC)

The American Legislative Exchange Council, (ALEC), is still another very well organized national consortium of current and previous federal and state politicians and powerful international corporations involving thousands of members. Although ALEC claims to be a non-partisan public-private partnership with both federal and state governments, they are clearly lobbying to increase corporate profits at public expense. Of the 104 members of ALEC who are active politicians, 10 are active Republican Senators, while only one member is a Democrat. Of some 64 active Republican Members from the House of Representatives, only one is Democrat, while of the 30 members that were previously members of the House, here again 29 are Republican and only one is Democrat. (See Appendix III page 254) ALEC serves as government consultants and lobbyists, creating self serving Bills that use their own federal and state legislative members to jointly prepare policies that powerful corporations and their lobbyists and special interest members have prepared for current state and federal House and Senate members to later approve as written by ALEC members. ALEC drafts and proposes legislation for each state, bringing together international corporations and their partisan Republican legislators to write and propose a variety of Bills — many dealing with gun laws, and voter suppression and union-busting policies as well as a whole series of self-serving and controversial legislation. ALEC's national network of state and federal politicians and powerful corporations is designed solely to increase corporate profits without ever being scrutinized by the public. In fact, the public no longer has very much to say about what their appointed representatives are secretly promoting

The Federal Reserve

Prior to the 1907 panic, the United States had no central bank, which forced Congress to create a National Monetary Commission. As previously stated this Monetary Commission was accomplished under the leadership of Senator Nelson Aldrich, which under Article I, Section 8, of the U.S. Constitution, granted the Congress the power to coin money and regulate its value. In 1913, this Commission recommended the creation of a Central Bank, and as a result, J.P. Morgan, John D. Rockefeller, Paul Warburg, Otto Kahn, and Jacob Schiff all played a major role in the establishment of the Federal Reserve System. Remember, the Federal Reserve is privately owned and is not subject to oversight by either the Congress or the President. The Rockefellers; J.P. Morgan; Carnegie; Rothschild; Lazard; Seiff; Loeb; and Sachs families all together owning controlling stock in this privately held Federal Reserve and their international banks, which make huge profits by lending fiat money, money without a gold standard, which they create by the stroke of a pen. Franklin Delano Roosevelt first took this country off the gold standard during the depression, and without the gold standard there is currently no way to protect one's savings should any type of inflation occur. Other countries have also floated their unregulated currencies, since our global currency is no longer backed up by any standard. And since a large share of the international market is owned by these same powerful *Money Barons,* the dollar is essentially regulated by the market. Gold had previously served as one's protector of property rights, but today's out of control deficit spending has essentially opened the door to this powerful *Money Barons* scheme of confiscating the vast majority of wealth, which they currently control. And since these banks establish their own policies the government has essentially relinquished their tax dollars and their interest income to the *Money Barons* privately held Federal and commercial banks. Once again, as previously discussed, the Federal Reserve pays the Bureau of Engraving and Printing approximately $23 for each 1,000 notes printed. One million dollars in fiat money cost the Federal Reserve $230 for which these *Money Barons* then secure a pledge of collateral equal to the face value from the U.S. government. The collateral is essentially our land, labor, and assets, which is conveniently collected for them by the government's IRS. By authorizing the Fed to regulate and create money, recessions, depressions and inflations — Congress has given these private international banks the power to create their huge profits at will.

Prior to Woodrow Wilson's appointment as President, he'd been persuaded at the Democratic Party headquarters in 1912, on the importance of supporting the proposed Federal Reserve Act, and this country's first income tax in 1913. A national income tax was previously declared unconstitutional in 1895 by the Supreme Court, so it required a constitutional amendment, which was proposed and questionably passed in Congress based on the efforts of Senator Nelson Aldrich. As presented to the American people it seemed reasonable enough — income tax on only one percent of income under $20,000, with the assurance that it would never increase, which of course never happened. More assuredly, John D. Rockefeller had once again found a way to be sure his loans would be paid, and this was actually the start of the Money Barons scam that has now taken over this entire country.

The Shrub Dynasty

Author Molly Ivins first coined the word *"Shrub"* to identify George W. Bush — however, the secret evolution of the *"Shrub Dynasty"* and its previous close ties to the CIA, the CFR, and the TC over some forty-years, actually poses a serious concern for this nation's Democracy. This *"Shrub Dynasty"* can be traced directly to the Bush family and President George H. W. Bush's open promotion and support for the NWO:
Prescott Bush:

> *"Prescott Bush, the late, aristocratic senator from Connecticut, and grandfather of George W. Bush, was a good friend of Allen Dulles, the CIA director, and the president of the Council on Foreign Relations as well as an international business lawyer. He was also a client of the Dulles' law firm. As such, he was the beneficiary of Dulles' miraculous ability to scrub*

the story of Bush's (Prescott's) treasonous investments in the Third Reich out of the news media, where it might have interfered with Bush's political career . . . not to mention the presidential careers of his son and grandson. (31)

As is the case with unscrupulous Bankers and industrialists whose only motive is greed, Rothschild's dynasties have reportedly sometimes financed both sides of a war. Such as in the case of WW II and Hitler's Third Reich, for example, one of their former clients, (along with grandpa Bush who also traded with the Nazis). It was certainly a winning strategy for war profiteers with no morals. They win no matter who loses the war. But only in a material sense. Just as the "death merchants" and their financiers of the wars of the 1990s did." (32)

President George H. W. Bush Sr. served as the Director of the CFR from 1977-1979, but failed twice in bids for the Senate and in his campaign for the Presidency in 1980, before he was finally appointed to head the CIA.

William Colby, a former CIA Director once said:

"The Central Intelligence Agency owns everyone of any significance in the major media." (33)

When George H. W. Bush Sr. was appointment as CIA Director — that was probably where the *Shrub Dynasty* took root. Then later, as Vice President under President Reagan and then President of the United States for one term, and *"Overlord" of the "Shrub Dynasty,"* he openly introduced to the public the term *"New World Order"* in his State of the Union Address, on January 29, 1991:

"What is at stake is more than one small country, it is a big idea - a new world order ... to achieve the universal aspirations of mankind ... based on shared principles and the rule of law ... The winds of change are with us now."

The question was, did he really believe the United States was a small and unimportant country?

President George W. Bush, in his attempt to accomplish what his father failed to accomplish, a war with Iraq, somehow effectively assured himself of being a two-term president by involving this country in two very questionable and simultaneous wars. Later, he also accomplished a budget breaking deficit with his *New World Order's* controversial tax reduction plan for the top one percent of the wage earners at a time when the former administration had for the first time in many years finally accomplished a $236 billion surplus in this country's budget. George W. has often been identified with what many have referred to as *"Our Puppet Government,"* which was behind the scenes entirely controlled by his far more experienced Vice President, Richard B. Cheney. CBS news reported on February 11, 2009, that the Times poll showed George W's approval rate at 22% and just before the November 2008 election only 20% of the public approved of the job he was doing as president — the lowest of any president since the Gallup began in 1938. Clearly, this has ranked George W. Bush as one of the worst presidents we've appointed to this important position.

A list of the close supporters of George W., and his tightly knit *"Shrub"* circle of powerful friends can be found in Appendix IV p. 258. As you will see in Chapter 10 and this Appendix, family nepotism played a major role in George W's election to the highest office in the world. Based on all the close ties that were developed with his father and grandfather over so many years — this should certainly caution us to be more discerning regarding future nepotistic appointments to the Presidency of the United States.

In the words of Phil Kendrick, he briefly outlines some of the nepotism in George W's preparation for his eventual appointment to the Presidency.

> *"In 1986, Bush's tiny Texas oil firm, Spectrum 7, was losing money and hopelessly in debt at a time when George W's father was Vice President under the Reagan administration. At that same time, Harken bought Spectrum 7 for the grossly inflated price of $2 million and put Bush on both its board of directors and the company's audit committee because, "His name was George Bush."(37)*

Yes, George W. Bush owed his early position at Harken, and his lucrative stake in that company's shares, not to his display of business acumen or personal merit, but to his close family connections, which were later strengthened by the time he was appointed President of the United States.

Close family and political ties far too frequently present political concerns, for example: Richard N. Pearl, the Zionist, also known as *The Prince of Darkness,* and co-author of *A Clean Break: A New Strategy for Securing the Realm,* served as George W's Assistant Secretary of Defense for International Policy. He was also closely identified with Conrad Black, the former chairman of *Hollinger International Incorporated,* which owns some 400 worldwide newspapers that trumpeted Pearl's anti-Saddam sentiments well before the unwarranted war with Iraq — a news-media that controls almost everything this powerful political inner circle wants us to read.

> *"... in 1913, the Schiff group (who also runs the New York Times among other media outlets) organized the "Anti-defamation League of the B'nai B'rith" commonly known as the "ADL" to serve as the Gestapo and hatchet-man outfit for the entire great conspiracy. Today the sinister "ADL" maintains over 2,000 agencies in all parts of our country and they advise and completely control every action of the "NAACP" or of the "Urban League" of all the other civil-rights organizations throughout the nation. In addition, the "ADL" acquired absolute control of the advertising-budgets of many department-stores, hotel-chains, and TV and Radio industrialist sponsors, and advertising-agencies in order to control practically all the mass-communications media and force every loyal newspaper to slant and falsify the news. In short, the B'nai Braith was established in 1913 to ensure that anyone who criticizes the Federal Reserve owners is labeled as an anti-Semite." (34)*

In William Blum's book, *Rogue State: A Guide to the World's Only Superpower,* he warns of how the media will make anything that smacks of *"Conspiracy Theory"* an immediate *"Object of Ridicule."*

> *"This prevents the media from ever having to investigate the many strange interconnections among the ruling class -- for example, the relationship between the boards of directors of media giants, and the energy, banking and defense industries."*

These unmentionable topics such as the questionable destruction of the Twin Towers in the 911 tragedy are usually treated with what Blum calls silence.

> *"... the media's most effective tool -- silence." But in case somebody's asking questions, all you have to do is say, "conspiracy theory," and any allegation instantly becomes too frivolous to merit serious attention."(35)*

Favoritism also usually runs unbridled where family ties take precedent, such as "Scooter" Libby who lied to protect Vice President Chaney and later received a presidential pardon from serving time in jail — or George Tenet, the CIA Director under George "W" who questionably was awarded the President's Medal of Freedom for counseling President George "W" regarding the one-sided war in Iraq, saying:

> *". . . only an all-out US military assault can realize American aims," (36)*

And as a possible precautionary note, it's possible that the NWO will in 2016 be looking for another Bush family member such as Jeb Bush to serve as the future Dictator of their rapidly growing *"Shadow Government."* — *The New World Order.*

---

1 Trilateral Commission (TC), http://www.4rie.com/rie%205.html
2 The New World Order," Pat Robertson, (p.102) Copyright 1991, Word, Inc., Dallas, Texas.

3 James Perloff, "The Shadows of Power," pages 154-156, Copyright 1998
4 Trlateral Commission (TC), p.2, http://www.4rie.com/rie%205.html

5 Ibid, p. 2

6 Ibid, p. 3

7 Ibid, p. 3

8 Terms and Organizations ©, p. 2, http://www.sanspap.com/terms.htm

9 Ibid, p. 2

10 Ibid, p.3

11 Treasonous agenda of the Trilateral Commission, by Devvy Kidd, June 24, 2005 http://www.worldnetdaily.com/news/article.asp?ARTICLE_id=44965

12 Ibid, p. 2

13 Ibid, p. 2

14 Ibid, p. 2

15 The trilateral Commission: World Shadow Government http://afgen.com/trilateral.html

16 Sen. Barry Goldwater, Trilateral Commission http://www.trilateral.org/about.htm

17 Devvy Kidd, *"Treasonous agenda of the Trilateral Commission,"* June 24, 2005, www.worldnetdaily.com/news/article.asp?ARTICLE_ID=44965 - 34k - Cached

18 Terms and Organizations © , p.2, http://www.sanspap.com/terms.htm

19 Blase, William. "The Council on Foreign Relations (CFR) and the New World Order," Website p. 1-2, http://www.conspiracyarchive.com/NWO/Council_Foreign_Relations.htm

20 Ibid p. 3

21 Ibid p. 6

22 Ibid p. 6

23 Ibid p. 6 & Curtis B. Dall, 1970, "FDR My Exploited Father-In-Law:" Washington D.C.: Action Associates.

24 The Council on Foreign Relations Website p 2, http://www.unc.edu/~ltolles/illuminati/cfr.html

25 John F. Kennedy, Speech, "The President and the Press," April 27, 1961, the American Newspaper Publishers Association meeting at the Waldorf-Astoria Hotel, New York, NY http://www.archive.org/details/jfks 19610427

26 Ibid p. 8 & Phyllis Schlafly, Chester Charles Ward, "Kissinger on the couch," Publisher: New Rochelle, N.Y. 1975

27 Ibid p.9 & Kingman Brewster, Jr., in "Reflections on Our National Purpose," the 50th anniversary issue of "Foreign Affairs," the official publication of the CFR.

28 Ibid p.9 & Council on Foreign Relations Website. http://www.cfr.org/about/mission.php

29 "To Conquer the World," p. 1 *http://www.maxexchange.com/ybj/chapter12.htm*

30 Devvy Kidd, *Treasonous agenda of the Council on Foreign Relations* p. 1-2 http://www.worldnetdaily.com/news/article.asp?ARTICLE_ID=44841

31 Alexander James, *The Hidden History of Money,*p.46 portland.indymedia.org/en/2004/03/282679.shtml - 532k - Cached

32 Ibid p 61-62

33 Ibid p 47

34 Ibid p 44

35 Ibid p 47

36 Bill Vann, US preparing full-scale invasion of Iraq, 10 July 2002 www.wsws.org/articles/2002/jul2002/iraq-j10_prn.shtml - 14k - Cached

4

The Great Cover Up

International globalization has presented and enormous fiscal and political obligation for the United States — while subtly allowing the *Invisible Money Barons* and their NWO to intentionally destroy our budget and financial reputation as they recklessly increase the size and cost of our government. Not one American can with any assurance explain what our real economic deficits are anymore, nor do they understand the size of the tax burden this wealthy cult has created for our children. Yet Americans blindly sat back and allowed several large tax reductions for the top one percent of the wage earners, while our infrastructure's huge financial warring deficits spiraled out of control. Isn't it foolish to believe our tax dollars support this nation, when we know full well we can hardly pay the *Money Baron's* rapidly escalating bank loan interest, as the working class reluctantly relinquishes their benefits to these profit seekers? For example: We've obligated ourselves to more than two trillion dollars in un-audited loan expenditures for the unjust Iraq war, and we can see no results that would even come close to justifying such exorbitant and uncontrolled spending. We're told we have to build and maintain the most powerful and expensive armed service in the world, when Congress and the Pentagon admit that *"terrorism can no longer be fought with conventional weapons."* And with all this budget breaking spending, we found that nothing meaningful was being done that adequately protected our troops during the Iraq war, or our borders, our port authorities, or the implementation of our homeland security report — for which we received a second failing grade. In just six short years, our administration took us from a $236 billion surplus to a deficit we've never seen before; a deficit that exceeds sixteen and a half trillion today and is still growing — and although the working class is screaming to the high heavens, nothing has even been attempted by our dysfunctional Congress to stop our reckless spending. Only after almost going "Over the Cliff," did we take back a small amount of the ridiculous tax reduction we foolishly granted to the very wealthy that are currently earning unheard of profits. Isn't it time we ask just where all this bank loan and interest money has gone? And just why has this country's interest debt increased to almost two billion dollars a day — an insurmountable figure by anyone's imagination? Here again, it all seems to be a big secret, and unless we carefully investigates the money trail, we'll never know. Should China call for the payment of their huge loans to us, which some believe to be more than $30 trillion dollars — or should we have to redeem our Social Security loans, which equals a similar amount, this nation is doomed to bankruptcy, and that's only if we're not totally bankrupt already. In fact, we now have to loan money just to pay our bills, and yet we offer to rebuild other countries, when far too many American paychecks are decreasing as favored executive benefits and corporate profits soar to unbelievable new levels. And yes, this country's workforce is the one that's obligated to pay for all this, while being forced into lesser paying jobs as these international corporations hire illegal foreign cut rate help while some of our children are bringing home their school lunch to help feed their family.

This country's trade deficits started to grow disproportionately as early as 1975, and over the years these deficits have been steadily climbing out of control, with no action being taken by our dysfunctional Congress.

For example:

- 1995 $180 billion

- 1996 $184 billion

- 1997 $198 billion

- 1998 $298 billion

- 1999 $372 billion

• 2000 $409 billion

• 2007 $830 billion

Worse yet, these huge trade deficits are continuing to grow while the off-shore tax fraud by these favored international corporations has been completely ignored. To date, the US has bought over 3 trillion dollars worth of foreign commodities with loans from these powerful international banksters — which are designed to intentionally level this country to that of others through the following ineptly administered agreements:

The General Agreement on Tariffs and Trade (GATT),

The World Trade Organization (WTO)

The North American Free Trade Agreement (NAFTA)

The Central America Free Trade Agreement (CAFTA)

The Free Trade Areas of the Americas (FTAA)

In fact, all these programs are actually stealing directly from our public treasury — and on top of all this, the international corporations are even more aggressively exporting our jobs from America, as they intentionally reduce average salaries across this nation.

Does this ridiculous dysfunctional Congress actually believe God has sent them on this mission to control the entire world while they acquiesce to this ridiculous NWO at the expense of the working class, while spending our tax dollar as if there's no tomorrow? Well let me assure you, there will be no tomorrow, if we continue to let these privately owned *Tri-lats* take over our once sovereign nation under their crazy privately run International Monetary Fund, their privately held Federal Reserve and World Bank, or their New World Order. And if you look at all the overwhelming facts, our dysfunctional Congress is certainly moving us much closer to a dictatorship, as they intentionally flatten the United

States to the same level as the rest of the world. Worse yet, this makes us easy prey for those countries that are now standing in the wings waiting to see this once great country fail. Isn't this playing directly into Al Qaeda and the terrorist's hands? Could it be that these financial geniuses are intentionally planning to bankrupt the United States, and then ultimately the entire world market as they seek to skillfully colonize the rest of the world? And all this is being done while these *plutocrats* maintain such a high level of terror and fear that we're all far less secure. Didn't the Napoleonic era in France, Caesar's Roman Empire, Russia, Spain, England, and more recently the Hitler Regime already try this? Emotion filled phrases like *"Weapons of Mass Destruction"* and a constant diet of terror alerts shouldn't disorient us when our appointed politicians do nothing to protect us, or fail to provide any hard evidence of destruction by anyone other than their NWO. This type of military science may perhaps blind some of the population for a time, but in the end, there will be a growing and dissenting workforce that can no longer be fooled by such tactics.

In studying this nation's financial dilemma, it's also time we start penalizing the International Industrial Complex and all their crooked CEO's who are getting into trouble because of these wealthy plutocrat's and their reckless corporate deregulation. We've constantly heard how so many corrupt executives have been investigated by the Justice Department; the Security Exchange Commission (SEC); Congress; the National Association of Securities Dealers (NASD) and Self Regulating Organizations (SRO) — and yet, we see only minimal evidence of justice to the working class who are always damaged by such illegal tactics. So as this deregulation of ethics and standards has fired up hundreds of corporate scandals, which we've identified as *"The Great Cover-Up,"* little is actually being done to stem this malignant narcissism that has stimulated far too many ruthless corporate executives into a false type of self-adoration — all resulting in what has become a host of grandiose implications that should result in hard jail time.

Enron, World Com, Adelphia, Global Crossing, and K Mart all sought protection through bankruptcy. And Arthur Anderson, City Corp, Merrill Lynch, Piper Jaffrey, and Xerox, and so many others that immediately settled potential law-suites just to get out of the lime light. As you may recall, far too many employees and stockholders of Arthur Anderson and Enron were totally destroyed by their shady dealings. And although numerous lesser fall guys have admitted fraud, and pleaded guilty — agreeing to cooperate with the government so they can eventually get the big crooks — only a few of the real top dogs are actually in jail today. Tyco, J. P. Morgan Chase, Dot Com, Quest, ImClone, Dynegy, CMS Energy, El Paso Corp, William's Cos, Schering Plaugh, Bristol Meyers Squibb, Johnson & Johnson, Rite Aid, AOL Time Warner, Goldman Sachs, Salomon Smith Barney, and more recently so many more International Investment Bank officials who are supposed to be investigated for their criminal acts — while few if any are ever jailed for their flagrant crimes.

The decentralization of this country's healthcare system into uncontrolled competitive HMOs and Managed Care Units, also resulted in far too many corrupt healthcare CEO compensation scandals. In 1996, the American Hospital Association exposed a study of salaries paid to HMO executives in their *Hospitals and Health Networks* magazine. The title of the news release was, "Study Finds HMO Execs Are In The Money." The article said:

> *"The 25 highest-paid HMO executives received a median salary of $4.8 million in 1996, according to a report by Families USA, a Washington-based consumer group. Topping the list is former Oxford Health Plans CEO Stephen Wiggens, who made $29.1 million, plus $82.8 million in unexercised stock options. Firms with the highest average pay per top executive were Oxford ($11.7 million), and CIGNA ($5.1 million). Families USA faults the executives for balking at spending pennies for enhanced patient protection when making millions. Meanwhile, New York's Gov. George Pataki has blocked Wiggens from receiving a $9 million severance awarded after he resigned ... State officials say the amount is inappropriate in view of Oxford's $292 million loss last year. (1)*

Our dysfunctional Congress also openly allows favored off-shore tax-free international corporations to bilk billions of dollars from our tax, again solely at the cost of the working class. And of even greater concern is that far too many members of Congress are obtaining lucrative positions on powerful corporate boards or as officers in favored corporations because they previously turned the right politician's head. Do you remember how the Security Exchange Commission was going to investigate our Vice-President, when it was reported that Mr. Cheney held stock in Halliburton while he was in a position to grant or influence substantial government no-bid contracts to his favored corporation. And yet nothing was ever really done even though this would have been illegal, unethical, and a clear conflict of interest. Former and current political appointees, like George H.W. Bush senior's closely knit Carlyle Group, and Cheney's Halliburton have openly and disgracefully ignored such blatant conflicts of interest as they boldly parlay their political clout into profits from defense, telecommunications and aerospace contractors. Former U.K. Prime Minister John Major, and former president of the Philippines, Fidel Ramos, have also been somehow associated with the Carlyle Group, which has made huge amounts of money off our wars. George Seros, Prince Alwaleed bin Talal bin Abdul Aziz Alsaud of Saudi Arabia, and Osama bin Laden's estranged family were all noted to be among the Carlyle high-profile clientele.

Here are a few more corrupt CEO's:

Lee Raymond, a former Exxon CEO, who in 2005 raked in 190K a day, receiving one of the most generous retirement packages in history, nearly $400 million, including pension, stock options and other perks, including a $1 million consulting deal, two years of home security and personal security, a car and driver, and use of a corporate jet for professional purposes.

Sam Waksal, the former CEO of IM Clone, pleaded guilty to insider information, while **Martha Stewart** went to court and was sentenced to five months in jail for trading four thousand shares of Omnimedia stock one day before the FDA registration rejected the drug TCA.

John Reges of Adelphia, the former CEO of # 6 cable Co., received personal loans of some one hundred seventy-four million dollars. His case involved a private golf course his family acquired through his company, and apparently some serious racketeering.

Dennis Kozlowski, the former CEO of Tyco, pleaded not guilty to evading tax on some six hundred million in lost charges. He was accused of having his company purchase valuable paintings, an umbrella stand valued at fifteen thousand dollars, a two thousand dollar waste basket, and two sets of bed sheets for five thousand nine hundred dollars for his own personal use. And although he's been sentenced and is serving time, he was released far too soon for his crimes.

Press lord Conrad Black, Radler and other top executives of Hollinger International, the owner of the Chicago Sun-Times and The Jerusalem Post looted some $400 million. Black and his wife spent $23.7 million for Gulfstream IV and Challenger jets; $1.4 million for chauffeurs and house staff; $90,000 to refurbish his Black's Rolls Royce; $42,870 for a birthday party for his wife Barbara; $24,950 for "*Summer Drinks*;" and $24,763 for handbags. Black was also a very close friend of Richard Pearl, who helped influence this country's unilateral aggression against Iraq.

Bernard Ebbers, the former CEO of World Com, and four other Telecom Execs improperly profited from some initial stock offerings by Smith Barney, in return for their investment banking business, and were prosecuted by New York State's Attorney General, Elliot Spitzer in September of 2002. Included in this action was **Philip Anschutz** of Quest, and **Joseph Nacchio**, a former CEO at Quest; **Alfred Taubman,** Southeby's once CEO; **Stephen Garofalo,** of Metromedia, the Fiber Networks chairman, and **Clark McLeod,** the former CEO of USA — and on and on.

Nobody wants "*Big Government,*" but we do need enough leadership in this country to protect our human services to the working class. ("*We the People*") Allowing our bridges, dams, and mines to self destruct because we need to take care of the *Money Barons,* makes no sense at all. If the average American will take the time to investigate all the red flags that are being raised, they'll soon realize that these *Invisible Money Barons* have gained total and complete control over the following:

- The world's most powerful Military Complex

- The world's most powerful Intelligence and Homeland Security System

- The world's most powerful International Banking System

- The world's most powerful News Media and Propaganda Network

- The world's most powerful Industrial Complex

Note: In addition to this, we've blindly favored the international industrial complex and their wealthy aristocracy by allowing huge off-shore tax benefits, as well as way too many un-audited and no-bid war contracts in return for far too many secretive favors that are regularly bestowed on this select NWO.

In 1910, the US government debt stood at about $1 billion ($12.40 per person), by 1920, the Federal debt had jumped to $24 billion, or $228 per person. And then by 1960, the Federal debt reached $284 billion, or $1,575 per citizen while our state and local debts began to spiral out of control. And now, the Federal debt has passed $16,432 trillion — but worse yet, it is still growing exponentially. As a result, this country's national debt equates to $44,900 per person /U.S. population, or $91,500 per member of the U.S. working population as of December 2010.

You need to recall that in 1913, Congress passed the Federal Reserve Act which created this nation's Central Bank as a private corporation which was supposedly established to control America's monetary system. And then when the stock market crashed in 1929, Congress passed the Glass-Steagall Act, which separated the commercial activities of banks, such as savings, checking, deposits and loans from that of investment banking such as stocks and bonds. And now while we're still suffering from the housing bubble bailout, we're heading directly into a huge bond bubble that will be far more disastrous than the banking bailout we just experienced. Yet, in 1999, the Federal Reserve and the Clinton Administration passed the Banking Modernization Act, which once again permits banks to enter the stock, bonds, insurance and real estate markets — essentially eliminating the Glass-Steagall Act of 1929. This has allowed the Money Baron's commercial banks to syndicate securities, sell personal and commercial insurance and real estate, and thereby create an even bigger monopoly or conglomerate worth trillions of dollars. Congress also passed the Gramm-Leach-Bliley Act in 1999, which amended numerous banking laws so that the Federal Reserve became completely responsible for our financial system, with almost no news media coverage. So, the issuing of money has now completely replaced our government with a private profit centered business.

And what's even worse is we will all inherit this pyramiding debt, when this *"fiat"* (paper) money inevitably becomes valueless. Yes, when we pay our hard earned taxes, we are actually paying these *Invisible Money Baron's* loans and interest through their privately owned central banks. And we will never be able to repay the total debt because the taxes we currently pay barely pays the interest we owe their banks now. And when all this paper money collapses, which it will do, the Money Barons will restructure our monetary system, or start another war with another impoverished nation or China who is not on good terms with their inner circle. Worse yet, we're paying interest to these plutocrats on money which they created from nothing, through the authority that was openly granted to them by this country's fraudulent legislators. In fact, it was our Government that forced us into this mess by violating four common fiscal and monetary rules, as outlined by Alexander James in his book *The Hidden History of Money:*

> "1. *No sovereign government should ever, under any circumstances, give over democratic control of its money supply to bankers. It is the job of the people's Treasury to create money interest-free and debt-free.*
>
> 2. *No sovereign government should ever, under any circumstances, borrow any money from any private bank.*

3. No national, provincial, or local government should borrow foreign money to increase purchases abroad when there is excessive domestic unemployment.

4. Governments, like businesses, should distinguish between 'capital' and 'current' expenditures, and when it is prudent to do so, finance capital improvements with money the government has created for itself." (2)

Many now feel this NWO intends to soon create a dictatorship under a President of their choosing by declaring Martial Law under the disguise of still another major terrorist disaster, such as an expanded war with Iran or North Korea, or even China — or the inevitable depression we are doomed to experience — which has been in their long range plan since they first took over in 1913.

Retired US Army Colonel De Grandpre said:

"The trigger for the 911 activity was the imminent and unstoppable worldwide financial collapse which can only be prevented temporarily by a major war, perhaps to become known as World War III. To bring it off one more time, martial law will probably be imposed in the United States."(3)

Therefore it's important to carefully review the recommended policy changes you need to demand from your legislature, which are described in greater detail in Section II of this book. If Americans do not take action now, the financial collapse of this great nation is very predictable, and this will prove to be extremely painful for the average American family. But even more frightening, should we continue to follow the lead of these *Invisible Money Barons* — it will be at the cost of our freedom, which we've enjoyed for more than two hundred and thirty-seven years. And remember — ***this time we have no place to run!***

Alexander James in his book, *The Hidden History of Money*, outlines numerous quotes that you should take time to read. I have summarized them in Appendix V page 266.

1 Families USA,"Study Finds HMO Exces Are In The Money," *Hospitals & Health Networks* April 20, 1998), 71.

2 Alexander James, *The Hidden History of Money*,p.4
portland.indymedia.org/en/2004/03/282679.shtml - 532k - Cached.

3 Ibid p. 3

5

The UN &
The NWO Crisis

The United Nations (UN) is an international organization that facilitates cooperation in international law, international security, economic development, social progress and human rights issues. It replaced the League of Nations in 1945, and their stated goal of avoiding wars.

The League of Nations was an international organization that was founded at the Paris Peace Conference in 1919. Its goals were disarmament, preventing war through collective security, settling disputes between countries through negotiation and diplomacy and improving global welfare. The League did not have an armed force, and depended on its members to enforce its resolutions and its economic sanctions, only providing an armed force if needed. After a number of successes and failures, and with the onset of a second World War, the League proved incapable of preventing aggression, and as a result, the United Nations Organization replaced the League after World War II. It began with some fifty countries signing the United Nations Charter. The five permanent members of the UN Security Council, and the victors of World War II, who have veto power over any UN resolution are the Peoples Republic of China; the French Republic; the Russian Federation; the United Kingdom; and the United States of America.

As of 2012, there are 193 United Nations member states, encompassing almost every recognized independent state. From its headquarters in New York, the UN and its specialized agencies decide on substantive and administrative issues at regular meetings held throughout each year. The organization is divided into administrative bodies that include:

- The General Assembly

- Security Council

- Economic and Social Council

- Secretariat

- The International Court of Justice (ICJ)

And the additional bodies that deal with the governance of all other UN agencies, such as the World Health Organization (WHO) and United Nations Children's Fund (UNICEF). The U.N inadvertently promotes what has been referred to as the New World Organization (NWO), which was first promoted by the Council on Foreign Relations (CFR). See:

http://en.wikipedia.org/wiki/United_Nations

Testifying before the Senate Foreign Relations Committee on Feb. 17, 1950, and as previously stated, James Warburg (brother of Paul Warburg, who was the head of the Federal Reserve in 1913) delivered the following ultimatum to the U.S. Senate:

> *"We shall have world government whether or not you like it. The only question is whether World government will be achieved by conquest or consent."(1)*

Richard Gardner, Professor of Law at Columbia University said:

> *"Instead of trying to make the U.N. a complete world dictatorship immediately, the establishment will identify different problems in different countries. Then they will propose a solution, which can only be achieved by some kind of international agency, so that each country concerned will be forced to surrender another segment of its national independence."(2)*

State Department Publication Number 7277, entitled, "Freedom From War: The United States Program for General and Complete Disarmament in a Peaceful World," states:

> *"The Nations of the world declare their goal to be the disbanding of all national armed forces and the prohibition of their reestablishment in any form whatsoever, other than those required to preserve internal order and for contributions to the United Nations Peace Force." (3)*

On September 1, 1961, the United States Government filed with the UN's Secretary General a plan to transfer this nation's military establishment to the UN. This State Department plan described the complete disarmament of every nation, including our own National Guard, while augmenting an international peace force under the United Nations, thereby making the United States subservient to the International Court of Justice. The idea was to reduce this country's military capability to zero, similar to the current failed Nonproliferation Treaty. Under this plan, the U.S. would be allowed to maintain a small federal army trained in counterinsurgency to put down civil strife, since the World Court and the UN Charter does not allow the UN to act on domestic matters. If you take a moment to study this document, which the Money Barons proposed, you will find:

> *"In 1943, there was the creation of the Informal Agenda Group, formed by Secretary of State Cordell Hull . . . The rest of the members of the group, besides Hull, were CFR members, and the concept for the United Nations was proposed here, by Isaiah Bowman, a founding member of the CFR . . . The United Nations sits today on land donated by the Rockefeller family . . . In the 1949 meeting in San Francisco that drafted the charter for the UN, forty seven of the US delegation were CFR members." (4)*

In essence, the UN Charter is suggesting the destruction of our country's sovereignty under the NWO, in spite of the United States Constitution and Public Law 495, Section 112, 82d Congress, which states:

> *"None of the funds appropriated in this title shall be used to pay the United States contributions to any organization which engages in the direct or indirect*

promotion of the principle of one-world government or one-world citizenship."(5)

According to the UN World Constitution:

"The age of nations must end. The government of the nations have decided to order their separate sovereignties into one government to which they will surrender their arms."(6)

What's so frightening about this proposal, which was written by the TC, is that these privately owned profit centered multinational banks, and David Rockefeller's CFR, only seek total control of the United States and all other nations — a tactic that far too many nations are already disgusted with. This is why China, Iran, North Korea, and now Russia and many other nations are challenging the NWO by building powerful armies while expanding or protecting their Weapons of Mass Destruction (WMD), which only undermine these international treaties and are in direct conflict with this human service mission of the UN.

So the question really is, has the U.S. Government decided to surrender our national sovereignty and our arms to this One-World Government? In the case of American Communications Association vs. Douds, the Supreme Court declared the function of the people to be:

"It is not the function of our Government to keep the people from falling into error; it is the function of the citizen to keep government from falling into error." (339 U.S. 382, 442) (7)

So just when will *"We the People"* take a stand against such irresponsible tyranny, whom the NWO will label as conspirators?

On September 11, 1990, President H.W. Bush declared:

"The Persian Gulf crisis is a rare opportunity to forge new bonds with old enemies . . . Out of these troubled times a New World Order can emerge under the United Nations that performs as envisioned by its founders." (8)

What George H.W. Bush failed to explain was that the privately owned CFR and the TC proposed this NWO, not our founders — and this order first came into being on October 24, 1945. Few Americans really appreciate that George H. W. Bush had previously served as the Director of the CFR from 1977-1979. Then once again later, on February 1, 1992, H. W. openly explained at the UN building:

> *"My vision of a New World Order foresees a U.N. with a revitalized peacekeeping function. It is the sacred principles enshrined in the U.N. Charter to which we will henceforth pledge our allegiance."(9)*

Did *"We the People"* really understand, or ever agree to President Bush's treasonous act of turning our nation's sovereignty and military over to the NWO?

Cicero once said:

> *"A nation can survive its fools, and even the ambitious. But it cannot survive treason from within. An enemy at the gates is less formidable, for he is known and he carries his banners openly. But the traitor moves among those within the gate freely, his sly whispers rustling through all the alleys, heard in the very halls of government itself. For the traitor appears not traitor; he speaks in accents familiar to his victims, and he wears their face and their garments, and he appeals to the baseness that lies deep in the hearts of all men. He rots the soul of a nation, he works secretly and unknown in the night to undermine the pillars of the city, he infects the body politic so that it can no longer resist. A murderer is less to be feared."(10)*

General MacArthur also long ago saw this enemy within and gave us his warning:

> *"I am concerned for the security of our great nation; not so much because of any threat from without, but because of the insidious forces working within . . . and restore government based upon truth."(11)*

Even Congressman John Rankin tried to warn us:

> *"The United Nations is the greatest fraud in all history. Its purpose is to destroy the United States."(12)*

In the Congressional Record of September 14, 1962, Senator Benton said:

> *"We are at the beginning of a long process of breaking down the walls of our national sovereignty." (13)*

In Senate Document No. 87, Congressman Bernard Kearney said:

> *"We signed the resolution [U.N.] believing we were sponsoring a movement to set up a stronger power within the United Nations for world peace. Then we learned that various organizations were working on state legislature and on peace movements for world government action under which the entire U.S. Government would be submerged in a super world government . . . Perhaps we should have read the fine print in the first place. We did not intend to continue in the role of sponsors of any movement to which undermine U.S. sovereignty . . . The Charter (U.N.) has become the supreme Law of the Land and the Judges in every State shall be bound thereby, anything in the Constitution or laws of any State notwithstanding . . ."(14)*

The League of Nations was the first attempt to create a One-World Government, which alarmed many Americans who objected to losing our sovereignty. At the World Government Conference in Copenhagen in 1953, the UN recommended the following:

1. *That the United Nations be made into a World Federal Government.*

2. *That there must be universal membership.*

3. *No right of secession*

4. *Complete and simultaneous disarmament, enforced by U.N. inspection and U.N. police powers.*

5.   *International courts, world legislature, world executive Council be established.*

6.   *World citizenship through U.N. Membership, with world law applicable to individuals. (15)*

And worse yet, can anyone explain why close to half of the financial support of the United Nations, at that time, was provided by the United States?

The United Nations Human Development program on June 1, 1994 called for a reenergized world court; a world police force; a world central bank and treasury; a world trade and production organization to regulate "free trade" and production quotas; a global tax on pollution, savings and income tax.   And as a result, several Presidents that preceded President Clinton, signed the following Executive Orders in preparation for the President to declare Martial Law:

EO 10995, *which takes over all communications;*

EO 10997, *which takes over all electric power, petroleum, gas, fuel, and minerals;*

EO 10998, *which takes over all food resources and farms;*

EO 10999, *which takes over all means of transportation, highways and seaports;*

EO 11000, *which drafts citizens into work forces under government supervision;*

EO 11001, *which takes over all health, welfare and education functions;*

EO 11002, *which empowers the Postmaster General to register all citizens nationwide;*

EO11003, *which takes over all airports and aircraft;*

EO 11004, which takes over housing and finance authorities, designates areas to be abandoned as "unsafe", establishes new locations for populations, relocates communities, builds new housing with public funds;

EO 11005, which takes over all railroads, inland waterways and public storage facilities;

EO 11051, which designates responsibilities of the Office Emergency Planning, gives authorization to put the above orders into effect in times of increased international tension or economic financial crisis . . .

And on June 3, 1994 ... President Clinton signed the following Executive Order:

EO 12919, "This order places all federal, state, and local law enforcement directly under the control of the President." (16)

We can only hope that some future *"Puppet Like President"* doesn't incite a revolution or disaster, or trump up another war where a President could invoke *Martial Law*, which would make them a *"Dictator"* overnight.

George W. Bush was quoted as saying:

"There ought to be limits to freedom!" – May 21, 1999

"If this were a dictatorship, it would be a heck of a lot easier, just so long as I'm the dictator." – December 18, 2000

"A dictatorship would be a heck of a lot easier, there's no question about it." – July 26, 2001 (17)

You should also know that this country's judges take an oath of office to *"Uphold and Defend the Constitution of the United States of America."* But now, more recently, they've also sworn allegiance to the United Nations, which is actually a treasonous act and a clear conflict of interest similar to politicians and government officials becoming members of private organizations like the CFR, the TC, and ALEC, who all benefit and capitalize on such informal and illegal memberships.

General Lewis Walt, one of the most respected four-star marines and former Assistant Commandant of the Marine Corps, in his book, *The 11th Hour*, had this to say about these no win UN wars like Vietnam, which only make privately owned multinational banks wealthy:

> *"I had to provide the Communist Commanders of the United Nations a 24 hour advance notice of my plans . . . The enemy knew my every move." (18)*

Yet, when the General decided not to give the United Nations advanced notice, he was relieved from his command. Walt's outstanding speech to Congress as recorded in the Congressional Record, March 15, 1978, can be found in Appendix VI, page 271.

In that the UN Charter was drafted by 47 members of the CFR, wouldn't it be appropriate that as a nation we redraft a more democratic charter that benefits the working class of every nation? Predictably the UN Charter will never be successful if it remains under the control of these powerful *Money Barons*, who have an inherent conflict of interest in both the purpose and mission of the UN.

So where does this leave us with the UN and the NWO?

Don't you think it's time to inform this NWO that we as a nation have no intent of losing our sovereign democracy? Don't you think we should tell them they will not be allowed to overthrow our democracy as we reclaim our Federal Reserve and our Banks? Don't you think it's time for the UN to assume its correct role of providing human services to the United States and the rest of the world, forcing these *Money Barons* out of this money seeking monopoly and back into a free and open competitive market. Don't they understand that the UN is also an organization of the people and should never be used as a shadow like dictatorship? But more importantly, don't you think it's time to admit that we've inadvertently allowed these *Money Barons* to destroy the sovereignty of the U.S. by letting them set-up a One World Totalitarian Order under our own powerful Military? And as a result, this once respected nation is now rushing headlong into a merger with the devil, and a skillfully executed healthcare, fuel and financial crisis that will make the Great Depression look like a picnic. In fact, if *"We the People"* do not wake-up from this nightmare soon, this NWO will absolutely emerge as our ruler. On January 30, 1976, the "Declaration of Inter-dependence" was signed by some 128 traitor like Senators and Representatives that absolutely conspired to destroy our sovereignty. On October 28, 1977 the passage of Public Law 95-147; 91 Stat. 1227, allowed some thirty or more Multinational and State banks, to act as the *"Overlord"* of the International Monetary Fund.

For more information on this topic please see:

http://en.wikipedia.org/wiki/World_Bank - which discusses Bush's appointment of Zionist Paul Wolfowitz to head the World Bank. And http://www.federal reserve.gov/pubs/frseries/frseri.html, and http://en.wikipedia.org/wiki/United _States Treasury Department

According to Senate Report No. 93-549, this International Organization now has total control over the financial well being of this once sovereign nation. And the President's Office now has in place the full capability to declare Martial Law via an Executive Order, simply by declaring a national emergency, which any *"Puppet like Leader"* could do. Was America sound asleep when all this happened? So don't you think it's probably time to admit that Jefferson was not engaging in idle rhetoric when he spoke of our revolutionary right to challenge such tactics? Yes, it's now time for us to wake-up the same sleeping giant that defeated our enemies of World War II — but this time the enemy is within our midst, destroying our freedom and liberties.

Kenneth Roth in *The Law of War in the War on Terror* said:

> *"What are the boundaries of the Bush administration's 'war on terrorism'? The recent battles fought against the Afghan and Iraqi governments were classic wars between organized military forces. But President George W. Bush has suggested that his campaign against terrorism goes beyond such*

conflicts; he said on September 29, 2001, 'Our war on terror will be much broader than the battlefields and beachheads of the past. The war will be fought wherever terrorists hide, or run, or plan.'. . . Bush, however, seems to think of the war on terrorism quite literally -- as a real war -- and this concept has worrisome implications. . . . The Bush administration has used war rhetoric precisely to give itself the extraordinary powers enjoyed by a wartime government to detain or even kill suspects without trial . . . But it has also threatened the most basic due process rights." (19)

Wake up America!

We are in a war between the "haves" and the "have-not's," disguised as a "war on terror," both having existed since the beginning of time. And once again, *"this time we have no place to run."*

1 http://www.maxexchange.com/civic/ybj/chapter12.htm - p.1.

2 Ibid p. 1

3 Ibid p. 2

4 Blase, William=*The Council on Foreign Relations (CFR) and the New World Order*-
The Courier 1995
http://www.conspiracy archive.com/NOW/Coubcil_Foreign_Relations.htm p8.

5 Ibid p.2

6 Ibid p. 3

7 Ibid p. 3

8 Ibid p. 3

9 Ibid p. 3

10 Ibid p. 3

11 Ibid p. 3

12 Ibid p. 4

13 Ibid p. 4

14 Ibid p. 4

15 Ibid p. 7

16 Ibid p. 15-16

17 gwbush.com web site May 21, 1999

18 http://www.maxexchange.com/civic/ybj/chapter12.htm - p.10

19 http://www.foreignaffairs.org/20040101facomment83101/kenneth-roth/the-law-of-war-in-the-war-on-terror.html p.1-2

6

The 9/11 Crisis

The words, *"New World Order,"* were first publically spoken by George H. W. Bush, the undisputed *"Overlord"* of the *"Shrub Dynasty,"* when he praised this country's victory over the *"Cold War,"* suggesting a better life ahead — one which would be based on *"order."* In his State of Union Message of 1991, he was far more open as he spoke about our *"small"* country:

> *"What is at stake is more than one small country, it is a big idea - a new world order ... to achieve the universal aspirations of mankind ... based on shared principles and the rule of law ... The illumination of a thousand points of light .... The winds of change are with us now." (1)*

In an article by John Pilger, "Hidden Agendas," dated December 12, 2002, Pilger said:

> *"Two years ago a project set up by the men who now surround George W Bush said what America needed was "a new Pearl Harbor."(2)*

Richard Pearl, Dick Cheney, Donald Rumsfeld, Paul Wolfowitz, I Lewis Libby, William Bennett, and Zalmay Khalizad, the Neoconservatives who surrounded George W. Bush, (the Shrub Dynasty) and who were also founders of the "Project for the New American Century" (PNAC) — shockingly proposed at this unusual time of peaceful world order, an increase in arms-spending by some $48 billion so that Washington could create, fight, and prolong multiple simultaneous major theatre wars. They also openly said, in the event George W. Bush is elected President, Iraq should be the next target, and alarmingly, Pilger's published article in the year 2002 came true the following year. Later, in a Pilger interview with Richard Pearl, Mr. Pearl described his idea of a war on terror:

> *"No stages,"*— *"This is total war. We are fighting a variety of enemies. There are lots of them out there. All this talk about first we are going to do Afghanistan, then we will do Iraq... this is entirely the wrong way to go about it. If we just let our vision of the world go forth, and we embrace it entirely and we don't try to piece together clever diplomacy, but just wage a total war... our children will sing great songs about us years from now."(3)*

However; the absence of some catastrophic and catalyzing event like the Lusitania or Pearl Harbor, did not support such a "Pearl Proposal." And because the NWO's slogan was *'World Trade through World Peace,"* selecting Iraq as the victim would require someone to somehow blamelessly maneuver the U.S. into such an aggressive attack on a small nation like Iraq. World War I, Vietnam, Cambodia, Laos, Philippines, Somalia, Haiti, Croatia, Bosnia, Chechnya, Albania, Kosovo, Serbia, Sudan, Afghanistan, East Timor had all previously served the NWO well in their money making interventions and civil war provocations, and now someone needed to create another annoyance to send a weakened U.S. Military into such a perpetual religious conflict in the Middle East.

Having reviewed hundreds of books and articles on the September 11th attack, as well as the 9/11 Commission's Report, I could find no reason that this provocation wasn't well planned by someone, and perhaps it was to support the eventual illegal and preemptive act of aggression against Iraq. Because a terrorist provocation would certainly create high shock value and certainly considerable news media visibility, could it be that these International Neoconservative Zionists may somehow have found a way that they could covertly influence a group of Arab/Moslems to perform a second attack on the Trade Center, thereby igniting a full scale war against Mideast terrorism? Although no American in their right mind would ever want to believe such, wouldn't it be important to at least have carefully investigated this attack. This chapter describes the obvious efforts made to avoid a thorough investigation of this horrific crime, as it also carefully attempts to summarize the facts based on the opinions of professionals and the candid observations of those that reported and recorded facts and photos of the incident, before, during, and after the tragedy. One thing for sure, the staging of the 9/11 incident had to be very timely, no matter how or who planned it. It was also very clear there was no unbiased or adequate crime scene investigation of the destruction of buildings 1, 2, or 7 of the World Trade Center. In any event, this type of provocation was certainly news worthy enough to provoke Americans into once again fighting and dying for freedom. Barry Silverstein, the leaseholder of these buildings, and his documented directive, "to pull WTC 7" (thought to mean take down by demolition) may someday still help to prove that WTC 1 and 2 were also intentionally demolished after they were hit by these two pirated commercial jets. Alexander James in his article, *The Hidden History of Money*, said:

. . ."*they will have to admit that the same happened to WTC 1 and 2.*"(4)

In evaluating and analyzing without bias, all the findings, the findings are truly overwhelming and they would normally demand further investigation be conducted under some form of open public scrutiny, rather than just closing our eyes in fear. And yes, we as Americans have that right and responsibility to question our government's actions, which is neither unpatriotic or a conspiracy type act as so quickly suggested by George W. Bush in 2001: (Please review the Declaration of Independence on p. xii)

"We must speak the truth about terror. Let us never tolerate outrageous conspiracy theories concerning the attacks of 11 September - - -malicious lies that attempt to shift the blame away from the terrorists themselves, away from the guilty." (5)

This *"kill the messenger"* statement would never have been necessary if we had been told the truth, and we as Americans must always feel free to seek the truth. Then perhaps we as Americans can speak the truth and tell no malicious lies — nor shall we *"shift the blame away from terrorists,"* or the guilty once we clearly and honestly understand the unvarnished facts about the destruction of the World Trade Center. In studying — 9-11 Research.com.wtc7.net, — there are hundreds of books and articles on this subject, and a few of the good books that best examined the forensics of the core of the attack and the destruction of the World Trade Center are the following:

Books Challenging the Official Account:

- The 9/11 Commission Report: Omissions and Distortions by David Ray Griffin

- Waking Up from Our Nightmare, the 9/11/01 Crimes in New York City by Don Paul and Jim Hoffman

- Christian Faith and the Truth Behind 9/11 by David Griffin

- The Hidden History of 9-11-2001 by Paul Zarembka

- Facing our Fascist State by Don Paul

- The New Pearl Harbor: Disturbing Questions about the Bush Administration and 9/11 by David Ray Griffin

- Painful Questions by Eric Hufschmid

- Inside Job: Unmasking the 9-11 Conspiracies by Jim Marrs

Books Promoting the Official Account:

- City in the Sky: The Rise and Fall of the World Trade Center by James Glanz and Eric Lipton

- Debunking 9/11 Myths by David Dunbar and Brad Reagan

Books Documenting the Attack and Aftermath:

- Mayday! Mayday! Mayday! by Steve Spak

- Who They Were: Inside the World Trade Center DNA Story by Robert C. Shaler

● Aftermath: Unseen 9/11 Photos by a New York City Cop by John Botte

We also know:

> *"On the morning of 12 September 2001, without any evidence of who the hijackers were, Rumsfeld demanded that the US attack Iraq. According to Woodward, Rumsfeld told a cabinet meeting that Iraq should be 'a principal target of the first round in the war against terrorism'. Iraq was temporarily spared only because Colin Powell, the secretary of state, persuaded Bush that 'public opinion has to be prepared before a move against Iraq is possible'. Afghanistan was chosen as the softer option." (6)*

In the Los Angeles Times, William Arkin also describes a secret army set up by Donald Rumsfeld, which Congress previously outlawed.

> *"This 'super-intelligence support activity' will bring together the 'CIA and military covert action, information warfare, and deception'. According to a classified document prepared for Rumsfeld, the new organisation, known by its Orwellian moniker as the Proactive Pre-emptive Operations Group, or P2OG, will provoke terrorist attacks which would then require 'counter-attack' by the United States on countries 'harbouring the terrorists' . . . This is reminiscent of* <u>Operation Northwoods</u>*, the plan put to President Kennedy by his military chiefs for a phony terrorist campaign - complete with bombings, hijackings, plane crashes and dead Americans - as justification for an invasion of Cuba. Kennedy rejected it. He was assassinated a few months later. Now Rumsfeld has resurrected Northwoods, but with resources undreamt of in 1963 and with no global rival to invite caution. You have to keep reminding yourself this is not fantasy: that truly dangerous men, such as Perle and Rumsfeld and Cheney, have power." (7)*

The following pages excerpt passages from the accounts outlined in *http://911research wtc7.net.com,* which pertain to the observations of numerous aspects of the destruction of the Twin Towers involving the following:

Regarding explosions, Dust Clouds, and WTC 7 collapse fore-knowledge:

On August 12, 2005, the *New York Times* released some 12,000 pages of oral histories in the form of transcripts conducted between 2001 and January of 2002 regarding the accounts of the attack. Some statements that you may find interesting can be found in Appendix VII, page 274.

Demolition Technology:
ww.911review.com/means/demolition/index.html suggests the explosive destruction of the Twin Towers (and the implosion of the Building 7, which few people have even heard about) clearly identifies the key features of controlled demolitions:

> *"The destruction of each building was systematic and thorough, leaving no large intact structures.*
>
> *The three tall buildings were brought down in a highly symmetric fashion, each tower depositing its mass in a radially symmetric pattern around its central axis. Bringing tall steel-framed buildings down into their footprints is a considerable engineering feat since it necessitates overcoming the natural tendency of such structures to topple. It is accomplished in conventional controlled demolitions by the synchronized detonation of numerous small explosive charges, placed adjacent to support columns throughout the building. Through precise timing of the detonations of the thousands of explosive packages, interior structures are destroyed ahead of exterior ones, pulling the exterior walls toward the central axis in a classic controlled demolition implosion. Presumably the detonations throughout the interior or exterior could be simultaneous, or marched up the building as it sinks into its footprint." (8)*

It's common knowledge that off-the-shelf computerized demolition using explosives that are detonated by computer via non-wired radio links could have been installed in these buildings. For Example:

HiEx.bc.ca sells the *TeleBlaster* "VHF or UHF telemetry [sic] blast initiation system intended for commercial blasting operations.

> *"... Each package would have a battery powered radio link that connected it to the main computer. This master computer would be able to detonate specific packages of explosives at specific times simply by sending signals to the packages. ... After determining that the airplane hit the 77th floor of the South Tower, the master computer would be set to detonate the explosives on the 77th floor, and then 250 milliseconds later the explosives on the 76th floor, then 180 milliseconds later the explosives on the 75th floor, etc."(9)*

This scenario is certainly not far-fetched, yet no one was specifically assigned to investigate computer demolition or the actual destruction of the World Trade Center Twin Towers. The suggestion that explosives could have been planted in the buildings raises the question of how anyone wanting to place explosives in the towers could have avoided the security checks, but this also was not investigated.

In evaluating WTC Security:

> *"This question brings us to a possibly relevant fact about a company---now called Stratesec but then called Securacom---that was in charge of security for the World Trade Center. From 1993 to 2000, during which Securacom installed a new security system, Marvin Bush, the president's brother, was one of the company's directors. And from 1999 until January of 2002, their cousin Wirt Walker III was the CEO (10)*

One would think these facts should have at least been made public---or been discussed in the 9/11 Commission Report.

> *Marvin Bush's role in the company is also mentioned in Craig Unger's book (11)*

Here are some additional reports given by people who had worked in the World Trade Center, which may be relevant:

> *"Some of them reportedly said that although in the weeks before 9/11 there had been a security alert that mandated the use of bomb-sniffing dogs, that alert was lifted five days before 9/11 (Taylor and Gardiner, 2001).*

Scott Forbes, who worked for Fiduciary Trust wrote on the weekend of September 8 and 9, 2001:

> *"there was a 'power down' condition in . . . the south tower. This power down condition meant there was no electrical supply for approximately 36 hours from floor 50 up. . . . The reason given by the WTC for the power down was that cabling in the tower was being upgraded . . . . Of course without power there were no security cameras, no security locks on doors [while] many, many 'engineers' [were] coming in and out of the tower. (12)*

Collapsing Buildings:

(http://911research.wtc7.net/wtc/analysis/collapse.html)   Points out that on September 11th, all seven steel beam World Trade Center buildings were either totally destroyed or in some way damaged. The 110-story WTC 1 and 2 buildings and the 47-story WTC 7 building were completely leveled, and WTC 3, 4, 5, and 6 all had some damage. No steel framed building 'has ever" been previously found to totally collapse into its own footprint due to any cause or combination of causes other than controlled demolition.   In fact steel beam buildings have survived severe fire, hurricanes, bombing and even earthquakes. None have ever just collapsed or pan-caked as seen in this disaster. Fires far more severe than those observed in building 7 had previously caused no damage of other steel framed buildings and in response to the FEMA report, David Ray Griffin, in "The Destruction of the World Trade Center: Why the Official Account Cannot Be True," said the following:

> *In 1988, a fire in the First Interstate Bank Building in Los Angeles raged for 3.5 hours and gutted 5 of this building's 62 floors, but there was no significant structural damage (FEMA, 1988). In 1991, a huge fire in Philadelphia's One Meridian Plaza lasted for 18 hours and gutted 8 of the building's 38 floors, but, said the FEMA report, although "beams and girders sagged and twisted . . . under severe fire exposures. . . , the columns continued to support their loads without obvious damage" (FEMA, 1991). (13)*

Buildings 1, 2 and 7 were the only permanent vertical steel structures known to man to have tidily fallen into their own foot print without toppling over, except in situations where carefully planned demolition was used. See Diagram 1.

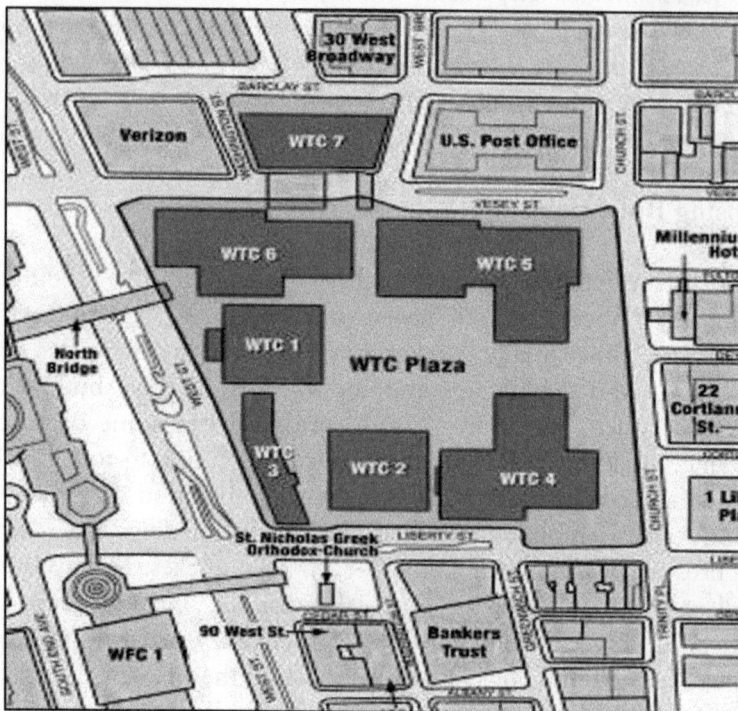

Diagram I

See http://911research.wtc7.net/mirrors/guardian2/wtc/WTC_ch1.htm p.4

Another interesting point is that none of the adjacent buildings surrounding the Trade Center complex were significantly damaged.

The North Tower - WTC 1:

911research.wtc7.net/wtc/attack/wtc1.html describes how the North Twin Tower 1 was the first to be hit by a 767 Jet (Flight #11) at 8:46 a.m.

on September 11th, 2001 — collapsing at 10:29 a.m. after surviving 1 hour and 43 minutes following impact. By tilting the plane on impact, the 767 tore a large hole in the northeast face of the tower, between floors 92 and 98, resulting in a huge external ball of fire and smoke. It was estimated that the plane was carrying approximately 10,000 gallons of jet fuel, and based on all observations it is thought that most of the jet fuel quickly burned inside the building. The impact was said to have swayed the upper floors, perhaps as much as 10 feet, yet three stairwells below the 92nd floor remained in use while the elevators became dysfunctional. The only piece of plane documented to fall from the North Tower was a small piece of landing gear — and what was thought to be (According to *ABC News* and the *Associated Press*) the unsigned and un-singed passport of hijacker Satam Al Suqami, which was found a few blocks from the North Tower. Although it was commonly claimed that Satam Al Suqami was supposedly on flight 11, this passport was later determined not to belong to Atta — suggesting the passport may have been planted as a prop to authenticate Arab involvement.

The evacuation of the North Tower proceeded efficiently after it was hit, via the three stairways, demonstrating that the stairwells were not filled with jet fuel as reported. In fact, the 143 minutes between the impact and collapse of the North Tower allowed a vast majority of its occupants below the crash zone to escape to safety, which indicates that the fire had not ravaged the lower section of the building. After the initial impact, fires could only be seen on several floors and around the entire perimeter of one floor for several minutes, while fewer flames could be seen from the north side of the building. During the first 18 minutes, the smoke was much darker as the jet fuel burned, and fires sporadically spread to new locations while burning out in others. Around 9:59 a.m. a large flame covering an area of about 40 feet appeared on the 104th floor just as the South Tower fell. Fires could also be seen in the windows on several floors of the upper section of the North Tower before it collapsed at 10:29 a.m. No one on the 91st floor or above is believed to have survived. The *New York Times* estimated that 1,344 people in that upper zone of the building perished. Smoke forced many to break the windows for fresh air, and it was confirmed that more than 37 people jumped to their deaths. A slight wind had kept the north corner of the roof clear of smoke, and helicopter rescues would have been possible, but the roof doors were locked. In less than fifteen seconds the huge permanent steel structure of the North Tower disintegrated from top to bottom into an exploding cloud of dust and rubble, leaving the unanswered question — do steel framed buildings really fall through themselves, turning into *"dust"* in seconds?

One hundred and twenty one Fire Department firefighters were killed when the North Tower collapsed, because their radios did not function adequately and it was stated that they did not hear the command to evacuate the building. Such a command should at least have been investigated as with any crime scene, since several reports indicate there was obvious foreknowledge of the collapse. When Mayor Rudy Giuliani, talked to Peter Jennings in a live interview on ABC News about his temporary emergency command center in building #7 at 75 Barkley Street, he said:

> *"I went down to the scene and we set up headquarters at 75 Barkley Street, [Building 7] which was right there with the Police Commissioner, the Fire Commissioner, the Head of Emergency Management, and we were operating out of there when we were told that the World Trade Center was going to collapse. And it did collapse before we could actually get out of the building, so we were trapped in the building for 10, 15 minutes, and finally found an exit and got out, walked north, and took a lot of people with us." (14)*

Giuliani has subsequently denied making this comment, which was recorded in his interview.

The South Tower – 2

(http://911research.wtc7.net/wtc/attack/wtc2.html) describes how at 9:03 a.m., a second 767 jet, (Flight #175) slammed into the southwest face of the South Tower on September 11, 2002 — collapsing the building at 9:59 a.m., surviving 56 minutes following impact. The jet hit the right side of the face at an oblique angle, creating a large hole that extended from the 78th to 84th floors. Upon impact, large fireballs emerged from the southwest, southeast, and northeast faces and the east corner where much of the fuselage emerged. It was again stated that the impact rocked the tower, causing it to sway several feet. It appears that a large portion of the estimated 10,000 gallons of fuel exited the southeast and northeast faces of the building in the fireballs that were observed. Unlike the North Tower, in which some fires were visible above the impact zone, the fires in the South Tower never spread beyond the impact zone. In fact the fires did not even appear to spread to the opposite side of the building, and these fires also appeared to be suffocated from the black smoke and soot that emerged from the point of impact. Before the building collapsed, firefighters were able to reach the crash zone, and they described seeing only *"two pockets of fire."* The elevators were working and the evacuation proceeded more efficiently than in the North Tower. Foolishly, someone on the PA system announced that the building was secure and people could return to their offices, which was fortunately ignored, saving hundreds of lives. However, when the jet hit the South Tower, it did leave at least one of the stairwells passable for the 30 floors above the impact zone, and the *New York Times* identified at least 18 people who escaped through that stairwell. Many people above the crash zone were not aware of this escape route, and at least 200 people climbed toward the roof in hopes of being rescued by helicopters, but again found the doors to the roof locked. The South Tower collapsed at 9:59 a.m. after a huge explosion of dust above the crash zone, and in less than 6.5-seconds, the top area was completely covered by the huge cloud of dust. Peter Jennings described the event as a controlled demolition. The whole sequences of destruction in both WTC 1 and 2 looked very similar, each falling in less than 15 seconds into their own footprint.

Building # 7

(http://911research.wtc7.net/wtc/attack/wtc7.html) Building # 7 was wedged between the Verizon building and the U.S. Post Office building, on the other side of Vesey Street, across from where building 6 was located. (See Diagram I, page 86) Surprisingly, neither of the adjacent buildings to building 7 was damaged by any falling debris. In fact, the collapse of Building 7 was remarkably tidy, and if you believe the FEMA report, building 7 was the only example in history of a steel framed building totally collapsing as a result of fire alone. There were twenty-four huge steel support columns inside WTC 7 as well as huge trusses, arranged non-symmetrically along with some fifty-seven perimeter columns, all arranged in an off angle building shape that defied any type of symmetrical collapse without the assistance of an implosion.

The 47 story skyscraper was occupied largely by government offices, and on the 23rd floor they'd previously completed 15 million dollars' worth of renovations including bullet and bomb-resistant windows; an independent and secure air and water supply; and the ability to withstand winds of 200 mph. This secure area was strategically designed for Mayor Rudolf Giuliani's emergency command center, but when the attack warnings were first given, Giuliani for some reason abandoned this special bunker that was designed precisely for such an event as described by the *New York Times*. Since Building 7 was not hit by an aircraft, it did not suffer the same damage that the Twin Towers did, and only a few small fires were observed in various parts of the building. In fact, these barely visible fires were not even hot enough to cause window breakage, yet the building was evacuated around 9 a.m.

Tom Franklin, a photographer said:

> *"Firemen evacuated the area as they prepared for the collapse of Building Seven."(15)*

Building 7 had a total structural collapse at 5:20 p.m.— also commencing suddenly and once again all over in seconds. After the penthouse dropped, the entire building began to drop, falling into its footprint in a precisely vertical fashion, looking exactly like a controlled demolition. Here again, after several huge explosions, only the rubble remained, with a few exterior wall sections on top. In fact, building 7 also sank at near free-fall speed, producing a cloud of dust the volume of the building, which is typical of conventional implosions. The entire collapse took only 6.5 seconds once the penthouse collapsed. A select group of volunteer engineers were asked by FEMA to investigate this collapse and in their report they outlined an absurd scenario, suggesting that fires caused the collapse of the building, but later admitting that their conclusion had a very low probability. If fires had leveled Building 7, it would have been the first case in history of fire alone causing the total collapse, or even the partial collapse of a steel-framed high-rise building. A rational look at the Twin Tower tragedy challenges the basic laws of physics, matter, and steel, as well as the design of these steel structured buildings. Structural engineers had previously determined these buildings could survive fires as well as the impact of a large 767 jet as validated by studies and interviews. British Steel and the Building Research Establishment (BRE) had also performed a series of experiments to study the behavior of steel frame buildings where the temperature of the steel beams reached 800-900° C (1,500-1,700° F) without collapsing. Some of the related facts that must be considered in the collapse of the Trade Towers include the following:

- The World Trade Center's designers anticipated jet planes of the size of the 767's could hit the trade towers and planned for this in their design. Their study included a 707 which is very similar in size to the 767.

- The fires in the North Tower diminished over time, and the fires in the South Tower were not considered severe before the towers collapsed. Building seven had only a few fires which were not either total or severe. Severe fires had never previously been known to bring down steel structured buildings in their foot-print; although steel framed buildings have been brought down in their footprint by skillfully planned demolition. More importantly, if a severe fire had brought down all three of these steel frame buildings, the buildings would have toppled over as the steel was weakened from the heat. However; this was not possible since the people exiting the lower part of the South Tower, as well as the firemen, had noticed no severe fires on the lower floors.

- Past experience with steel structured buildings suggests that in a collapse due to extreme temperatures, the collapse remains localized to the area that experienced the high temperatures.

- The kind of low-carbon steel used in buildings bends rather than shatters when heated. Steel strength is a function of temperature, and is expressed in degrees Celsius (C). At temperatures above 800° C structural steel loses 90 percent of its strength. If part of a structure is compromised by extreme temperatures, it may bend in that region, conceivably causing a large part of the structure to sag or topple, but not shatter. In fact, heated steel beams have never been known to disintegrate into piles of rubble.

• As stated over and over in the interviews, (See Appendix VII, page 274) the towers underwent explosive disintegration, supporting the controlled demolition theory.

• Steel structures are normally designed to withstand five times the anticipated static loads and 3 times anticipated dynamic loads. With these buildings the critical load ratio was designed to be well over 10 with an even greater measure of reserve strength.

• The fires in the South Tower were observed to diminish in severity, due to the jet fuel being exhausted within a very short time frame. Since kerosene (jet fuel) has a low boiling and a low flash point it would have evaporated or caught fire quickly. Subsequently the fires dwindled rapidly as observed.

• The fires in all three buildings were also not hot enough to produce significant window breakage in either tower. Window breakage is a common occurrence in large office fires where temperatures exceed 600° C.

• At temperatures above 700° C, steel glows red hot, a feature that is visible in daylight, but not observed in the collapse of these buildings.

• At least 18 survivors were evacuated from above the crash zone of the South Tower through a stairwell that passed directly through the crash zone, and none of those survivors reported extensive heat around the crash zone.

• Communications revealed that firefighters had reached the 78th floor of the South Tower and were implementing a plan to evacuate the people after putting out two pockets of fire, just before the tower collapsed

• Oxygen-starved fires (un-combusted hydrocarbons) produce dark smoke and soot, which because of its high thermal capacity robs fires of heat, and this was observed in the Twin Towers fires.

• The Twin Towers' totally collapsed virtually unimpeded. The speed of fall can also determine the mode of destruction. The Twin Towers both fell completely with everything but the dust reaching the ground in around ten seconds based on seismic measurements. Video evidence of the North Tower collapse suggests that it took close to 15 seconds for all the debris to reach the ground, which is comparable to the controlled demolition time for a building of that size. The CNN live video clip shows the mushrooming North Tower dust cloud reaching the ground at about 13 seconds, and a free fall object was later measured to take 9.2 seconds. If the building pan-caked, as suggested by FEMA, the falling rubble would have to crush every floor below the crash zone – tearing down the steel beams of the outer walls and the core structure which was observed to be intact. The idea of a steel frame building crushing itself as suggested by FEMA, would not even come close to 15 seconds in total fall time.

• The volume of the dust clouds also suggests the demolition of both of the Twin Towers, which exploded and immediately expanded to five times the volume of the towers within 30 seconds. If the collapses were merely gravity-driven, the clouds of debris would normally occupy the same amount of space as the buildings before they were slowly dispersed into the surrounding air. The massive dust cloud was a direct result of a very rapid expulsion of air, releasing heat and energy from an explosion. This question was discussed in quantitative detail in a

paper entitled, *"The North Tower's Dust Cloud: Analysis of Energy Requirements for the expansion of Dust Cloud Following the Collapse of 1 World Trade Center,"* by Jim Hoffman, on October 16, 2003 [Version 3.1]
http://911research.wtc7.net/papers/dustvolume/volumev3_1.html

Mr. Hoffman's paper shows that the energy required to produce the expansion of this huge dust cloud in less than 30 seconds was much greater than the gravitational energy available from the buildings elevated mass, and it uses basic physics to determine this. Only the detonation of large quantities of explosives could have driven this kind of cloud expansion. An anonymous author calculated that it took 14 tons of the high explosive amatol to produce this type of rapid expansion, which was incompatible with the official FEMA explanation.

The Science Committee of the House of Representatives said the FEMA-controlled operation actually restricted independent investigation. Steel beam evidence was immediately removed from the crime scene, denying the Building Performance Assessment Team (BPAT) access to vitally important crime scene evidence. FEMA also required BPAT members to sign confidentiality agreements, and then denied them the necessary building documents, which defeated any effort to accomplish an unbiased and independent study.

The Editor of *Fire Engineering Magazine,* Bill Manning, highlighted concerns among the firefighting community over the barring of investigators from the crime scene:

> *"Fire Engineering has good reason to believe that the 'official investigation' blessed by FEMA and run by the American Society of Civil Engineers is a half-baked farce that may already have been commandeered by political forces whose primary interests, to put it mildly, lie far afield of full disclosure. Except for the marginal benefit obtained from a three-day, visual walk-through of evidence sites conducted by ASCE investigation committee members described by one close source as a 'tourist trip' -no one's checking the evidence for anything."*

Manning also emphatically condemned the destruction of structural steel, declaring:

The destruction and removal of evidence must stop immediately."(16)

Manning also indicated:

"the destruction of the steel was illegal, based on his review of the national standard for fire investigation, NFPA 921, which provides no exemption to the requirement that evidence be saved in cases of fires in buildings over 10 stories tall." (17)

"On September 26th, Mayor Rudolph Giuliani banned photographs of Ground Zero." (18)

Did Explosives Destroy the Twin Towers?

Numerous Engineers suggest that Thermite (or similar reactions) was used exclusively or in combination with other methods to demolish the Twin Towers. Aluminothermic reactions are exothermic chemical reactions that oxidize aluminum and another metal at high temperatures. Thermite, is the reduction of powdered aluminum with an iron oxide. Because aluminum has a greater affinity for oxygen than iron, oxygen is transferred from the iron oxide to the aluminum, releasing a great deal of energy, instantly leaving molten iron and aluminum oxide.

A photograph from Dr. Jones report clearly shows yellow white hot liquid metal dropping from the South Tower, still hot as it nears the ground.

Journal of 9/11 Studies — September 2006/Volume 3
http://www.surfline.com/home/index.cfm p.12

In a well documented research article entitled, *"Why Indeed Did the WTC Buildings Completely Collapse?"* Journal of 9/11 Studies, September 2006/Volume 3
http://www.surfline.com/home/index.cfm - page 5 *(19)*

Dr. Steven E. Jones, a noted Physicist and Archaeometrist at BYU — calls for a serious investigation of the study committee's hypothesis that WTC 7 and the Twin Towers were brought down by impact damage and fires, rather than the use of pre-positioned cutter-charges. He presents evidence suggesting that a controlled-demolition hypothesis can be tested scientifically, and that the destruction of the Trade Center has not yet been properly analyzed in any of the reports funded by the US government. As a result, Dr. Jones has been put on paid leave pending further investigation of his study. In his research, he reviews thirteen reasons to challenge the government-sponsored reports and to investigate the controlled-demolition hypothesis. The thirteen points are summarized as follows:

1. Molten Metal: Flowing and in Pools
2. Observed Temperatures around 1000°C and Sulfidation in WTC 7 Steel
3. Near-Symmetrical Collapse of WTC 7
4. No Previous Skyscraper Collapse Due to Fires
5. Squib-timing during the Collapse of WTC 7
6. Early Drop of North Tower Antenna
7. Eyewitness Accounts of Flashes and Loud Explosions
8. Ejection of Steel Beams and Debris – plumes from the Towers
9. Rapid Collapses and Conservation of Momentum and Energy
10. Controlled Demolition "Implosions" Require Skill
11. Steel Column Temperatures of 800°C Needed: A Problem in the Argument of Bazant and Zhou
12. Problems in the NIST Report: Inadequate Steel Temperatures and Tweaked Models
13. NIST's Failure to Show Visualizations

Insurance Payouts

Author Don Paul investigated the insurance money flow surrounding WTC 7, saying:

"In February of 2002 Silverstein Properties won $861 million from

Industrial Risk Insurers to rebuild on the site of WTC 7. Silverstein Properties' estimated investment in WTC 7 was $386 million. So: This building's collapse resulted in a profit of about $500 million." (20)

By following the insurance money trail further suggests a far greater purpose behind Silverstein's order to take down WTC 7, in that Silverstein Properties was also the new majority owner of the Trade Center at the time of the incident. Silverstein Properties had just signed some 25 temporary insurance policies with multiple carriers on July 24, 2001, just two months prior to the Trade Center's destruction. Less than one month after the attack, the *Bloomberg News* reported Silverstein Properties commenced litigation against its insurers, claiming it was entitled to twice the insurance policies' value because the two hijacked airliners struck the twin towers in separate occurrences, entitling them to collect twice on the $3.6 billion in policies — and yes, the jury actually awarded the insurance holder double on their claim. On top of that, the leaser persuaded the city to dispose of the wreckage, excavate the site, and plan its replacement on the site.

The stock market also suggests foreknowledge of the trade towers destruction. Financial transactions suggest that selected investors reaped huge profits due to insider information. The following was observed:

- *Huge surges in purchases of put options on stocks of the two airlines used in the attack -- United Airlines and American Airlines*

- *Surges in purchases of put options on stocks of reinsurance companies expected to pay out billions to cover losses from the attack -- Munich Re and the AXA Group*

- *Surges in purchases of put options on stocks of financial services companies hurt by the attack -- Merrill Lynch & Co., and Morgan Stanley and Bank of America*

- *Huge surge in purchases of call options of stock of a weapons manufacturer expected to gain from the attack -- Raytheon*

• *Huge surges in purchases of 5-Year US Treasury Notes (21)*

Resurrected Hijackers

Of the 19 hijackers allegedly identified by the FBI as dead, the following were later reported to be alive: For more information see Appendix VIII, page 294.

> Abdulaziz Alomari
> Saeed Alghamdi,
> Salem Al-Hamzi
> Ahmed Al-Nami
> Waleed Alshehri
> Abdulrahman al-Omari
> Ameer and Adnan BukhariIn *(22)*

There is far more 9-11 information available, which will only prove overwhelmingly what took place — however, Americans have an obligation and a right as citizens of the United States to demand an unbiased investigation of this crime scene, even though much of the evidence has been manipulated and intentionally destroyed.

1 Alexander James, The Hidden History of Money, p. 61
http://portland.indymedia.org/en/2004/03/282679.shtml

2 John Pilger, *Hidden Agendas,* dated December 12, 2002-p.1
http://www.redandgreen.org/War_and_Peace/Pilger/Hidden_Agendas_Pilger.htm

3 Ibid p.1

4 Alexander James, The Hidden History of Money, p. 61
http://portland.indymedia.org/en/2004/03/282679.shtml

5 David Ray Griffin "The Destruction of the World Trade Center: Why the Official Account Cannot Be True, p 2, http://911review.com/articles/griffin/nyc1.html

6 John Pilger, *Hidden Agendas,* dated December 12, 2002-p.1-2
http://www.redandgreen.org/War_and_Peace/Pilger/Hidden_Agendas_Pilger.htm

7 Ibid p2
8 http://www.911review.com/means/demolition/index.html

9 Ibid p. 2

10 Burns, Maggie, 2003. "Secrecy Surrounds a Bush Brother's Role in 9/11 Security," American Reporter

11 Unger, Craig, 2004, p. 249, House of Bush, House of Saud: The Secret Relationship between the World's Two Most Powerful Dynasties. -New York & London: Scribner

12 Forbes' statement is posted at: *www.apfn.org/apfn/patriotic.htm*

13 David Ray Griffin, "The Destruction of the World Trade Center: Why the Official Account Cannot Be True," p. 7   http://911review.com/articles/griffin/nyc1.html

14 www.wireonfire.com/donpaul &
http://www.whatreallyhappened.com/wtc_giuliani.html

15 http://911research.wtc7.net/wtc/analysis/collapses/explosions.html, Collapsing Buildings, Building 7- p.1-2

16 'Burning Questions...Need Answers': FE's Bill Manning Calls for Comprehensive Investigation of WTC Collapse, *FireEngineering*, 1/4/02 [cached]

17 Experts Urging Broader Inquiry in Towers' Fall, *New York Times*, 12/25/01 [cached]

18 City: No more photographs of World Trade Center site, *AP*, 9/26/01 [cached]

19 Dr. Steven E. Jones *"Why Indeed Did the WTC Buildings Completely Collapse?"* Journal of 9/11 Studies — September 2006/Volume 3 http://www.surfline.com/home/index.cfm page 5

20 http://911research.wtc7.net/wtc/background/owners.html

21 http://911research.wtc7.net/sept11/stockputs.html

22 http://911research.wtc7.net/disinfo/deceptions/identities.html

7

The Oil, Water, Infrastructure, & Population Crises

Oil

Since this country's oil was one of the first natural resources that was placed on the competitive open market, it's important to briefly review what has actually happened to this natural resource over the last century. Oil has certainly had a profound impact on the United States as well as the world, and these same powerful plutocrats that now seek to control healthcare and the global economy, also control most of this country's natural resources, which originally belonged to the people when we first created this great nation. To better understand the fraudulent tactics the Rockefeller *"Robber Barons"* used in the oil industry, one needs to examine the history of the Rockefeller Dynasty, which established the first oil monopoly in this country — a monopoly that is still very much alive and well.

John Davison Rockefeller, Sr., was born on July 8, 1839 and died May 23, 1937 — 26 months shy of his 100th birthday. He was born in Richford, New York, and in 1853 his family moved to Strongsville, Ohio, where as an industrialist he sought to monopolize the oil industry — eventually becoming the world's richest individual and the first billionaire. In 1864, he married Laura Celestia Spelman, and had four daughters and a son named John D. Rockefeller, Jr. John, Junior would later marry Abigail Greene Aldrich, the daughter of Nelson W. Aldrich, one of the most powerful leaders in the United States Senate, inheriting much of that family's fortune in addition to managing the Rockefeller Foundation.

John Senior first founded Standard Oil in 1862, and rapidly became the most profitable oil distributor in Cleveland. Then in 1867, he and his brother William formed a company called Rockefeller, Andrews & Flagler, which added a silent partner in 1870 by the name of Stephen V. Harkness, before eventually incorporating the Standard Oil Company, with John D. Rockefeller as president. Cleveland was one of five major oil refining centers in the U.S., which included Pittsburgh, Philadelphia, New York, and Pennsylvania, where most of the oil was processed at that time. The Rockefeller Standard Oil's success was largely attributed to a secret rebate Rockefeller had negotiated with the railroad companies, helping Standard Oil become one of the largest distributors of oil and kerosene in the nation. And as expected, other oil distributors quickly asked for these same rebates, forcing the railroad companies to form the South Improvement Company, in a weak attempt to stabilize freight rates. Although oil would eventually have a huge impact on numerous human services, such as food, employment, military, trucking, the automobile and the airline industries, Rockefeller selfishly forced this natural human resource into the unregulated open market where the business of distributing oil could become both decentralized and competitive. No one even gave it a second thought that oil was a natural God given resource that originally belonged to the people, and required some level of regulation as an important resource to humankind. Because Rockefeller was the largest distributor, he agreed to support the railroad cartel if they gave him preferential treatment as a high volume shipper for all of the Rockefeller products. Part of his scheme was to increase freight charges for his competitors, which created a significant amount of complaint, once they discovered how Standard Oil was in bed with the railroad companies. A major New York refiner, by the name of Charles Pratt and Company, headed by Charles Pratt and Henry H. Rogers led this opposition, eventually forcing the railroads to back off. In the meantime, Rockefeller was acquiring many other competing refineries, while receiving discounts on their oil shipments through his under the table railroad deal. By 1872, Standard Oil had absorbed some 22 competitors, making it impossible for the other companies to compete against Standard Oil; and by 1874, he even acquired Pratt and Rogers. In fact, Rogers eventually became one of Rockefeller's key men; and Pratt's son, Charles Millard Pratt eventually became the Secretary of Standard

Oil. In that Standard Oil had now gained complete control of almost all oil production in America, and since this monopoly had drawn a considerable amount of unfavorable attention, the United States finally filed a sizeable anti-trust movement aimed at breaking up Standard Oil. However, in 1882, Rockefeller created a partnership that centralized all their holdings under what was called the Standard Oil Trust. But it wasn't until 1892, when Ohio utilized its long standing state anti-trust laws, to force a separation of Standard Oil of Ohio from the rest of the company, finally leading to the dissolution of the Standard Oil Trust. However, in spite of all this, Rockefeller continued to consolidate his oil interests.   Then by 1896, he was at long last forced to reduce his management role in Standard Oil; however, he did retain his title as president and kept all his stock. Then in 1899, New Jersey allowed the re-creation of a Standard Oil Trust in the form of a holding company, and this drew even more attention to Rockefeller's monopolistic practices. The 1904 publication of *The History of the Standard Oil Company,* by Ida Tarbell presents one of the more effective attacks on Rockefeller and his firm — and finally in 1911 the Supreme Court of the United States held that Standard Oil was an illegal monopoly, controlling almost 65% of the market and ordered it to be broken up into some 34 new companies.

A few of the name changes that occurred were as follows:

Continental Oil became Conoco
Standard of Indiana became Amoco
Standard of California became Chevron
Standard of New Jersey became Esso – later became Exxon
Standard of New York became Mobil
Standard of Ohio became Sohio

Since Rockefeller still owned stock in all these companies, he decided to become a philanthropist, so he could reduce his guilt, skirt taxes, and make even more money through his privately owned bank loans. Now all he had to find was a way to be sure his loans would be paid by promoting this country's first income tax in 1913. It's always interesting to watch the wealthy aristocracies attempt to make up for their ruthless tactics through philanthropy rather than paying their taxes, as they sit back and let their wealth work for them while they skillfully steal directly from the public treasury.

> *"A national income tax was declared unconstitutional in 1895 by the Supreme Court, so a constitutional amendment was proposed in Congress by none other than ...Senator Nelson Aldrich. As presented to the American people it seemed reasonable enough: income tax on only one percent of income under $20,000, with the assurance that it would never increase." (1)*

As described by Gary Allen in his 1976 book *The Rockefeller File*, this tax was to be a graduated tax which was designed to "soak the rich," but the rich had other plans. There was no way they were not going to devise a scheme for protecting their wealth.

> *"By the time the (16ᵗʰ) Amendment had been approved by the states, the Rockefeller Foundation was in full operation ... about the same time that Judge Kenesaw Landis was ordering the breakup of the Standard Oil monopoly ... John D ... not only avoided taxes by creating four great tax-exempt foundations; he used them as repositories for his 'divested' interests ... making his assets non-taxable so that they might be passed down through generations without...estate and gift taxes ... Each year the Rockefellers can dump up to half their incomes into their pet foundations and deduct the 'donations' from their income tax.*
>
> *Exchanging ownership for control of wealth, foundations are also a handy means for promoting interests that benefit the wealthy . . . With the means to loan enormous sums to the government* (the *Federal Reserve), a method to repay the debt* (income tax), *and an escape from taxation for the wealthy,* (foundations), *all that remained was an excuse to borrow money." (2)*

Monopolies that control the use of tax dollars through philanthropy, only diverts their tax burden to the working class, reducing the workforce human services and benefits programs. And although the Rockefeller Foundation may have accomplished some important philanthropic projects, there still remains a great deal of blood on Rockefeller's hands. In fact, the Rockefeller philanthropy was and is still often looked at as "*tainted money*" which was so vividly described in a 1910 *Puck* cartoon that portrayed Rockefeller trying to purify his money through some type of foundation machine. James Alexander summed it up very well in several statements in *The Hidden History of Money*. He said:

> *"By the way, all the silver and gold (REAL MONEY) from the U.S. is presently in Switzerland, guarded for the 'Illuminati Bank of Rome' by the Swiss Guard. Switzerland has served as a neutral meeting place for the world-wide Illuminati plotters and banking since at least 1812 when Switzerland declared neutrality."*

How convenient to become a neutral zone for the world's dirty business. Alexander also quotes the United Nation's World Constitution adding:

> *"...The age of nations must end... The governments of the nations have decided to order their separate sovereignties into one government to which they surrender their arms. . . ."*

Going on to say:

> *"Maybe Milosevic, the power-thirsty Communist banker, who bullied his way into 'Serbian presidency, figured out who really runs the American plutocracy masquerading as democracy – the men and women from the Council on Foreign Relations (CFR) and the Trilateral Commission (TLC).' . . . Barry Goldwater (a John Bircher) said that the Trilateral Commission was 'David Rockefeller's latest scheme to take over the world, by taking over the government of the United States' . . . David Rockefeller, . . . is sort of the 'Big Cheese,' the grand patriarch of the American foreign policy, who 'owns' people around him. Using the CFR and the TLC as instruments of power, Rockefeller and his associates have nearly all the political and media bases covered. In the end, it does not matter whether Republicans or the Democrats win. Either way, it will be the (Rockefeller) 'insiders' who will run the show in Washington. Which makes the 'world's greatest democracy' a little more than an intra-squad competition with the score always predetermined by the 'Big Cheese' and his cohorts!" (3)*

As a result of the Rockefeller's ruthless business tactics, this country will never forget the many violent labor struggles during the first part of the

20th century, which resulted in the appointment of a federal Commission on Industrial Relations in the year 1913. This was just before the southern Colorado coal strike erupted into what was eventually termed "*The Ludlow Massacre*," where three women and eleven children were killed the night before Easter in the year 1914 by the Rockefeller Robber Barons, at a mining encampment in Ludlow, Colorado. The *New York Times* vividly described John D. Rockefeller, Jr. and his disgusting attempt at denial of their brutal actions against the Ludlow strikers. Needless to say, the Ludlow massacre sent chills across the entire nation after the commission exposed the many horror stories about the brutality and greediness of this large Rockefeller owned Colorado Fuel and Iron Company. John, Sr. died on May 23, 1937, at his luxurious home in Ormond Beach, Florida, while this country was in the total grips of the depression – and in spite of all his philanthropic endeavors, he will be most remembered for his long and controversial career, where many of his former competitors were driven to ruin by his infamous, "*Robber Barons.*" Yes, John D. Rockefeller ruthlessly stole this country's rich oil and coal deposits from every American, and his fortune was estimated at $1.4 billion at the time of his death, placing his net wealth among the very wealthiest in history.

Biographer Allan Nevins concluded:

> "*The oil fortunes of 1894 were not larger than steel fortunes, banking fortunes, and railroad fortunes made in similar periods. But it is the assertion that the Standard magnates gained their wealth by appropriating 'the property of others' that most challenges our attention.*"(4)

Biographer Ron Chernow wrote of Rockefeller:

> "*What makes him problematic—and why he continues to inspire ambivalent reactions — is that his good side was every bit as good as his bad side was bad. Seldom has history produced such a contradictory figure.*" (5)

In an excellent documentary by Ronan Doyle entitled *Smoke and Mirrors*, which was distributed on October 5, 2006 and can be viewed on www.OilSmokeAndMirrors.com, he makes the following points about oil:

- Oil extraction quality is dropping significantly each year and is becoming slow and tedious to obtain at a high quality level, using more and more deep-water and costly soil extraction.

- Currently the world is using three times more oil than we discover, reaching close to eighty-four million barrels per day.

- Oil production has been estimated to reach a peak capacity of approximately ninety-five to ninety-six million barrels per day maximum sometime between the year 2010 and 2015.

- Once peak capacity is reached, it is anticipated that oil production will decrease two percent per year from that point forward, while human demand for this natural resource continues to escalate dramatically.

Although many people want to ignore these signals from the earth, and our one time God given gift of fossil energy to the people on this planet — we as a nation should at least be studying and investigating the human impact any reduction in oil may have on our human services to the working class of the world. One thing for certain, an oil decline is unavoidable.

Scientists have already concluded that *"World Peak Oil"* and the exploring for oil is no longer the solution with nine out of ten wells ending up dry holes, while perhaps only one in a hundred wells ever becoming a significant find. They know full well that drilling deeper than 15,000 feet is not the answer since 7,000 to 15, 000 feet is where oil is found in what's called the oil window, where the organic-rich soil sediments are hot enough to change into oil molecules — while drilling deeper, like 15,000 feet, the oil becomes so hot that the oil molecules are changed into natural gas. And every one of our politicians have been told that if we started today we could still not produce significant oil within ten years, which falls well after the shortage we're already experiencing. Yet these plutocrats have done nothing about it, and we'll need to someday hold them accountable, because they knew we have no renewable combination of energy sources that can replace the energy we get from oil. And yes, we need to take some type of legal action against these powerful plutocrats so they will never do this again, or perhaps change the Constitution, so we can get these dysfunctional two party politicians that are in eternal conflict out of office — maybe permanently.

The problem is, that all our current renewable energy combined cannot even begin to produce even a small fraction of today's industrial or technological energy required. And worse yet, if we continue to remain insensitive to this looming disaster, our debt-based economy that depends on economic growth to survive will soon be gasping for air because this finite global resource is someday going to run out. In fact we've allowed our current carbon emissions and air pollution to result in a rise in carbon emissions to a level of 390 parts per million globally, as compared to 280 parts per million prior to the start of our industrial revolution.

Mr. Michael Meacher MP, the former UK Environment Ambassador suggests that oil depletion can and will have a dramatic effect on industry, agriculture, transportation and travel by cars, planes and trucks, as well as this country's military ability to fight wars. Trucks stalled on the highway, rather than transporting food to the shelves of our super markets will someday have a dramatic effect on jobs and the world economy as a whole. In fact, any depletion of this natural resource may well promote the one event or conflict that will create an enormous economic shock, a shock that will inevitably increase competition and conflict amongst the major powers of the world. Doesn't this suggest an international conference rather than these wars to control the Caspian Basin, which is the second largest oil resource in the world? Could it be that these *Money Barons* see the control of this natural resource as their most effective way of controlling the world economy?

An article written by Edmund L. Andrews on March 29, 2007 entitled, "Ex-Auditor Says He Was Told to Be Lax on Oil Fees," explained the following:

> *"A former top auditor at the Interior Department accused senior officials ...*
> *of prohibiting him and other investigators from recovering hundreds of*

millions of dollars in underpayments from oil and gas companies that drill on federal land and in federal waters.

There's hundreds of millions of dollars, billions of dollars out there, and I don't think we should be scared of the oil companies,' said Bobby L. Maxwell, a former senior auditor who, as a private citizen, sued the Kerr-McGee Corporation, claiming it intentionally cheated the government of royalties for oil and gas it produced in the Gulf of Mexico.

In February, a federal jury in Denver agreed with Mr. Maxwell and ruled that Kerr-McGee had underpaid the government by $7.5 million. Under a law intended to encourage whistle-blowers, the company could be liable for more than $30 million . . .

C. Stephen Allred, Assistant Interior Secretary for land and minerals management, defended the Bush administration's enforcement efforts. 'I am convinced, after my review, that the M.M.S. is collecting the royalties that are set forth in the legislation' . . .

According to Interior Department data, enforcement revenue averaged well over $100 million a year during the 1990s, peaking at more than $331 million in 2000. In the six years since then, enforcement revenue has averaged about $46 million a year. In December, the inspector general of the Interior Department scathingly criticized the department's dwindling use of detailed audits and its growing reliance on softer 'compliance reviews' that rely primarily on company statements rather than sales records.

The inspector general estimated that the Interior Department had reduced the number of auditors by 15 percent since 2000 and was completing about 22 percent fewer audits than it did six years earlier.

'It does appear that we're getting ripped off, plain and simple,' said Representative Nick J. Rahall II, Democrat of West Virginia and chairman of the House Natural Resources Committee.

The Interior Department fired Mr. Maxwell in early 2005, one week after his lawsuit against Kerr-McGee became public." (6)

Infrastructure, Water, Carbon Emissions and Population

We as a nation do not understand what we're doing to our environment, and future generations will bear the consequences of our dysfunctional politician's failure to even attempt to meet this country's carbon reduction requirements and the need to halt the growing carbon emissions in our atmosphere. And because of this, we're seeing all kinds of warnings, like weather extremes and climate changes, temperature increases, and far more floods and storms. And with the world's exponentially growing population of seven billion human beings we're rapidly becoming seriously out of balance with the finite number of global resources this planet can ever provide. It is projected that the global population will reach 13 billion by 2075, and 26 billion in 2145, which is a population well beyond the earth's capability to support — however, this will never happen since humanity will have ceased well before that, unless we find another planet to over-populate. And since Americans are watching the roads and bridges in the United States disintegrate right before their eyes, perhaps it's time we stop playing these ridiculous money kickback games with our Congress, and direct some of the one percent profits to this nation's road and bridge repair. Worse yet, the world's water shortages are becoming extremely critical and yet Washington doesn't even want to talk about them. Isn't it time we at least begin to search for uncontaminated deep spring water, dig wells that aren't contaminated by pesticides and fertilizers, and help solve this growing water shortage and water contamination crisis? Yet, these dysfunctional politicians don't even want to look at a Master Plan for this nation's water or environment problems because they are too busy looking for donations from their favored entrepreneur. Water usage has tripled since 1960, with this nation's current demand for freshwater already requiring more than 64 billion cubic meters a year. By 2030 it is estimated that some 3.9 billion people will be living under severe water stress, and this nation's agriculture and animal and plant life are already being threatened, while adequate soil for plant growth has also been trending in the wrong direction. Because our politicians refuse to implement even reasonable carbon reduction requirements, melting glaciers and ice caps are dangerously depleting so much of our fresh water that it is becoming even more worrisome than our current energy crisis — and as a result, many of our lakes and rivers are already drying up. As glacier water turns into salt water, our shorelines will in the not too distant future be covered by as much as eight feet of sea water, reducing even further the amount of land for our ever growing population. Studies are also showing serious statistical links with water contaminants and neurological diseases, which have been estimated to increase to one in every three people over the next 20 years. We've already determined that residents who consume private well water and live within 500 feet of farmland where pesticide are used are almost twice as likely to acquire some type of neurological disorder. Paraquat was banned years ago by the European countries, but not in United States. And the widespread use of pesticides and weed killers such as Bromacil, Diuron, Simazine, and Atrzine have all been banned in Europe while they are still the most widely used herbicides in the United States. Why? Because, once again, our politicians don't want to put a damper on those huge kickbacks the very profitable corporations provide them. Sure we know which chemicals are the culprits, but what's the government doing about it — nothing! So currently we have no transition away from water like there may be from fossil fuels, such as wind, solar or other energy sources — however, we have no replacement for water. And we can't forget that water also has an enormous impact on food and soil irrigation. Therefore, the United States and the rest of the world all find themselves in a sustainability crisis that will inevitably destroy the ecological balance of humankind if mankind doesn't decide to act soon, by challenging these powerful plutocrats that represent us and are intentionally ignoring the entire world's global environment with complete disregard for the following:

- Air quality and climate

- The misuse of our environmental energy, water and the food chain

- The world's population crisis

- And the destructive deregulating and decentralizing of our transportation, education, retirement and healthcare systems

(1) Blase, William. "The Council on Foreign Relations (CFR) and the New World Order" The Courier. 1995. p. 3
http://www.conspiracyarchive.com/NWO/Council_Foreign_Relations.htm

(2) Ibid p. 3-4

(3) Alexander James, *The Hidden History of Money, See*
http://portland.indymedia.org/en/2004/03/282679.shtml p. 62

(4) John D. Rockefeller: Robber Barron or Industrial Statesman?, by Latham, Earl, ed. 1949, p.104

(5) Titan: The Life of John D. Rockefeller, Sr. Warner Books (1998). ISBN. Online Review

(6) Edmund L. Andrews, "Ex-Auditor Says He Was Told to Be Lax on Oil Fees,"March 29, 2007 http://www.nytimes.com/2007/03/29/business/29royalty.html

8

The Healthcare Crisis

Since healthcare was the first human service that was placed on the competitive open market, it's important to also review what has actually happened to this human service over the last century. Perhaps then one can better understand how this NWO intends to pillage this human service to the point where it will eventually collapse. Yes, oil as a natural resource and then healthcare as a human service is where it all started.

During the depression, no one openly disputed the need for FDR's healthcare reform proposal, but behind the scene, the rhetoric of the have's clearly opposed FDR's *New Deal*. In fact, they openly lobbied organized medicine's Republican and Southern Democrats to squelch any debate on healthcare reform by attaching the slogan *"Socialized Medicine"* to FDR's healthcare reform package. And because Roosevelt could not risk losing his Social Security program, healthcare reform was dropped from the Social Security package. However; FDR continued to support the opportunity for every citizen to enjoy good health by assisting selected states to establish private nonprofit prepayment programs under a single private organization called Blue Cross. This nonprofit prepayment program was initially operated under state enabling legislation that clearly declared Blue Cross *"not to be"* a profit insurance company, placing it under strict state and public regulation. Initially, Blue Cross paid only the hospital's bills, but then later, under considerable public pressure, they established Blue Shield to pay physicians. The *Blues*, as they were called, had two missions: The first was to pay hospitals and doctors adequately, and the second was to provide universal healthcare equally for the greatest number of people. As a nonprofit organization, the *Blues* had certain privileges; hence they paid no federal income tax, and in many of the states no taxes on the premiums they collected.

"Community rating was the trademark of the Blues." (1)

This meant that everyone in the community paid the same rate, regardless of age, sex, where one lived or how sick they were. The *Blues* program was an enormous success because there was a professional incentive to make equal quality care available to all without discrimination. By the mid-60s, some 82 million Americans were covered through more than 75 local Blue Cross and Shield plans, and for more than thirty years the *Blues* served as this country's only prepayment program. Over five billion dollars in healthcare was provided annually, and the program was eventually so successful it expanded to Canada, Puerto Rico and Jamaica. During that period, the *Blues* preserved confidentiality of patient information; they treated all patients fairly; and they and the healthcare field had cost containment programs that effectively helped to control healthcare costs.

In 1909, the Carnegie Foundation had commissioned Abraham Flexner to study this country's healthcare problems and present recommendations. And although the Flexner Report was a shocker, it helped tremendously in establishing the Blue Cross standards.

The Flexner report said:

> *"Medical education in this country has hitherto been such as not only to commercialize the process of education itself, but also to obscure in the minds of the public any discrimination between a well-trained physician and the physician who has had no adequate training whatsoever." (2)*

Flexner had recommended the medical profession rise above the consideration of personal and professional gain, and that's exactly what the *Blue's* program was attempting to accomplish. It also stressed the development of medical patriotism on the part of the physician, which was defined as:

> *"The duty of loyalty to the standards of common honesty, intellectual sincerity, and scientific accuracy. That sense of responsibility for its efficiency*

which will enable members of that profession to rise above the consideration of personal and professional gain." (3)

But many physicians still preferred the unscientific view of medicine as an art form without rules, regulations, formal education standards or laws, largely because there were none. Some practitioners viewed their license to practice medicine as immunity to any regulation whatsoever — but, the Flexner report stated it well:

"As a rule, Americans, when they avail themselves of the services of a physician, make only the slightest inquiry as to what his (or her) *previous training and preparation have been." (4)*

Flexner also recommended educational standards in medicine, suggesting that the moral attitude of the medical profession toward medical standards was seriously lacking, referring to it as:

"Scandalous." (5)

But more importantly, it strongly addressed the danger of competition in a human service, which has spiraled healthcare costs out of reach today. Flexner indicated that medicine required reconstruction in line with the highest professional ideals of efficiency and in accordance with the finest conceptions of public service, suggesting:

"When the uncontrolled proliferation of unqualified physicians, advertising, competition and money incentives occur, the whole plane of professional conduct is lowered in the struggle which ensues, each man (person) *becomes intent upon his* (their) *own practice. Public health and sanitation are neglected, and the ideals and standards of the profession tend to demoralization." (6)*

And this is exactly what is happening today. The report went on to describe:

"Promotion of medicine as a business rather than an ethical profession resulted in the general interest of the public being lost." (7)

Wars Change Healthcare

Almost all of the soldiers that returned from World War II experienced the terrible aftermath of killing and trauma, and vowed that war should only be a last resort after all other alternatives were exhausted. The wounded veterans then, as today, found that long term care in the United States was terribly inadequate and the required numbers of beds were just not available to care for so many wounded veterans of World War I and II. The Federal Hospitalization Act of 1919 was one of the first programs to assist in providing funds to care for World War I veterans, yet by the end of World War II, only fifty-nine percent of the necessary hospital beds were available. In fact, it was not until the advent of FDR's federal Hill-Burton Program that the Hospital Survey and Construction Act of July 1, 1944 passed. Prior to that time, hospitals were referred to as *"Pest Houses"* because they dealt primarily with epidemics and contagious diseases, and proper sanitation was unheard of as patients went un-bathed and bed linens were seldom changed. Most patients stricken with catastrophic illness or injury were terrified when they were required to go to the hospital, hopelessly resigning themselves to die there, while the wealthy were treated in their homes — usually by the most qualified physician available. Clearly healthcare in the United States was a two level system, one for the have's and one for the have-not's.

And to make things worse, the American Medical Association (AMA) at that time remained totally unregulated since regulation meant control, and standards were thought to be too restrictive. Colleges and universities had yet to define a clinical curriculum even though they were public service corporations supported by taxation. And although Flexner had recommended many basic educational standards in his report — his major objective was that all patients would someday receive *"equal care"* from properly trained physicians — which has yet to be accomplished. At that time, indigent patients, and injured soldiers received less than quality care, perpetuating a two level system. In fact, healthcare really didn't gain much momentum until FDR's government programs were implemented. Then when FDR died in 1945, profit insurance and the drug industry saw a huge market potential and immediately manipulated our politicians into passing the McCarran Ferguson Act — an Act that was designed to deregulate, decentralize, and derail this nation's once world-renowned single nonprofit prepayment program, which was then ranked 1st instead of today's 37th in the world by the World Health Organization (WHO). The McCarran Ferguson Act actually allowed profit insurance to unequally compete with the *Blues* — by allowing profit insurance to be totally unregulated and exempt from all anti-trust laws. Behind the scenes, the NWO had successfully bought off our politicians back then just as they have today, so they could move this human service into the competitive open market, where they could steal directly from the working class through their public treasury.

With this Act, profit insurance bought themselves a sweetheart deal, and as long as they were free to lobby congressmen, they were untouchable, essentially remaining free of all state and federal healthcare regulations. This Act dangerously set a precedent and opened the door for other profit seeking industries to invade the public treasury and lobby other human services such as our utilities, our highways, our education, transportation and our environment – while Congress blatantly ignored those that voted them into office by accepting so many gifts and benefits from corporations they became dysfunctional. By 1965, profit insurance was:

"skimming the best risks from the Blue's pool by offering lower premiums than the Blues charged," (8) — under a community-rated system.

Profit insurance offered groups of younger, low risk employees, lower premiums in this new profit seeking healthcare market. The strict state nonprofit enabling acts couldn't touch these private profit seeking insurance companies that could function without any regulation at either the federal or state level. Healthy individuals and working groups, tempted by immediate financial gain, ignored their community rated programs and were easily persuaded to buy cheaper, low-risk *"group tiered"* insurance policies from these totally unregulated insurance companies — a process that was termed, *"Bait and Switch."* Yes, these profit insurance companies sold *"group rating"* as though it was the same as *"community rating."* Of course the gullible public sought a cheaper rate, not understanding that each group would eventually increase in cost as its member's aged and required increased healthcare. Permitting profit-oriented insurance to compete with our community-rated prepayment plan was short-sighted to say the least, destroying all cost containment efforts and standards previously accomplished by the *Blues*. As profit insurance companies enjoyed these profits with minimal risk, they intentionally and methodically raised premiums for their high risk clients, who were slowly becoming uninsurable. Because of this, the *Blues* were increasingly forced to cover more patients with health problems, which profit insurance intentionally dumped by increasing their premiums to unrealistic levels. As a result, many of the Blue Cross and Blue Shield plans were forced to become commercial insurance companies in order to survive and avoid the state regulations they previously lived under. And because of this, many of the *Blues*,

"lost their tax exemption from the Federal Government,"(9)

thereby abandoning their mission to provide equal healthcare to everyone under their community-rated system.

Later, those clients that had jumped ship were stunned when they eventually became undesirable under what was called the *"Death Spiral."* In insurance jargon, the *"Death Spiral"* was commonly used to describe the results of group pool rating. Under group pool rating, the insurance company sells a policy for a year or two, creating a pool of policy holders. After a while, this group was closed, and from that point forward no new clients were allowed to come into that pool. The company would then sell the next group pool in a process called *"Tiering."* As those in the older pool slowly aged, the number and size of their insurance claims inevitably increased, allowing the profit insurance company to uncontrollably jack up that individual pool's rates. Healthy clients could leave a pool to get lower rates, but older clients, women of child-bearing age, and those in poor health couldn't obtain new policies to cover preexisting health problems. Eventually, the premiums in this group pool were raised so high (sometimes thousands of dollars a month) they were forced to quit and become members of the increasing number of uninsured, thereby entering the *"Death Spiral."* Within a very short time this country suddenly had over forty-seven million people uninsured, while another sixty million stood in the wings waiting to lose their coverage when they became uninsurable. After paying into a program for so many years, policy holders eventually found themselves on the outside looking in, without any control or regulation, and this is what eventually happened to almost everyone. Worse yet, the NWO and most of the Republican Party and a few southern Democrats now want to take Medicare and Medicaid away from our sick and indigent.

And more recently, the pharmaceutical houses have also joined this shadow government, as they ruthlessly market our sick and disabled who have little choice in what they receive for their dollar. In fact, these pharmaceutical houses spend more by constantly bombarding us with their advertising than the drugs cost themselves — and yes, here again we indirectly pay for that added advertising burden. Advertising in healthcare was once considered unethical, back when the *Blues* regulated this human service to the working class. A study by Sharon L. Davis, a Budget Analyst in the U.S. Department of Commerce, confirms the seriousness of this problem, as she documents the unbelievable percent of markup in drugs in the United States, which ranged from a high of 80,362% to 2,898%. (See Appendix IX, page 296) Canada buys drugs at a lower cost because they have a single prepayment system negotiating the cost, while we pay a far greater price in today's open and confusing decentralized market.

Following World War II, FDR's publicly financed Hill-Burton program had provided $850 million of our tax dollars for the construction of medical facilities, all coordinated by the federal government. The primary thrust of this Hill-Burton program was to assist in construction of public, nonprofit, community healthcare facilities, providing adequate hospital and clinic services. Under this program the government assisted healthcare facilities in obtaining forty-year loans for construction at one percent interest per year, to be matched with federal funds. However, the government only provided matching funds to nonprofit institutions that agreed to the stipulations of the Act, which required they comply with their then available "Area-Wide Planning and Cost Containment Programs" for healthcare facilities. Local area-wide planning agencies were established to review and enforce facility and equipment standards within each tax supported area, and this is the type of local involvement that is so desperately needed today. As a result, clinic and hospital construction has become haphazard and is currently in a costly and competitive state of disarray. But in spite of all this, the Hill-Burton program truly did advance hospitals remarkably, by setting standards and trying to treat patients equally.

The Veterans Administration (VA) also developed very costly and comprehensive healthcare facilities following World War II, again at the tax payer's expense. These facilities included comprehensive hospital, nursing home, domiciliary, and outpatient medical and dental care — operating 172 hospital medical centers, 27 domiciliaries, 260 outpatient clinics, 122 nursing homecare units, and almost 200 outreach centers throughout the United States, the Commonwealth of Puerto Rico, and the Republic of the Philippines. These facilities provided improved service to 27.5 million World War II veterans and 76.4 million of their dependents until these services were intentionally cut by our dysfunctional Congress in 1988. These facilities and services also assisted in the education of physicians, dentists and many other healthcare professionals, which suggests that the VA system could have been easily expanded to a comprehensive program for all U.S. inpatient care. These outpatient services also efficiently ringed these medical centers that were strategically located so that they were within convenient driving distance to almost every location throughout the United States. All these facilities were a graphic demonstration of the base hospital concept; efficient patient referral; and cost-effective treatment. Together, these VA facilities constituted the largest healthcare system in the free world, but as peace prevailed and the United Nations came into being, the need for soldiers to risk their lives defending their country diminished, that was until our most recent unilateral acts of aggression.

It should also be noted that the United States Air Force maintains more than sixty hospitals, medical centers and regional centers, and the United States Army, Navy and Coast Guard provides even more healthcare facilities for those who are serving their country. The United States Public Health Service Indian Hospitals number more than forty, along with four Penitentiary Hospitals and a Penitentiary Medical Center, all providing healthcare benefits to those to whom the country has provided a service, as well to those who have done a disservice to the country. All paid for by you, even though most people don't have a clue of how much they are really paying for healthcare over and above their direct cost, which has now become totally out of control. Even the Abu Ghraib prison is financed by our tax dollar. Had the VA system been properly coordinated with the Blue Cross and Hill-Burton programs, as originally planned, they may well have expanded into an outstanding cost effective single comprehensive nonprofit healthcare service to all humanity.

The Healthcare Fraud

Prior to 1945, most Blue Cross and Blue Shield members received partial coverage through Medicare and Medicaid and their fringe benefits from their job, while World War II soldiers, government employees and our dysfunctional Congress and prison inmates, received full healthcare benefits from the government. For example: The United State's House of Representatives and Senate receive and enjoy comprehensive government health insurance benefits under the Federal Employees Health Benefits Program (FEHB) and are individually able to select from among several health benefit plans. Participation in their FHEB program is on a voluntary contributory basis, and based on the Health Care Benefit program the individual congress member selects, they will currently pay the lowest rates of any other health care program in the nation. This however, still leaves a sizable gap in the number of citizens that can afford healthcare coverage, and those that cannot.

President Harry Truman, in order to solve what had become known as *"The Gap"* — on September 6, 1945, proposed a Universal Healthcare Plan that included an Economic Bill of Rights for every American. Like Franklin Roosevelt, and almost every president since, he described every citizen's right to adequate medical care:

> *"The right to enjoy good health ... and the right to adequate protection from the economic fears of sickness." (10)*

But once again the profit insurance lobbyists, with the help of organized medicine launched a very expensive campaign against Truman's *"Gap"* proposal, using the phrase *"Socialized Medicine,"* as threats of communism ravaged the country at that time, along with the steady diet of fear tactics used today. Truman and everyone that supported the reform were all identified as left-wing communists trying to create a socialistic state. Of course Truman lost the battle, and the term *"Socialized Medicine"* rather than *"Employee Benefit"* has been permanently fixed to healthcare reform ever since.

President Lyndon B. Johnson, had also tried to fill the *"Gap"* by signing into law several amendments to the Social Security Act of July 30, 1935. This amendment established Medicare and Medicaid as a partial federal healthcare program specifically for persons over 65 years of age, including the disabled and elderly that were not employed and couldn't afford coverage. Medicare (Title XVIII of the Social Security Act of 1965) is funded through Social Security contributions, monthly premiums from its members, and general revenue — all paid by the taxpayer. Hospital coverage (Part A) provides short-stay hospital care, limited post hospital care in skilled nursing facilities, and home healthcare services. Supplementary care (Part B) helps to partially pay physicians, outpatient, hospital, home health, and ambulatory care. In 1972, a cost control amendment set reasonable cost-control measures for hospitals due to the unanticipated growth in the program. Then in 1979, the Carter Caps Amendment placed fixed limits on payments, requiring local Professional Standards Review Organizations (PSRO's) to review the necessity and appropriateness of hospital patient care, and these committees were shocked by the amount of abuse they found. Next, competition for reducing cost was promoted through the Tax Equity and Fiscal Responsibility Act of 1982, but most noteworthy among all hospital cost containment programs was the 1983 amendment altering Medicare payments to hospitals from a cost-based reimbursement system to a prospective payment system based on Diagnostic Related Groupings of Diseases. (DRGs) Surprisingly, this amendment set cost standards for the first time based on patient diagnosis, treatment and prescription orders. This author served on the first DRG committee in Washington D.C. and these initial DRG standards actually enabled Medicare to determine the cost of a patient product in advance for a given diagnosis — something organized medicine really didn't want to see. However, DRGs did open the door to a potentially powerful new concept, that of setting clinical standards for the treatment of patients. Another dramatic expansion was the Medicare Catastrophic Coverage Act of 1988, which required beneficiaries to pay the full cost of expanded benefits via an income-related tax surcharge and a flat premium — substantially reducing abusive patient and physician overuse. Out of fear for losing physician support, the Congress hadn't previously focused on problems dealing with physician reimbursement until 1984, when the Deficit Reduction Act froze maximum payments to physicians and introduced the idea of Participating Physicians accepting the allowable fee as full payment for all Medicare claims for a one-year period — and you can imagine how that went over. Since the number of participating physicians was in the minority, the freeze ended in 1987. Far too many uncooperative physicians refused any form of control as they either cheated on the system or did not participate in the Medicare program. Rather than solve this problem, our Congress backed off, as physicians intensified their political pressure. In the long run, Medicare and Medicaid had actually benefited the profit insurance business tremendously by acquiring their costly high-risk patients, thus allowing profit insurance to become even more profitable, under the same old two level systems.

Medicaid, Title XIX of the Social Security Act was established as still another means-tested entitlement program to provide medical assistance to low-income persons who were aged, blind, disabled, pregnant, or members of families with dependent children, and each state designed and administered its own program. Under this program, the state was required to meet standards set by the Federal Government before they'd be reimbursed for 50 to 80 percent of their costs, depending on the average income for each state — and once again this was paid by the tax payer. Under this program, the states covered hospital and physicians' services; care in skilled nursing facilities; home health services; family planning; and the early and periodic screening, diagnosis and treatment of Medicaid patients under the age of twenty-one. Care of the mentally retarded was provided in an Intermediate Care Facility (ICF). Medicaid also emerged as an important source of coverage for patients with

Acquired Immune Deficiency Syndrome (AIDS), as well as nursing home care for the aged. Amendments to the Social Security Act in 1972 limited expenditure increases and extended coverage to the Supplemental Security Income (SSI). Recently the mentally retarded (ICF) program has been substantially reduced by Congress, placing thousands of mentally ill patients on the street amongst the growing homeless — resulting in the many recent crimes like the recent "Sandy Hook Elementary School Shooting." In 1984, concern for infant mortality resulted in the extension of coverage to pregnant women and infants below the poverty line. Under the Medicaid program, more than 25 million people receive medical services, and in 1998, there were still some 38 million beneficiaries enrolled in Medicare. President Lyndon Johnson referred to the Medicare and Medicaid programs as:

> *"The largest management effort this nation had undertaken since the Normandy invasion."*(11)

The younger population praised the universal aspects of Medicare because it provided security for their parents and themselves someday, but it certainly hasn't been without problems. Far too many physicians openly boycotted and cheated on the program, while some physicians boldly refuse to accept Medicare and Medicaid patients, a discrimination that contravenes our democratic principles as well as the physician's own Hippocratic Oath. In fact, refusing Medicare patient's equal access to healthcare clearly violates this country's anti-discrimination and equal rights principles. In challenging Medicare, physicians challenged the people, creating a double standard of care that takes patients back to the nineteenth century, rather than negotiate an adequate reimbursement for the physician.

President Richard Nixon was also very much aware of healthcare reform, by forcing it to the forefront when he said,

> *"We face a massive crises in [health] . . . a breakdown in our medical care system. Things do not have to be this way. We can change these conditions — indeed we must change them — if we are to fulfill our promise as a nation. Good healthcare should be readily available to all our citizens."* (12)

123

These comments resulted in the House Ways and Means Committee holding extensive hearings in 1971, but organized medicine and profit insurance once again moved to prevent what they had identified as *"Socialized Medicine"* instead of a working class *"Benefit."* The politician's primary excuse for their inaction at that time was the need to wait until the inflationary spiral in healthcare was brought under control, knowing full well that any control at all was impossible under today's decentralized and deregulated system.

President Ronald Reagan openly discouraged the concept that healthcare was a right rather than a privilege, even though the workforce pays for all these programs. Faithful to the Republican Party, he promoted competition, deregulation, and decentralization, while his concern over the deficit deflated any further discussion of domestic-policy or social incentives. His words, *"Big Government,"* were as effective as *"Socialized Medicine,"* and his corporate welfare attitude soon replaced the workforce's *Benefits* — thereby, discouraging the social justice efforts of Lyndon Johnson. It wasn't "Big Government," it was "Profit Insurance" and the powerful "Pharmaceutical Houses" that replaced our once internationally renowned Nonprofit Prepayment Benefit System, which was once ranked 1st instead of 37th in the world.

President George H. W. Bush, on February 6, 1992 announced his "Comprehensive Health Reform Program," which was to guarantee access to affordable healthcare coverage through transferable health insurance tax credits for the poor and a tax deduction for the middle class. He stated that these credit certificates could be used to buy insurance, just as if it wasn't our money in the first place. His administration intensely lobbied to transfer the entire healthcare system to these decentralized competitive profit-oriented managed care monopolies in the open market. These Bush tax deductions were supposedly going to provide individuals and families with additional funds to purchase coverage without even looking at the out of control healthcare cost that was already ravaging every family. But here again, budget reductions took precedent, and once again nothing was done.

President William Clinton in January 1993, proposed a Bill he submitted to the 103d Congress, 1st Session known as:

"The 1995 Health Securities Act." (13)

But it also was quietly and quickly tabled in its proposed form, and was essentially dead because both the Senate and the House were already bought off by the *"Shadow Government"* (the NWO). Although a modified version was to be presented for discussion in 1995, that Bill was also conveniently tabled without a vote. Then on August 1997, President Clinton signed a very secretive balanced budget agreement that piggy-backed major changes to Medicare. The interesting thing about this agreement was a provision allowing physicians, hospitals and other healthcare providers to form "Provider Sponsored Organizations," (PSOs). These PSOs were to contract directly with the government to care for Medicare members, which again provided the many profit seekers a direct tap into the public treasury. The reason Congress was pressured to approve PSOs was to lure more Medicare patients out of Medicare and into Managed Care Organizations, which was the NWO's plan all along. What the government disregarded was that these PSO organizations were monopolies. The law suggested the PSOs would take on the financial risks under state and federal regulations, however, these regulations had yet to be defined. In other words, managed care was put in place without public approval or understanding, and these PSOs were to manage risk in such a way that their plan would not collapse under the weight of excessive claims, unnecessary hospitalizations and unforeseen costs. Yet, at no time previous or during the entire history of healthcare have these Money Baron's been able to set limits on their own income, so this was very much like a child putting their hand in the cookie jar. Once again, the consumer was blindly required to delegate all their responsibility to the provider of the service, thereby creating a monopoly. And as a result, what was created was a large and unappetizing blend of organizations that were identified by an endless list of acronyms, many of which have confused and angered patients and frustrated physicians. The marketing of HMOs; PSOs; PPOs; IPAs; POSs; PHOs; PPMs and many more mumbo jumbo terms, which are seriously confusing and disorienting the consumer on a daily basis. This decentralized form of healthcare actually defies any form of comprehensive cost control, regional planning, or public understanding. Each managed care organization suggests it will take care of the patient's healthcare dollar more efficiently, yet none of them have clearly defined the complex standards required to efficiently run a comprehensive and well managed system. These confusing provider acronyms are described in greater detail in Appendix X, page 298.

Now, add to this more than eighty competing profit insurance companies and one begins to recognize why the public is disgusted with what's happening to their healthcare dollar in this fraudulent out of control competitive, decentralized and commercialized monopoly. As a result, the consumer tax payer is saddled with paying for three conflicting and costly systems through direct payment, employment benefits, and tax. No other healthcare system in the world has placed this type of ridiculous boondoggle on the consumer. Today's un-auditable healthcare system includes the *"Private Pay System,"* the *"Employer System,"* which includes two systems known as the *"Play"* or *"Pay,"* and the *"Government System,"* which provides comprehensive healthcare to the armed forces; federal employees; the Indian Health Services; Welfare; Medicare/ Medicaid; the Veterans Administration; the penitentiary programs; and the very same politicians that refuse to discuss healthcare in America, all comprising more than twenty healthcare programs that are crying out to be brought under one roof. These decentralized organizations control the product, they establish what is charged for the product, and they collect from the working class directly through their public treasury without any compunction or form of control by the purchaser. And since patients are a captive audience, they have little choice in the care they receive. Usually, when the consumer buys a commercial product, they at least have a choice in what they are buying, but for some reason this matter of choice does not hold true when the consumer purchases a non elective human service for the sick and disabled.

President George W. Bush, in 2004, planned a health care program that covered ten million people who lacked health insurance at a cost of $102 billion over the next decade. He also supported the expansion of Medicare to cover prescription drugs using private insurance through the

Medicare Part D program. His plan was to support entitlement reform and privatization of Social Security by allowing individuals to set up personal retirement accounts, saying he understood financial affairs if they were projected to have a negative impact on the economy. In 2008, Bush said:

"Our aim should not be more government. It should be smarter government."

During the beginning of his first term, Bush also enacted substantial corporate tax cuts for the wealthy in the hope that the economy and jobs would flourish. He supported major bailout plans for mortgage lenders and auto makers who were facing bankruptcy, and then supported and enacted the first major economic stimulus in the face of a failing economy on the 2007 down-turn, handing free checks to all private tax-paying citizens.

In the meantime, healthcare costs continued to grow faster than the national income, while service has only improved slightly for a larger number of patients under the Obama Presidency. So as a result, profits continue to skyrocket totally out of control under today's decentralized and deregulated profit seeking healthcare system — now ranked 37th by the WHO.

"Total health expenditures are estimated to be $2.16 trillion in 2006, and are projected to rise to over $4 trillion in 2015." (14)

Per person health spending was $7,960 in 2009

It's shocking to look back to a time when this kleptocratic aristocracy was not in control, in the year 1960, when annual expenditures were $27.1 billion, and per person cost was only $143.00 dollars a year?

"As a share of the economy, health care has risen from 7.2% of GDP in 1965 to over 16% of GDP today, and it is projected to reach 20% of GDP in just 10 years from now." (15)

During the many years that profit insurance and managed care have been toying with this country's once number one healthcare system, they've accomplished the following:

- *Decentralized the healthcare system into competitive units.*

- *Reduced the government's and the people's role in healthcare.*

- *Taken over the licensed physician's clinical decision making under the profit seeking corporate insurance practice of medicine.*

- *Violated patient's rights and responsibilities.*

- *Replaced a nonprofit system with a profit system*

- *Increased healthcare costs to meet their profit incentives from the sick and disabled who tax support healthcare and have no choice in the price they pay for the product they receive.*

- *Reduced professional healthcare standards and cooperative community and regional planning programs.*

But more importantly, today's *Invisible Money Barons* have taken healthcare and its working class back in time more than a hundred years, to the same profit seeking, advertising, marketing and competition that existed in the 1890's — creating the same professional and ethical fraud that both Flexner and Hippocrates tried to warn us about.

Cost reduction through competition and decentralization has clearly proven unsuccessful, and today's huge fraudulent profits have been completely disregarded as a potential cost savings under a comprehensive nonprofit system. Mixing profit with professional clinical judgment is like trying to mix oil and water.

At a special eight hour meeting with former President Ford in the late 70's, this author asked for his advice regarding the take-over of our once nonprofit healthcare system. And as they left their meeting President Ford put his arm over my shoulder and whispered: *"I believe the healthcare system will have to collapse before this congress will change anything."*

Then as he paused a moment, he continued. *"Or it will take a revolution of the people before they'll change."*

And perhaps that's what is needed.

Whether it is government or private, or both, Americans will someday have to stand up and demand their benefits back under a single cost effective, comprehensive and manageable nonprofit prepayment program for our sick and disabled, based on professional standards rather than profit.

1 "Blue Cross and Blue Shield — Abandoning the Mission," Consumer Reports Vol. 55 #8 (August 1990): 543.

2 Abraham Flexner, *Medical Education in the United States and Canada* — (Published by the Carnegie Foundation, 1907), x.

3 Ibid xiii.

4 Ibid xiv-xvi

5 Ibid

6 Ibid

7 Ibid

8 "Blue Cross and Blue Shield — Abandoning the Mission," Consumer Reports Vol. 55 #8 (August 1990) : 543.

9 Ibid 30

10 Rashi Fein, "Prescription for change," *Modern Maturity* August September, 1992), 24

11 Ibid p.30

12 Ibid

13 Health Securities Act, 103d Cong.,1st Sess.151—183 (1993).

14 Borger et al., op cit; CMS National Health Statistics Group, NHE summary including share of GDP, op cit. p 1

15 Ibid

9

The Anti-American &
Anti-Semitic Bigotry

In going to war with Iraq, America inadvertently chose to support the
Shrub Dynasty's proposed NWO and this country's alliance with Israel,
the American Israel Public Affairs Committee (AIPAC) and their Likud-
Zionist Prime Minister, Ariel Sharon — generating a new frontier of
worldwide anti-Americanism and anti-Semitic bigotry of global
proportions. It also suggests that many Republican conservatives and
Democratic liberals were unknowingly forced into this predictably
unsuccessful alliance with little or no understanding of the complex
conflict that was raging between Judaism and Zionism; nor the religious,
racial, and ethnic issues that are currently disrupting the entire Muslim
and European cultures throughout the world. Here are some of the
deceitful lies used to push the *Shrub Dynasty's* agenda:

- *Iraq is reconstituting its nuclear weapons. (10/07/02)* — *Bush*

- *Saddam Hussein is seeking quantities of uranium from Africa.
(10/28/030)* — *Bush*

- *Saddam has reconstituted nuclear weapons. (03/16/03)* — *Cheney*

- *The CIA has solid reporting of senior-level contacts between Iraq and al-
Qaeda going back a decade. (10/07/02)* — *Tenet/Bush*

• *Iraq has trained al-Qaeda members in bomb making and poisons and deadly gases, and their alliances with terrorists could allow Iraq to attack America. (10/07/02)* — Bush

• *Iraq has a growing fleet of manned and unmanned aerial vehicles that could disperse chemical or biological weapons. (10/07/02)* — Bush

• *We have seen intelligence over many months that Iraq has dispersed chemical and biological weapons, and that command control arrangements have been established. (02/08/03)* — Bush

• *Our conservative estimate is that Iraq has a stockpile of between 100 and 500 tons of chemical weapons agents to fill some 16,000 rockets. (02/05/02)* — Powell

• *We know where Iraq's WMD are, around Tikrit and Baghdad and east, south, and north somewhat. (03/30/03)* — Rumsfeld

• *We found a biological laboratory in Iraq, which the UN prohibited. (06/01/03)* — Bush (1)

And there are many other lies that have yet to be investigated, such as:

• The Scooter Libby's lies to a Grand Jury.

• Blaming Iraq for the Trade Center destruction

• And what the "Top Gun" said on the deck of the USS Abraham Lincoln under a banner saying *MISSION ACCOMPLISHED:*

> *"The tyrant has fallen and Iraq is free . . . Major combat operations in Iraq have ended . . . The United States and our allies have prevailed . . . And now our coalition is engaged in securing and reconstructing that country."*

...and on and on!

Although our national security interests relating to the destruction of the World Trade Center certainly suggested some form of retaliation against terrorism, perhaps without having the facts it was irresponsible for this country to add to the fear, anger, and resentment between Judaism and Zionism, which has been a serious but completely different problem. A problem, which has been rapidly gaining more and more momentum in Iraq and its neighboring states of Iran, Afghanistan, Turkey, Libya, Syria, Lebanon, Jordan, Egypt, and Saudi Arabia, as well as Germany and France. And in that Iran now controls the Shiite population in both Iran and Iraq, they will inevitably blame the resulting religious war on America. A religious war called the "Rapture" or the "Apocalyptic Event" in which God will destroy the ruling powers of evil. In other words, they believe that all these suicidal bombings we see are acting in behalf of God — and that these protagonist will go to heaven in an unending war that culminates with the end of the earth.

Most of the world, outside of the United States, now recognizes the Iraq war was not a matter of *"win or lose,"* and we're just now realizing that it was a huge mistake for the United States to ignore the real terrorist, Al Qaeda's Osama bin Laden. Yet, our President at that time suggested, *"we're going to stay the course,"* not even having a clue of what the course involved in this endless religious conflict. Could it be that George W. Bush was trying to prove his father failed where he planned to succeed at all cost. Even a few ethical politicians have been asking themselves — *"Just how could we have been so stupid as to authorize an illegal unilateral act of aggression without a clear understanding of the facts?"* Before this Iraq war, the most strongly oriented Zionist-neoconservatives, Richard Pearl and co-author Douglas Feith had just completed writing *A Clean Break: A New Strategy for Securing the Realm,* and these two Zionists retrospectively played a major role in influencing the start of our religious war with Iraq. Pearl and Feith had also previously presented this document to the former Israeli Prime Minister, Netanyahu for his approval, long before the Trade Center's destruction in New York. Their strategy called for the elimination of Israel's enemy *"Saddam Hussein,"* and the September 13, 1993 *"Oslo Accord,"* which defined the interim self-government arrangements between the Palestinian Liberation Organization (PLO), and Israel. Pearl also proposed to install a Hashemite monarchy in

Baghdad to destabilize the governments of Syria, Lebanon, Saudi Arabia, and Iran — recommending a regional dominance by Israel over that entire area, which he referred to as *"The Greater Israel."* Of course Iran would have none of this, and is currently prepared to reach heaven by dying in an Apocalyptic War if necessary. So, instead of hunting down terrorists like Osama bin Laden — on the advice of Karl Rove, Richard Cheney, Donald Rumsfeld, Paul Wolfowitz, I. Lewis "Scooter" Libby, Richard Pearl, Douglas Feith, and George Tenet — President Bush chose to take steps toward promoting a Zionist state called *"Greater Israel,"* which they actually believed would soon become the sole power in the Middle East. Yes, it was this small group of Neoconservatives that played a major role in this unilateral and still potential criminal act of aggression in Iraq — who was Israel's arch enemy. Worse yet, they did this without the real support of any of the neighboring countries, the United Nations, or the Muslims, estimated to be between 1.2 to 1.4 billion people throughout the world's almost seven billion population. Since the start of this war, the Institute for Advanced Strategic and Political Studies (IASPS), a Pearl organization, has been trying to explain to the press and the bewildered public why the United States spent more than two trillion dollars instead of the originally projected $50 to $80 billion to fight this war that promoted *"Greater Israel."* And more recently, Israel continues to defiantly and intentionally escalate its perpetual religious conflict with Lebanon and Jerusalem. And as a result, no one is able to currently resolve this dangerous Zionist Israeli conflict with Judaism that we have inadvertently created throughout the entire Islamic world — or the anti-Americanism and anti-Semitism that has been on the rise throughout the Middle East, Germany, France, as well as the entire world.

The World of Islam

To better understand this serious issue, one needs to understand what "Islam" is all about. The word "Islam" means peace and the Islam religion means the submission to one God, as well as to live in harmony with other people and the environment. A Muslim is one whose obedience, allegiance and loyalty are to God, Lord of the Universe, and one who strives to live in accordance with God's laws. Muslims may be Arabs, Turks, Persians, Indians, Pakistanis, Indonesians, Europeans,

Africans, Americans, Chinese or any other nationality not limited to race. Yet, far too many Americans are still under the impression that Judaism and Zionism are synonymous, believing that being a Jew means to be a Zionist, which implies a certain loyalty to the State of Israel. What's not understood are the terms Judaism and Zionism are completely incompatible. Jews are not a religion, a nation, or a race. According to their own belief they are the "Chosen People," but they are not chosen for domination; they are not elected to rule over people; they are chosen to serve the Creator of the Universe and the Father — thereby serving all of mankind. According to the Jewish faith, there are only seven laws that are binding, and they follow some 613 commandments that were derived from the Five Books of Moses, constituting the Rabbinic and Halachic literature, which is obligatory to everyone born of a Jewish mother or one who has accepted the Jewish faith. Political Zionism only started in Europe in the 1930s in response to anti-Semitism, and is a complete departure from Judaism. The aim of the Zionists is to provide a country for the Jewish people, where they can speak Hebrew under a government or nation, which can have an army, navy and air force. Yet, this entire concept defies the Jewish faith. The creation of *"Greater Israel"* as a secular Jewish State is treason to the Jewish people that were constituted on Mount Sinai. By supporting *"Greater Israel"* in its quest to establish and control Iraq and its neighboring Jewish nations, the United States has blindly waded right into the middle of a perpetual religious conflict with Judaism, and as a result, Jewish people, as well as Russia and China actually believe we are becoming a *"Dictator State,"* which they must protect themselves from. In other words, if we'd have left them with their own dignity and some respect, we may have had no problem. The last country to consider the Jews a race was the Nazis, whose irrational racism and dictatorship attempted to annihilate an indefinable culture of perhaps a billion or more Jews, all under a Dictator that left a scar on humanity, which will long be remembered. The United States can only hope that this nation has not created another form of bigotry that we may someday regret, just as Germany now regrets Hitler's atrocities. By foolishly embracing Israeli Zionism through wars that are intended to create a *"Greater Israel,"* this nation has revealed an abysmal ignorance of Jewish history, which could eventually rekindle anti-Semitism and anti-Americanism to a level never before seen throughout this world.

The use of such bully like fear phrases as: *"Axis of Evil"* — *"Shock and Awe"* — and the constant reminder of the *"WMD threat,"* fails to recognize that our wars have killed, injured, and disrupted the lives of millions of innocent human beings and their families in both the United States and Iraq and Afghanistan — as well as the numerous other skirmishes we've been involved in. As a result of the Iraq war, two million Iraqi's have left Iraq, and 1.8 million have relocated, with estimates of Iraqi's killed exceeding 655,000. Here again, we really don't know, nor do we even seem to care. And as the United States continues to support the realm for Israel, it can be expected that we will certainly kill and injure many more as these seemingly out of control unilateral acts of aggression now mushrooms throughout the Middle East.

The Cost of Violating International Law

Yes, it's now time for our Congress to face up to the many terrible blunders they've made. In fact the entire world is becoming exhausted by our pathetic and dysfunctional political rhetoric that prevents any unbiased investigation of our country's War Crimes and our violation of international law, which has included:

- Any unilaterally act of aggression without being attacked.

- Any bombing of the Iraqi people with radioactive material.

- Any prisoner torture tactics.

Yes, these bully like *"War Crimes"* have embarrassed the United States throughout the world. And none of these acts fall within sound political judgment, such as Saddam Hussein's trial and hanging, which should have been reviewed by the International World Court in *"The Hague"* — just as this country once demanded in the Nuremberg Trials that were held from 1945 to 1949, involving the Nazi Holocaust and the corrupt German officers of World War II. In retrospect, it's now very obvious that the United States has failed the world, by pushing our close allies to ignore the Geneva Convention, as well as all six of the previous Geneva related agreements we've signed. Just how could we as a leading nation stand by and allow our country to openly degrade our once flawless image? Aren't we even angered by this nation's definition of torture? Aren't we even embarrassed in that we've also demanded absolute immunity for all U.S. Military personnel and civilian officials prior to involving ourselves in the Iraq war? — Just so we could remain free from prosecution for war crimes by the International Criminal Court. Hasn't the Patriot Act taken us back to the Alien & Sedition Act of 1796, where the Federalist elite previously attempted to take full control of our government, using the threat of attack by hostile forces as the excuse to enact the Sedition Act, which at that time established the following laws?

- *branded their political opponents as traitors*

- *made it a crime for American citizens to "print, utter, or publish . . . any false, scandalous, and malicious writing" about the Government*

- *imprisoned their most outspoken verbal critics*

- *allowed aliens to be imprisoned or deported at the whim of the president*

- *had the intent of keeping the Federalists in power indefinitely, perpetuating its control of the government (2)*

Wasn't this similar to some of our present policies and the Patriot Act, which attempts to brainwash the working class into believing that our appointed tribunals can convict people on circumstantial evidence? Should any free nation ever use *"Gestapo"* like tactics to torture victims into false confessions?

The infamous Hitler Storm Trooper "Hermann Goering" said it very well at the Nuremberg Trials after World War II:

> *"Why of course the people don't want war ... But after all, it is the leaders of the country who determine the policy, and it is always a simple matter to drag the people along, whether it is a fascist dictatorship, or a parliament, or a communist dictatorship . . . Voice or no voice, the people can always be brought to the bidding of the leaders. That is easy. All you have to do is to*

tell them they are being attacked, and denounce the pacifists for lack of patriotism and exposing the country to danger."(3)

The *Financial Times* of London published a commentary on July 2, 2002 under the headline "US Takes Chance to Target Peacekeeping," saying:

> " ... *Condoleezza Rice, Bush's national security advisor at that time, spelled out her outlook in an article in Foreign Affairs magazine, saying:*
> *The president must remember that the military is a special instrument. It is lethal and is meant to be. It is not a civilian police force. It is not a political referee. And it is most certainly not designed to build a civilian society."' (4)*

Our Congress has also promoted and passed, "The Netherlands Invasion Act," which allows our U.S. Military to rescue any U.S. Personnel brought to trial in *"The Hague."* Doesn't this expose the complete lack of equality for other nations, while destroying the very basic freedoms so many of us once fought for? Has it been so long ago that we can't recall our nation once set an example to others, rather than this steady diet of embarrassing acts and preemptive wars that we're all ashamed of?

During World War II, those veterans that returned, all experienced the terrible aftermath of killing and vowed that war should only be a last resort after all other alternatives were exhausted. So isn't it time we carefully evaluate why our twentieth century closed with almost thirty-five thousand American-air sorties bombing Serbia and Kosovo, under the direction of the United Nations? And although those particular acts of war may have been justified, they destroyed almost all of the Yugoslavian power and water filtration plants, railroads, bridges, and a majority of their petroleum reserves — essentially annihilating the Yugoslavian culture and its small industrial and social infrastructures for years to come. Paradoxically, the twenty-first century started with a similar destruction of Afghanistan — and more recently, the United States unilaterally initiated this ridiculous preemptive act of religious aggression against Iraq, a country of less than twenty-six million people, with Lebanon, Jerusalem, Iran, and Syria and the entire region of the Middle East all next in line. As a result, North Korea, China, and even Russia are all taking steps to protect themselves from this country's apparent worldwide colonization and policing tactics. Yes, America is once again becoming very familiar with the scars of war — scars that will never heal for the thousands of families both here and abroad that have been touched by death or injury, all because of our many reckless decisions to take this country to war before all other efforts were exhausted. However, none of this seems to bother the *Shadowed Money Barons* that most likely welcome these endless skirmishes so they can both control a country's natural resources and make their huge profits. Current estimates for rebuilding all these countries exceed trillions of dollars per state, which is far more than any of these now dependent colonies can ever afford. And since their GNP has dropped so dramatically, the United States, and particularly *"We the People,"* the working class, will never be able to regain the minimal prosperity we once enjoyed. Therefore, our tax dollars will play a major role in each country's recovery well into the twenty-first century. But worse yet, while we as Americans are spending enormous amounts of tax dollars on revitalizing and redirecting all these other countries, we're not revitalizing our own floundering economy, which is currently riddled with corrupt un-audited no bid contracts for these wealthy *Money Baron's* corporations; trillions of dollars in loans and deficits; the decentralization of human services to humankind — and the obvious deregulation of standards and the decentralization of our human services, while our dysfunctional government aggressively attempts to over regulates its own citizens. And since all these small foreign states were actually stripped of their sovereignty, our military occupation will also be required for years to come, as more and more American soldiers are being forced to leave their families and perhaps even die to protect the almost eight hundred military basis we currently operate in other countries — countries that aren't very happy that we Americans are even there. Iraq, the Middle East, France, Germany, Russia and China, all wonder if the United States isn't unilaterally deploying this country's military force for geopolitical and economic advantage. And many now question this unrealistic quest for *"Worldwide Freedom,"* under this ridiculous *"One World Order"* when we know full well that these Invisible Money Barons are only interested in their profits and the total control of the other countries rich mineral deposits in the Middle East. An article entitled "US preparing full-scale invasion of Iraq" by Bill Vann on July 10, 2002 stated:

> *"Vice President Cheney, Defense Secretary Donald Rumsfeld and Assistant Defense Secretary Paul Wolfowitz, reportedly were in agreement with the Israeli regime of Ariel Sharon that the US military force can effectively subjugate Iraq, providing the US with an alternative to Saudi Arabia as a source of oil and a site for our military bases. CIA Director George Tenet reportedly warned this administration that, "there was little or no chance of a successful coup against the Iraqi leader," counseling that, "only an all-out US military assault can realize American aims."(5)*

And this was reported well before the Trade Center bombing and the Iraq war ever began. In any event, all this nation's perpetual skirmishes are becoming more and more difficult to identify as wars, when in actuality they massacre thousands. Isn't it becoming obvious that when a hostile conflict occurs between a super-power and a small state like Iraq, it's just not appropriate to call it a war — more likely it becomes a massacre, where the smaller nation can only attempt to defend itself? And the political price that's paid for this type of super power aggression is the deterioration of our once respected image.

Former Secretary of State, Lawrence Eagleburger said it very well:

> *"We've presented to the rest of the world a vision of the bully on the block who pushes a button — that's going to haunt us in terms of trying to deal with the rest of the world in the years ahead, a fact that carries with it a serious political price."(6)*

What Eagleburger was referring to was this *"Big Bully Syndrome"* we've recently taken on. Even "The United Nation's Security Council," as well as much of the world, no longer supports our preemptive and unilateral tactics that inflict irreparable damage to others. Why can't we meet face to face and pressure troubled states like North Korea, Iran and Syria into a solution, rather than threaten war? Perhaps it's because too many insiders, like Halliburton and the Carlyle corporations become wealthy when we foot the bill. After all, why should they care if they provoke a growing mass of humanity to cry out against these senseless acts of totalitarianism? Many feel the world would anxiously unite, if we'd only ask them to help fight terrorism, rather than pursue all these self-serving interests like marketing war materials, gaining control over oil, or creating strategic air bases. Americans have seldom been unsupportive of a just war — but Christianity, Authoritarianism, the Inquisition, the Crusades, the bloody Reformation and Counter Reformation and the past persecutions, purges, heresy, Witch burnings, religious tribunals of penance, self immolation, flagellation, and mass murders of uncounted millions of indigenous people under the guise of some form of religious, political or anti-Semitic conflict have plagued humankind for centuries. And yet, the United States intentionally plunges our politicians, the fundamentalists, and the religious right into an era of universal religious strife between Judaism and Zionism. Force-feeding Israel's Zionist theocracy into both Iraq and American politics also defies the separation of church and state, which both liberal and conservative politicians have long held sacred. And yes, our once respected two party system needs to expel these theocratic issues from politics, if sanity is to ever return to America — or perhaps we need to change our entire two party system.

So Why Was Iraq Invaded?

The U.S. and the U.K. had been bombing northern and southern Iraq since 1991, and although these *Invisible Money Barons* knew that our sanctions and containment efforts were working — they were well aware that these sanctions were soon going to be lifted, with Saddam still in charge. In other words, the *Money Barons* stood to be shut out of getting any financial benefit at all. Also the Food for Oil program had switched to the Euro in November 2000 — and Saddam Hussein would be selling his oil for Euros when these sanctions were lifted. Everyone knew Saddam was sitting on top of the second largest oil reserves in the world — and because the US was a debtor nation, meaning their currency was no longer backed up by the gold standard, their currency would most likely shift confidence in the dollar if a very solid commodity like oil was traded in Euros. That's why one of George Bush's first executive order signed in May, 2003 changed trading of Iraq's oil back to the dollar, as these *Money Barons* took over Iraq's Central Bank and shrewdly bought Iraqi companies at a penny on the dollar.

On the flip side, the Shrub Dynasty was also no longer on good terms with Saudi Arabia, since the questionable death of Salem bin Laden, Osama bin Laden's oldest brother, who was an investor in George W's oil company. Salem died in an unexplained airplane accident outside of San Antonio, Texas on May 29, 1988. On top of this, the *Invisible Money Barons* were very dissatisfied with the Saudi's restrictions on US bases in Saudi Arabia, which they desperately needed, to secure the energy resources in that region.

1 Christopher Scheer, AlterNet 6/27/03 Ten Appalling Lies Were Told About Iraq
http://www.alternet.org/story/16274

2 Alexander James, The Hidden History of Money p. 6
http://portland.indymedia.org/en/2004/03/282679.shtml

3 Ibid p. 6

4 Bill Vann, US pushes Europe to the brink on international court, 4 July 2002
www.wsws.org/articles/2002/jul2002/icc-j04.shtml - 24k - Cached

5 Bill Vann, US preparing full-scale invasion of Iraq, 10 July 2002
www.wsws.org/articles/2002/jul2002/iraq-j10.shtml - 22k - Cached

6 Robert Elias, Professor of sociology , University of San Francisco, California-
Terrorism and American Foreign Policy, ,September 25, 2001
http://www.tanbou.com/2001/fall/USForeignPolicyElias.htm

10

The President

Has this nation's dysfunctional Congress totally relinquished its responsibility to the NWO for placing a qualified candidate for President that represents the people in this important Democracy of the People? Shouldn't each party be required to screen mentally healthy candidates who they can recommend and that they feel the world will trust, and who's not tainted by this powerful invisible government's nepotism? Shouldn't they be required to recommend a President who understands the long range impact of war and at least has some experience with such conflicts — one who will not squander the prestige our soldiers have earned from this nation's humanitarian role in two previous World Wars? Shouldn't they run someone that can be tough as well as prudent in face to face meetings with other troubled nations, rather than someone who openly labels other nations as being evil, which only generates more fear and resentment? Don't these parties appreciate we need someone who understands that wars kill and injure huge numbers of people?

Isn't it also time for *"We the People"* to demand that our leaders at least understand who they represent, and that they are vested with the responsibility of protecting this nation's working class, their human services and benefits, and their open and free world market? And shouldn't the Presidents also be required to meet some level of basic job description criteria, education, and leadership capability? Wouldn't it also be prudent that every President also be required to have a psychological evaluation before they are placed in this most demanding office? Shouldn't the Republicans and Democrats have a well defined method for evaluating their candidates for President before any name is placed on the ballot? Could it be that the NWO is in total control and intentionally selects a puppet like leader they can control — keeping our great nation in a constant state of fear and apathy through their ridiculous lies, deceit, and war crimes?

Since George W. Bush was acknowledged to be one of this nation's worst Presidents, let's take a moment to really analyze this particular President's history and his involvement in wars and what happened during his term in office. Perhaps then we can determine why this nation is now caught up in such a costly preemptive and un-winnable religious war with some 1.2 to 1.4 billion Islam's. Perhaps then we can determine if and how politicians are bought off by those that can afford to do so.

For Example:

A cursory psychological evaluation of George W. Bush can be found in the following two books — even though nothing was done to really evaluate this man's credentials and history and obvious nepotism before his party allowed him to become a candidate for the highest and most important job in the entire world:

Dr. Justin Frank, in his 2004 book, *Bush on the Couch - inside the Mind of the President*, offers an in-depth personality profile of President George W. Bush, through applied psychoanalysis in which teams of psychiatrists had previously utilized a vast reservoir of clinical data involving many other world leaders. Dr. Frank utilized massive amounts of video footage on the President, as well as autobiographical and biographical data from many of his most intimate associates, including members of his family, as well as other clinical data not often available on other leaders in developing the more recent George W. Bush's profile. This book is a devastating psychological dossier on the 43rd President, as well as a compassionate profile of a human in need of care. In this book, Dr. Frank indicates that:

> *"Bush is clearly a puppet of Cheney, but one who carries out his Presidential decisions with a clear conviction that he is the real power, or the ultimate decision maker with a megalomaniacal conviction that he is the king of the roost."*

Dr. Frank also describes a man suffering from a number of serious psychological disorders. Among them:

> *Attention Deficit Hyperactivity Disorder (ADHD); untreated and uncured alcoholism (a dry drunk); an omnipotence complex paranoia; an Oedipal Complex; sadism; and a mild form of Tourettes Syndrome, with a diminished capacity to distinguish between reality and fantasy, all resulting in a diminished ability to manage anxiety." (1)*

John P. Briggs, MD, and J.P. Briggs II, PhD, in their book entitled, *Bush and the Psychology of Incompetent Decisions*, writes:

> *"President George W. Bush prides himself on 'making tough decisions.' But many are sensing something seriously troubling, even psychologically unbalanced, about the president as a decision-maker. They are right ... His continued, almost obsessive, attempts through the years to emulate his father, obtain his approval, and escape from his influence are extensively recorded ... Being 'born again' also allows the president to present himself as having relegated to the past all those previously inadequate behaviors of his younger days: the poor academic performance, the drinking, and the failed businesses. He's a new man, no longer incompetent but now supremely competent as a result of his faith. ... Bush's mother, Barbara (sarcastic, mean, disciplinarian, always with an acid-tongued retort), is probably the model for another major defense Bush deploys to defend himself against feelings of inadequacy. Much of the world outside the US considers Bush a bully ... 'You're either with us or against us' is a bully's threat that anyone can recognize. The Bush doctrine of pre-emptive strikes is a bully's doctrine. They suggest a desperate uncertainty about everything that the president reflexively seeks to hide by taking absolutist, rigid positions about 'victory,' 'success,' 'mission accomplished,' 'stay the course,' 'compassion,' 'tax cuts,' 'no child left behind,' and a host of other issues. Thus, instead of focusing on the process needed to arrive at a decision, Bush marshals his defenses in order not to feel incompetent. That doesn't leave much room for exploring the alternatives required of competent decision-making. Not interested in discussion or detail (where the devil often lies), he seeks something minimal, just enough so he can let the decision come to him; it's his 'gut' (read 'God') that will provide the answer. But these gut feelings are the very feelings*

associated with his deep sense of inadequacy and his defenses against those feelings. So while he brags that he makes the 'tough decisions,' psychologically, he's defending himself against the very feelings of uncertainty that are the necessary concomitant to making tough decisions. His tough decision-making is a sham ... We don't dare to really confront the scale of his incompetent behavior, because then we would have to face what it means to have such an incompetent and psychologically disabled decision-maker as our president."
(2)

Perhaps this Brigg's analysis helps to explain why President George W. Bush deceived Congress — or why the Republican Congress doesn't want to be held responsible for their selection of Bush as a candidate for President

So who is George W. Bush?

George W. Bush was the 43rd President of the United States, and was born in New Haven, Connecticut, not Texas, on July 6, 1946. He was initially sworn in as President of the United States on January 20, 2001, and appointed to a second term as President in January 2005. He received a bachelor's degree in history from Yale University in 1968, and in 1975 he received a Masters of Business Administration from Harvard. He avoided the military-draft and active military duty by being selectively chosen to serve in the Texas Air National Guard during the Vietnam War. Only a few documents could be found to attest to his service in the Guard, and many important records were missing regarding his appointment. Several key individuals have stated that nepotism played an important role in his appointment to the Guard; however, this was quickly and diplomatically concealed from any public scrutiny. The CBS newscaster, Dan Rather and his staff were in fact fired after years of honest and ethical reporting when they attempted to expose the truth about the Bush service appointment to the public. Their firing was a direct result of undue influence, which spurred Mr. Rather's decision to file a $70 million lawsuit against CBS and its former parent company. On September 20, 2007 Mr. Rather said on CNN's *Larry King Live*:

> *"Somebody, sometime has got to take a stand and say democracy cannot survive, much less thrive with the level of big corporate and big government interference and intimidation in news."*

In June 1977, at the age of 31, George W. Bush incorporated an oil drilling company called Arbusto Energy Inc. in Midland, Texas. (*"Arbusto"* is the Spanish word for *"Bush."*) *The Wall Street Journal* and several other reputable publications reported that James R. Bath, a friend and neighbor helped George "W" obtain his initial Arbusto oil company's financing from two Saudi Sheiks — Salem bin Laden, Osama bin Laden's older brother, and Khalid bin Mahfouz, all occurring while his father, George senior, was the Director of the CIA. *The Houston Chronicle* reported that, "Salem bin Laden had signed a trust agreement with James R. Bath, as his representative in Texas in 1976," and the *American Free Press* later confirmed this in an October 7, 2001 article entitled,

> *"Bush & Bin Laden — George W. Bush had Ties to the Billionaire bin Laden Brood."*

It should be noted that Mahfouz was one of the richest men in the world at that time, serving as controlling shareholder of the Bank of Credit and Commerce International (BCCI). The BCCI was started in Pakistan with funds from the CIA, then under George senior, and funds from the Bank of America. When the Soviets invaded Afghanistan in 1976, the CIA helped supply the Afghani resistance with weapons through the BCCI and a closely interwoven Pakistan agency called Inter-Service Intelligence (ISI). The founder of BCCI, Agha Hasan Abedi, also dealt directly with the Bush run CIA. In 1980, George senior ran for President, and lost to Reagan, at which time William Casey, the next head of the CIA, continued to work directly with Abedi and the BCCI. Then in an unusual turn of events, George senior was selected to serve as Reagan's Vice-President. The BCCI had financed operations in Afghanistan, brokered weapons and supplies, and acted as paymaster according to an article in *The Outlaw Bank,* by Beaty & Gwynne. BCCI also helped fund the covert CIA and U.S. military operations in Afghanistan, helping to train Osama bin Laden's Al-Qaeda terrorists, while supporting this drug and money laundering operation, which was fronting as a bank. *The San Francisco Chronicle* reported:

> ". . . *the dealings between the Bank of America and the BCCI reached $1 billion-plus a day.*"

In the September 1991 issue of *Time* magazine, they described the BCCI as

> "*a vast stateless multinational corporation that deploys its own intelligence agency, complete with a paramilitary wing and several enforcement units, known collectively as the Black Network.*"

This Black Network had at times been linked to numerous suspicious deaths for which no attempts to even investigate had been made. (See Appendix XI, page 299) *The Outlaw Bank* also quotes John Moscow, the Assistant D.A. in Manhattan, as saying:

> "*You are never going to understand BCCI if you persist in thinking of it as a bank.*"

The BCCI was later shut down in 1991 with some $10 billion in losses. In any event, it should be noted that the BCCI factored significantly into *The Shrub Dynasty's* inner circle, including numerous executives, their lobbyists, and the submissive and dysfunctional politicians who were all on the receiving end of some type of political favor. (See Chapter 4, page 48 - The Shrub Dynasty) At this same time, it should be noted that the United States was working closely with Iran.

During George senior's Vice-Presidency, there were many rich Texas business connections seeking to exploit the Bush name. One of them was Bill DeWitt a part owner of Spectrum 7, who was somehow persuaded to acquire George W's failing Arbusto oil business. Later, De Witt sold his holdings at an inflated price to a company called Harken Energy. In this deal, George "W" received stock in Harken in trade for the Bush name, agreeing to serve on the Harken Board of Directors. At that time, Robert Stone, an oilman and a long-time supporter of George

Bush senior and the Republican Party, controlled the Harvard Management Corporation (HMC), an investment committee at Harvard University. In 1986, the Harken Energy Company was struggling to pay off two of its major loans with The Bank of Boston, and First City Bankcorp — and it was highly unlikely that the HMC, together with a billionaire financier by the name of George Soros would voluntarily come forward to rescue two failing corporations like Spectrum 7 and Harken, without the *Shrub Dynasty* connections. With this new backing from HMC, First City was easily persuaded to refinance the Harkin loans, according to an article in the October 9, 2001 *Wall Street Journal.* The *Harvard Watch*, a coalition of Harvard students and alumni, which monitors governance at the Harvard University, published a series of reports that documented the way in which this Ivy League school helped Harken and Enron fashion deals that hid debt and artificially elevated earnings. They also documented the close ties with both the Bush and Clinton administrations. The *Harvard Watch* reported:

> *"Harvard and another shareholder loaned Harken $46 million in May, 1990, to help them escape from a severe liquidity crises."*

In December 1990, HMC and Harken also established a partnership known as the Harken Anadarko Partnership (HAP), to help hide the Harken Company's financial difficulties. HAP was created with some $64.5 million worth of property contributed by Harvard and $26.1 million worth of drilling operations contributed by Harken. At a Harken board meeting, it was recorded that George "W" made the motion to create this Partnership called HAP. Because Harken carried $20 million in debt and liabilities, their net investment in the partnership was less than twenty percent — and because of this, Harken was not required to include this unusual partnership in their financial statements. The basic idea was to shift debt off of the company's balance sheet to improve reported earnings and elevate share values. The *Harvard Watch* reported:

> *"While the stock value of Harken had fallen to a low of $1.25 in late 1990, it now soared to a high in 1991 with the creation of HAP, thereby misleading investors regarding Harken's actual profitability. Harvard used this bubble to sell 1.6 million of the Harken shares."*

An article entitled, *"How George W. Bush Made His Millions,"* by Joseph Kay, on August 1, 2002, states:

> *"In the early 1990s Bush made hundreds of thousands of dollars in a deal that reeks of the same illegal insider trading and accounting fraud he as President later claimed to oppose."*

Since then, the powerful entrepreneurial controlled media has paid very little attention to what George "W" did with the $850,000 he made through the sale of what should have been restricted Harken stock options. Nor have they really openly reported on the manner in which George "W" then transformed this windfall into more than $13 million dollars through the Texas Rangers baseball team. George W's purchase and sale of the Texas Rangers baseball team has also revealed many identical characteristic of this same nepotism, which involved the plundering of public assets for private gain; the confluence of political and economic power; and the defrauding of the American people.

In any event, in 1989, Bill De Witt offered George "W" a chance to bid for ownership in the Texas Rangers baseball team. This deal was made with the help of Richard Rainwater, a wealthy Texas financier, who joined George "W" and several others in buying the Rangers. George "W" bought only a two percent share, financed with a $500,000 loan from a bank he'd previously served on as a board member, eventually repaying this loan from his sale of Harken stock. His new title with the Rangers was to be the Managing Partner, which required he attend the home baseball games to present a public face, while Edward Rose, a Texas investor and associate of Rainwater, became responsible for the business operation of the team. The top priority of these new owners was to increase the value of their holdings by building a new stadium. Since they had no intention of paying for the stadium, they threatened to move the team if the Arlington community did not foot the bill. In 1990, the city government agreed to pay $135 million of the estimated cost, which was $190 million. The remainder was to be raised through a ticket surcharge, requiring the local taxpayers to finance the entire remaining cost of the stadium. The original owners were then allowed to buy back the stadium for $60 million, which was to be deducted from ticket revenues at a rate not to exceed $5 million a year. This tightly knit *Shrub* clique was then somehow magically given an unusual property tax exemption, and a sales tax exemption on products purchased for use in the stadium — again requiring City residents to pay a higher local tax. Later, George "W" and this wealthy Texas inner circle successfully sold back to the voters what was referred to as, *"an unbelievable boondoggle,"* — earning some $250 million without putting down a penny of their own money. As a part of the deal, they also got a sizable chunk of the land, which had substantially increased in value with the new stadium's construction. According to documents obtained by the Center for Public Integrity, the owners previously located this piece of land and offered a price far below the market value, and if the owners refused, they planned to bring in the ASFDA to condemn the land. Bush admitted to a reporter at the *Fort Worth Star-Telegram*,

> *"The idea of making a land play — that's kind of always been the strategy."*

Joe Conason writes,

> *"Never before had a municipality authority in Texas been given a license to seize the property of a private citizen for the benefit of other private citizens."*

Thomas Hicks, a rich financier, and one of the wealthiest buyout specialists in Texas, serving as Chairman and Chief Executive of Hicks, Muse, Tate & Furst, bought the Texas Rangers for $250 million in 1998. This should have given George "W" a return on his investment of a little more than $2 million; however, it was presumed that another under the table deal may have significantly played a role in increasing George W's return, since he actually netted more than $13 million on the deal. When Bush cashed out of the Texas Rangers in 1998, his return on a $600,000 investment was 2,400 percent as reported by the Center for Public Integrity, in an article written by Joe Conason in the February, 2000 *Harpers Magazine*. This was also confirmed in the July 16, 2002 *New York Times*, in columns by Paul Krugman and Nicholas Krist. In any event, by using his family connections and allowing rich Texas businessmen to exploit the Bush name, George "W" was suddenly propelled from failed oilman to wealthy corporate executive almost overnight. On November 8, 1993, with the stadium being readied to open the following spring, George "W" announced that he would be running for Governor in the state of Texas. He didn't even appear ashamed when he proclaimed,

". . . his campaign theme would demand self-reliance and personal responsibility rather than dependence on government."

After George "W" won the gubernatorial election, Hicks quickly transferred his allegiance from Ann Richards, the previous Democratic Governor, to George "W" — giving him a $25,000 campaign contribution a full month after his election. Bush later appointed Hicks and several other Regents to the University Of Texas Board Of Regents, which gave Mr. Hicks substantial latitude to use the University's public funds to invest in ventures of his own choosing. George "W" accomplished all this by next establishing the University of Texas Investment Management Company (UTIMCO) — similar to what he'd worked with at Harvard under the HMC. Nine billion of the Texas school's assets were then handed over to UTIMCO for investment. Unlike the Texas Board of Regents, UTIMCO was organized so that it was not required to open its meetings or publish its activities. In fact, they were totally free of any public oversight, thereby becoming the first external investment corporation ever formed by any public university. UTIMCO also controlled the General Endowment Fund and extensive land and oil holdings that were valued at more than seven billion dollars. In 1995, UTIMCO invested $10 million in the Carlyle Group, which also had very close ties to the Bush family. The Chairman of Carlyle was Frank Carlucci, the former Secretary of Defense under Reagan. Also linked to Carlyle is James Baker the III, the former Secretary of State under George W's father. Even George senior once worked for Carlyle, and in the 1990's, George "W" served on the Board of Directors of Caterair, a company that had earlier been acquired by Carlyle in 1989. Carlyle, the 11th largest defense contractor in the United States, quickly took its crown jewel of defense; a company called, "United Defense," public in less than a month after U.S. Troops invaded Afghanistan. The fact that this company was even able to go public was testimony to

Carlyle's pull in Washington. United Defense manufactured the controversial Crusader, a 42-ton, self-propelled howitzer, that moved like a tank, while lobbing ten 155-mm shells per minute some 40 kilometers. This unit was considered *"a relic of the cold war, who's time had passed,"* according to Steve Grundman an aerospace consultant at the Charles River Associates. In awarding this unusual contract, it would be hard to ignore that Mr. Carlucci and Mr. Rumsfeld were good friends and former wrestling partners from their undergraduate days at Princeton University. According to Greg McCarthy, a spokesperson for Representative J.C. Watts Jr. (R: Oklahoma), whose district is home to one of the Crusader's assembly plants, the Carlyle Group's influence was indeed felt at the Pentagon and perhaps the White House itself. UTIMCO also invested $50 million in the KKK 1996 Fund, a subsidiary of Kohlberg Kravis Roberts, a leveraged buyout firm that left targeted companies nearly bankrupt during the 1980's. Henry Kravis, the company's founding partner was the financial co-chairman for George senior's campaign in 1992. In addition to all this, UTIMCO also invested $20 million in a deal involving the Bass family, another family that significantly increased its wealth through the help of Richard Rainwater. The Bass family had earlier helped George "W" finance his preliminary exploration for oil in Barhain, a small island off the coast of Saudi Arabia, by obtaining the oil drilling rights for Harken Energy, who'd never drilled an off-coast oil well before. This close Saudi/Harken tie shocked the entire professional oil drilling community when their supposed competitive bids and experience were essentially ignored. It should also be noted that the Bass family has been one of George W's largest career patrons, all helping him to become very wealthy.

Prior to George W's Presidency, he served for 6 years as the 46th Governor of the State of Texas. In 1988, he'd previously elected to help with his father's Presidential campaign. During this time, George "W" unquestionably gained many inside connections, while gaining substantially in his own political might through his father's numerous contacts and long political career.

George senior had previously served as a Texas Representative to Congress, Ambassador to the United Nations, Chairman of the U.S.

Liaison Office to the People's Republic of China — but most importantly, he served as the Director of the Central Intelligence Agency (CIA) before becoming Reagan's Vice-President in 1981, and finally President from 1989 to 1993. George senior also had some very significant lows during his career — one being when he served as a Navy pilot during World War II, when he bailed out of his plane while his crew of two crashed and died in the Pacific Ocean. Bush senior, also previously failed twice in bids for the Senate, and in 1980 he'd lost in a campaign for the Presidency against Reagan. And although he was not elected for a second term as President, he was very instrumental in moving healthcare into the profit oriented open market that has now spiraled healthcare cost to a level that is no longer affordable. With George W's two terms in office, added to his powerful father's political and industrial career, the Shrub Dynasty's tightly woven web of inside connections and political power played a key role in the personal wealth of George "W" as well as his rapid ascent to the Presidency of the United States — much of it being at the expense of public asset manipulation. Over the last fifty years, the Zionist fundamentalists, the neoconservative politicians, the *Invisible Money Barons,* and a select group of wealthy international industrial executives have all benefited from their ties with the *Shrub Dynasty.*

An important reminder: The danger of placing any type of imperialistic dynasty in the White House is why a term limit was established for the President in the 1940's. Consequently, it's very important for the people of this great nation to not allow any inner circle of power; wealth; family; religion; or political party — to ever control this Republic of the People.

Therefore, we do not need any more family dynasties in the White House. We'd also be very wise if we'd set term limits for all Congressmen and Senators.

1 Dr. Justin Frank, in his book, "Bush on the Couch - inside the Mind of the President" http://www.powells.com/biblio?show=TRADE%20PAPER:NEW:9780060736712:14.95#synopses_and_reviews

2 John P. Briggs, MD, and J.P. Briggs II, PhD, "Bush and the Psychology of Incompetent Decisions," http://www.truthout.org/docs_2006/011807J.shtml

Section II

HOW TO RECOVER OUR DEMOCRACY

In order of priority, you will find twelve policies in Section II that if implemented will help to change the dangerous direction this country has taken since it sanctioned the unjust religious war this nation started in Iraq. Following World War II, this nation unanimously felt they should never go to war again unless our country was attacked, and yet we have been involved in some seventeen conflicts in which we were the aggressor. Why? Because the NWO makes money under this nations fallacious policing of the World, which our working class pays for while this powerful organization's earnings spiral to the highest level in our history. But the hard fact is, we can no longer afford to pay for this United Nation's responsibility — and if we demand our dysfunctional politicians in Washington implement these twelve policies, it will help change the wrong direction these international banks and corporations have forced us to take under the erroneous title of globalization. Yes, the upper crust's selfish control and money seeking schemes must be stopped if we are to remain a democracy under this government of the people. This Section also recommends international policy

POLICY 1

Donations to Politicians

The United State's House of Representatives and Senate salaries and benefits have been a source of taxpayer unhappiness for years and it's time every citizen of the United States understands why:

The United State's House of Representatives and Senate Annual Salaries

- Basic House and Senate – $174,000

- Majority and Minority Leaders in the House and Senate and the Chief Administrative Officer – $193,400

- President Pro Tempore and Speaker of the House– $223,500

- Vice President (President of the Senate) – $230,700

A cost-of-living-adjustment (COLA) automatically takes effect annually if not repealed by Congress, and the United State's House of Representatives and Senate Members are free to turn down these COLA increases, which a few have actually done. It should also be noted that the median personal wealth for a member of Congress has grown from $785,515 in 2008 to $911,510 in 2009 and all members have seen their overall personal wealth grow by more than 16 percent since the Great Depression. Shockingly, this country has some 261 millionaire members of the United State's House of Representatives and Senate according to the Center for Responsive Politics. It should also be noted that substantial pay increases have frequently occurred during this country's worst economic downturns, according to several financial studies. And although this salary and benefit program is administered by the U.S. Office of Personnel Management, the program is based solely on the United State's House of Representatives and Senate's own Congressional decisions, which unquestionably constitutes a serious conflict of interest. As a result of this self-administered program, this nation's representatives inherently feel free to spend far too much time in managing their reelection, and their own salary and benefit programs instead of doing the work they were elected to do.

Retirement

Prior to 1984, the United State's House of Representatives and Senate paid no Social Security taxes and therefore were not eligible to receive Social Security benefits — however, their retirement was at that time covered by a government pension plan called the Civil Service Retirement System (CSRS). Then in 1983, an Amendment to the Social Security Act required all Members of Congress pay into Social Security even though they still do not receive Social Security benefits — and since the CSRS was not designed to coordinate with Social Security, in 1986 Congress created the Federal Employees' Retirement System Act (FERS) for all new Members. So as a result, all United State's House of Representatives and Senate Members elected since 1984 are all covered by FERS and those elected prior to 1984 by CSRS. However, more recently, all members have been given the option of remaining with CSRS or switching to FERS. It should also be noted that all Members of Congress fund their retirement through a combination of tax money and their own contributions and that their retirement becomes fully vested after five years of participation. Today, Members of Congress under FERS contribute 1.3 percent of their salary into their retirement plan and still pay 6.2 percent of their salary to Social Security Tax. Perhaps this is why so many politicians are so very anxious to privatize Social Security. After a Member of Congress has completed 20 years of service, they become eligible for a pension after they reach the age of 50, or at any age if they've completed 25 years of service or have reached the age of 62 — and all Members must have served 5 years to be eligible for a pension. Their amount of pension depends on their years of service and the average of the highest 3 years of salary — however, the starting amount of a Member's retirement annuity may not exceed 80% of their final salary. According to the Congressional Research Service, as of October 1, 2006 — some 413 retired Members of Congress were receiving federal pensions based on their period of congressional service. Of this number, 290 had retired under CSRS and were receiving an average annual pension of $60,972, while a total of 123 Members under both CSRS and FERS, or just under FERS alone, were receiving an average annual pension of $35,952.

Health Insurance

The United State's House of Representatives and Senate receive and enjoy comprehensive government health insurance benefits under the Federal Employees Health Benefits Program (FEHB) and are individually able to select from among several health benefit plans. It's important to note that this program is a government program that will not be transferred to some profit insurance corporation as being suggested for Medicare and Medicaid. Participation in their FHEB program is on a voluntary contributory basis, and based on the Health Care Benefit program they select they pay the lowest rates of any other health care program in the nation. Perhaps this single cost effective nonprofit prepayment program should be considered for our future universal health care system, or perhaps the Members of the United State's House of Representatives and Senate should be limited to what every citizen is currently provided. It certainly seems strange that so many Members of Congress seek to privatize our current Health Benefits program, while there is no mention of changing their own.

Life Insurance

The United State's House of Representatives and Senate are all eligible to participate in a very cost effective Federal Employees Group Life Insurance Program. The amount of coverage for personal insurance is determined by a formula based on the coverage they select. It also seems strange that this nation's Working Class, the backbone of America, can only buy profit centered insurance benefits in the open market.

Allowances

The Members' Representational Allowance (MRA) is calculated based on three components:

- Personnel
- Official Office Expenses
- Official (Franked) Mail

These three components all result in a single MRA authorization for each Member, which can then be in turn used to pay for any of these three official expenses. All allowances are authorized from January 3 of each year through January 2 of the following year, and these allowances are created by written statute and are regulated and adjusted by the Committee on House Administration. Funding is provided within each member's salary and expense account. The average allowance ranges from $1,356,975 to $1,671,596 per member, with an average MRA of $1,446,009. These allowances vary based on size of the United State's House of Representatives and Senate member's state, which include:

Personnel Allowance

The member's total number of employees has ranged from as low as 26 to a high of 60, for both Washington and the United State's House of Representatives and Senate's district offices. Pay per employee has gone as high as $156,848; however, employee annual salaries are not to exceed $168,411.

In a Representative's Washington, DC district office each member may employ no more than 18 permanent employees. However, as many as four additional employees may be designated by a member, if they fall into one of the following categories:

- Part-time employees
- Employees drawing compensation from more than one
Member's employment

- Interns receiving pay
- Employees on leave without pay
- And temporary employees

Expense Allowance

The Representative's expense allowance varies with each member and is based on population and location of their state and covers all office stationary, business cards, newsletters, travel, communications and general office expenses, as well as their office space based on the cost of office space in that area, which is based on the dollar equivalent to 2,500 square feet multiplied by the applicable rental rate per square foot charged federal agencies by the administrator of the General Services Administration in a member's district. This official office expenses allowance may also be used for travel, office equipment lease, district office rental, stationery (paper, envelopes, and other supplies), telecommunications, printing, postage, computer services, and other expenses. The individual mileage component also varies from member to member due to variations in the distance between their district and Washington, DC. Mileage allowances between Washington, DC, and the furthest point in a member's district, plus 10% — is provided each member. The minimum mileage amount paid is $6,200.

Rate Per/Mile for Mileage between Washington, DC, and the Furthest Point in any District

Fewer than 500 miles	$0.96
500 to 749 miles	$0.86
750 to 999 miles	$0.71
1,000 to 1,749 miles	$0.61
1,750 to 2,249 miles	$0.51
2,250 to 2,499 miles	$0.48
2,500 to 2,999 miles	$0.43
3,000 miles or more	$1.32

In addition, all foreign travel is covered; and free use of any available military air craft is also available to all United State's House of Representatives and Senate Members.

Franking Privilege

This policy allows for mail to be sent free of postage so long as it involves correspondence with a citizen of the United States. Official mail allowance also varies based on the number of non-business addresses in a member's district. All Representatives are authorized the privilege of sending mail as franked mail in the conduct of official business to assist them in their duties. The franked mail postage component of the MRA is based on a formula in which the rate of a single piece of first class mail is multiplied by three, and the resulting figure is multiplied by the number of non-business addresses in a Representative's district. Administration set the 2010 official mail allowance for each Member at 45% of the calculation based on the above described formula. This allowance may be used to pay the costs of first, third, or fourth class franked mail, but may not be used to pay for certain specified mailing costs such as express mail. Since the official mail allowance is combined with the personnel and office expenses allowances, the amount of money a member can spend on franked mail is limited only by the total of the combined allowances. A base allowance of $256,574 was authorized for each member in 2010.

Other Allowances

The United State's House of Representatives and Senate Member's also have other allowances available to support them in their official representational role to the districts they were elected, and this averages $944,671 for each member. Overall representational allowances are not to be used to defray any personal, political, or campaign related expenses. A member also may not use campaign funds to pay for expenses related to his or her official and representational duties; may not use committee funds to pay for official representational expenses; may not use an unofficial office account to support official and representational duties.

Outside Earned Income Limits and Prohibition on Honoraria

The Ethics Reform Committee reduced the limit on honoraria to 27% of salary and permissible "outside earned income" for the United State's House of Representatives and Senate, which is limited to 15% of the base annual pay level of the Executive Salary Schedule. Certain types of outside earned income are prohibited:

- A member may not receive compensation for affiliating with or being employed by a firm, partnership, association, corporation, or other entity providing professional services involving a fiduciary relationship.

- A member's name may not be used by such a firm, partnership, association, corporation, or other entity; practicing a profession involving a fiduciary relationship.

- A member may not serve as a member or officer of the board of an association, corporation, or other entity.

Note: This membership restriction clearly was intended to include the American Legislative Exchange Council, (ALEC), and the Trilateral Commission, (TC), which are both very well organized national consortiums of current and previous federal and state politicians and powerful international corporations involving thousands of members. Although they claim to be non-partisan public-private partnerships with both federal and state governments, they are clearly lobbying to increase corporate profits at public expense. Of the 104 members of ALEC who are active politicians, 10 were active Republican Senators, while only one member is a Democrat. And of some 64 active Republicans from the House of Representatives, only one is Democrat. Of the 30 members that were previously members of the House, here again 29 are Republican and only one is Democrat. (See Appendix III, page 254) Both ALEC and TC serve as government consultants and lobbyists, creating self serving Bills that use their own federal and state legislative members to jointly prepare policies that powerful corporations and their lobbyists and special interest members have prepared for current state and federal House and Senate members to later approve as written. ALEC drafts and proposes legislation for each state, bringing together international corporations and their partisan Republican legislators to write and propose a variety of Bills —

many dealing with gun laws, and voter suppression and union-busting policies — as well as a whole series of self- serving and controversial legislation. ALEC's national network of state and federal politicians and powerful corporations is designed solely to increase corporate profits without ever being scrutinized by the public. In fact, the public no longer has very much to say about what their appointed representatives are secretly promoting.

• A member may not teach without prior notification to and approval of the Senate Select Committee on Ethics for Senators, or the House Committee on Standards of Official Conduct for the House of Representatives.

• Members of the House of Representatives and Senators are also prohibited from accepting honoraria.

Outside Earned Income means, wages, salaries, fees, and other amounts received or to be received as compensation for personal services actually rendered. This does not however include copyright royalties, which are received from established publishers under usual and customary contractual terms.

Tax Deductions

Members are allowed to deduct from income tax, living expenses up to $3,000 per annum, while away from their congressional districts or home states.

Government Publications

Each Representative is entitled to receive certain government publications and printed products including: Copies of the daily Congressional Record, one copy of Deschler's Precedents, various manuals and directories, online Publication of Disbursement Records and public document franked envelopes.

Travel Allowance for Organizational Caucuses or Conferences

Each member-elect and one designated staff person may receive one round trip between their places of residence in the district and Washington, DC, for the purpose of attending a caucus or conference, which is reimbursed on a per diem or other basis for expenses incurred in connection with their attendance.

The Legislative Assistance Allowance for all Senators.

The total amount available in each Senator's Official Personnel and Office Expense Account (SOPOEA) is the sum of the two personnel allowances (administrative and clerical assistance and legislative assistance) and the office expense allowance. The components of the SOPEOA can be interchanged. In other words, office expenses can be used to pay office personnel salaries. Mass mailings may not exceed $50,000 per fiscal year. The Administrative and Clerical Assistance Allowance Component of the SOPOEA is allocated according to the population of a Senator's state. Preliminary allowance figures have varied from $2,361,820 for a Senator representing a state with a population under 5 million to $3,753,614 for a Senator representing a state with a population of 28 million or more. All components of the SOPOEA are interchangeable. The Legislative Assistance Component of the SOPOEA is $477,874, which is equivalent to three positions paid at $159,291.

Senate Interns

Senators may employ interns and determine their own financial arrangements.

Office Space in States

Each Senator is authorized to secure suitable office space in federal buildings in the state they represents. In the event suitable office space is not available in a federal building, a Senator may lease privately owned office space. The cost of private space is not to exceed the highest rate per square foot charged by the General Services Administration (GSA).

The aggregate square footage of office space that can be secured for a Senator ranges from 5,000 square feet, if the population of the state is less than 3 million, to 8,200 square feet, if the state's population is 17 million or more. There is no restriction on the number of offices. A Senator is also entitled to lease one mobile office for use only in the state they represent and are reimbursed for rent and non-personnel costs of operating the office. There are limitations on the terms of the lease, the maximum annual rental payment, and reimbursable operating costs. No reimbursement is to be made for expenses incurred during the 60 days preceding a contested election.

Each Senator is authorized furniture and furnishings from an approved list. Furniture and furnishings are supplied and maintained by the Architect of the Capitol (for spaces in Senate office buildings) and the Senate Sergeant at Arms (for offices in the Capitol). Additional furnishings can be purchased through the Senate stationery store. Each Senator is authorized $40,000 for state office furniture and furnishings for one or more offices, if the aggregate square footage of office space does not exceed 5,000 square feet. The base authorization is increased by $1,000 for each authorized additional incremental increase in office space of 200 square feet, and this allowance is automatically increased at the beginning of each Congress to reflect inflation. The aggregate dollar amount is the maximum value of furniture and furnishings to be provided by GSA for state office use at any one time. Furniture and furnishings remain GSA property. Each Senator may use certain basic office equipment allocated in accordance with the population of the state he or she represents and other factors that have been stipulated by the Senate Committee on Rules and Administration.

Congressional Salaries and Allowances Congressional Research Service shows a range of $2,960,726 to $4,685,279, depending on the state. The average allocation was $3,206,825.

Politicians set their own benefit programs for their very comprehensive single prepayment type Government Healthcare Plan and a very lucrative Retirement Plan. In essence, *"We the People"* have essentially condoned a situation that promotes corruption. In fact the United State's House of

Representatives and Senate currently spend so much time administering their Salary, expense and benefit programs as well as their current out of control election donations that they no longer have time to deal with the major issues confronting our nation. Therefore an unbiased administrative committee for *"We the People"* needs to set future policy that should be considered when calculating the overall compensation a Senator or a member of the House of Representative receives. Today's dysfunctional two party political system has failed remarkably and urgently needs to be revised so it fairly represents the people, rather than the powerful wealthy of the New World Order who have bought off our politicians through Citizens United or the more recently created Super PACS along with all their other self administered financial gifts and benefits. This country needs a more transparent and simpler system that constantly reminds the government representatives that they actually do represent *"We the People"* and not some powerful privately owned International Investment Banking System or some International Corporate Monopoly. Therefore it is recommended that the following Policy be implemented and enforced.

Proposed Policy 1

All members of the United State's House of Representatives and Senate and this government's Administration should be restricted by an unbiased administrative committee of *"We the People"* from accepting any corporate employment or position, stock, or direct or indirect donations, campaign donations, subsidies, gifts, outside benefits or membership during their tenure in office and for a period of five years following their term in office, thereby utilizing their substantial retirement programs, which were designed to protect them from this type of conflict of interest or outside influence. As a result, the United States Government will therefore be required to grant adequate public campaign subsidy for all approved government candidates running for public office.

POLICY 2

Change the Tax System

It is questionable that the working class really understands that our Federal Reserve Bank System is privately owned and is not subject to oversight by either the Congress or the President. When the Federal Reserve Act was passed in 1913, the people of the United States did not perceive that a world banking system was being established by a few very powerful international bankers and industrialists that intended to eventually control the United States Government. Lending money was primarily how these powerful privately owned international investment banks made their huge profits, and since these banks established their own policies and owned controlling stock in the Federal Reserve System, the working class inadvertently and really unknowingly relinquished their tax dollars and their interest income to these privately held Federal and Commercial Investment Banks. Some of these wealthy family stock holders included the powerful J.P. Morgan; Carnegie; Rothschild; Lazard; Seiff; Loeb; Sachs and Rockefeller families. Prior to Woodrow Wilson's appointment as President, he'd been persuaded by these same powerful bankers on the importance of supporting the proposed Federal Reserve Act, and our country's first income tax that was approved in 1913. A national income tax had previously been declared unconstitutional by the Supreme Court in 1895, so it required a constitutional amendment, which was proposed and passed in Congress based on the efforts of Senator Nelson Aldrich, who was John D. Rockefeller Junior's father-in-law. Coincidentally, World War I began in 1914, and as with all wars, it produced a large national debt and huge profits for these closely knit *Money Barons.* Baruch, the head of the War Industries Board; the Rockefellers; Cleveland Dodge, who sold munitions to the allies, the Rothschild's, and J.P. Morgan who loaned hundreds of millions, all benefited enormously with the U.S. entry into a war. And just as planned by these multinational entrepreneurs, the national debt suddenly went from $1 billion to $25 billion. Both Baruch and Rockefeller were reported to have earned more than $200 million in interest alone during World War I. However, in spite of that and as presented to the American people, it seemed reasonable enough to pay income tax on only one percent of income under $20,000, with the assurance that it would never increase — which never happened. But more assuredly, John D. Rockefeller and J.P. Morgan had obviously found a way to be sure their loans to the Government would be paid by tax, thus supporting the same Money Baron's scam that has once again taken over our entire country by way of today's dysfunctional Congress. It does not take a Genius to understand that budgets require adjusting both income and expense up and down to be kept in balance, and those that think otherwise are clearly heading into troubled waters. The oath of office, which is taken before undertaking the duties of any office in our government, certainly constitutes a statement of loyalty to the constitution of the United States, and it should certainly be considered treason or a high crime to betray a sworn oath to such a high office.

For example:

> *I do solemnly swear that I will support and defend the Constitution of the United States against all enemies, foreign and domestic; that I will bear true faith and allegiance to the same; that I take this obligation freely, without any mental reservation or purpose of evasion; and that I will well and faithfully discharge the duties of the office on which I am about to enter.*

Based on their Oath of Office, how dare any newly elected or previously elected official even think of violating their responsibility. Signing the Norquist pledge, which cannot even be printed without authorization, should clearly be considered a treasonous act and should be prosecuted to its fullest extent. Budgeting is a responsibility that requires the ability to increase or decrease both income and expense as required and every Republican who signed the Norquist Tax Pledge as far back as 1990 clearly violated their Oath of Office when they signed another conflicting oath that they will "never" allow a tax increase. Some 238 Republican members of the House and 41 senators, along with hundreds of state Republican officeholders have signed such a pledge, and this Taxpayer Protection Pledge has obviously been the cause for today's dysfunctional Congress by advancing the political gridlock in Washington as well as every state capitol. Without a doubt, no elected representative should ever be allowed to sign any pledge other than their Oath of Office. To support this, surveys show that some 85% of the electorate, *"We the People,"* and some 77% of the Republican voters think the Norquist pledge was a bad idea.

Since the Clinton era had produced a budget surplus, George W. Bush felt it was time to revise the United States tax code by signing into law the following:

- The Economic Growth and Tax Relief Reconciliation Act (EGTRAA) of 2001.

- The Jobs and Growth Tax Relief Reconciliation Act (JGTRRA) of 2003.

- The Tax Relief, Unemployment Insurance Reauthorization, and Job Creation Act which was signed into law in 2010.

These Tax Cuts had sunset provisions that made them expire at the end of 2010, however, these sunset provisions were extended for two years by President Barack Obama in 2010, because the 2001 and 2003 Acts were incorrectly thought to have significantly reduced the marginal tax rates for almost all U.S. taxpayers. However, this was not the case, and there was a great deal of controversy as to who actually benefited from these Bush tax cuts, or if they were effective in creating both jobs and economic growth. The proponents of lower taxes argued that the Bush tax cuts increased the pace of this nation's economic recovery and job growth — while the critics said the tax cuts had clearly failed to encourage growth and increased the budget deficit by shifting the tax burden from the rich to the middle class — which actually did happen, thereby increasing income inequality by shifting the burden of taxation away from upper-income groups to the wage-earning households of the lower and middle class, while skyrocketing the top 1% of wage earners income to historic levels. Another problem involved the previously established Alternative Minimum Tax (AMT) of the Internal Revenue Code, which had inadvertently not been adjusted to match the lowered rates of the 2001 and 2003 acts. In actuality, this caused the working class to pay higher taxes, thereby reducing the benefits of the two acts for the middle class wage earners who paid for dependents and both state and local income taxes as well as property taxes. The Internal Revenue Service tax rate reductions for the top 0.1% had been dropping steadily from the year 1945 to 2005 from 60 % to 21% while the top .01% dropped from 55% to 24% for that same period. Since 2005 both categories have had a slight increase for the 0.1% to 24% and the .01% to 26% in 2010. Despite the extension of the Bush tax cuts in 2010, it should be noted that the unemployment rate was 4% in 2000, increasing in 2003 to 6.1% and 10% in 2010, which indicates the unemployment rate increased instead of creating jobs because of the Bush Tax cuts. And now that the sunset provisions have finally been reinstated in the 2013 tax year, there will finally be a tax increase for the top 0.1% tax bracket to 39.6% — close to where it was when this country had a budget surplus for the first time in many years under the Clinton administration. However, now that the United States has returned to tax increases for the wealthy as of January 2013, the unemployment rate is only slowly starting to decrease to 7.9 % according to the U.S. Bureau of Labor Statistics. The Bush tax cuts were clearly the single biggest cause for the current deficit, reducing revenues by about $1.8 trillion between 2002 and 2009. The Bush tax cuts (EGTRRA and JGTRRA) also added about $1.6 trillion to our debt between 2001 and 2011, excluding interest. The Democrats have suggested that couples with incomes less than $250,000, not be subjected to tax increases, while the Republicans wish to add $3.3 trillion in loss of taxes to the national debt, plus another $0.66 trillion for interest and debt service costs, which all points out the need for major tax policy changes if we are ever to get our federal government back on course. And on top of all this, we now know full well that the U.S. needs to increase current revenues substantially above current levels, while decreasing spending by at least some four trillion dollars over the next ten years.

Proposed Policy 2

The United States shall develop and implement a single Tax Standard, which is adequate to meet all of this country's financial needs, and which is proportionate to every citizen's earnings and purchases in the open market. All other Federal tax, including tax-exempt foundations that serve as repositories for divested interests that make one's assets non-taxable to avoid estate and gift taxes, should also be brought to an end.

POLICY 3

Protect Working Class Benefits

After experiencing the largest budget breaking period in this nation's history, this country's working class is beginning to wonder if they'll ever be able to protect their non-elective human Entitlement Services, which our elected politicians are trying so hard to take away. In fact, these elected politicians are actually trying to force the average American's job related benefits into the open competitive market. Worse yet, if the working class is ever going to be able to protect these work benefits, it will require a knowledgeable and just leadership that is capable of differentiating between an *"Open Market"* and our once protected *"Noncompetitive Market,"* which is essential in maintaining a healthy and productive workforce. By allowing the working classes' human services to be placed in the open market arena, these puppet plutocrats have allowed this New World Order to actually steal directly from our public treasury; thereby callously challenging the equality of this country's middle class. Yet, we as a nation have allowed these invisible banking aristocracies to do exactly that. Allowing Congress to pass the McCarran Ferguson Act of 1945 was their first attempt to seek profit from this nation's healthcare entitlement program — and as we now know based on actual experience, profit insurance has spiraled healthcare cost to an unbelievable level, thereby changing this nation's healthcare system from number one in the world to 37th. Now Congress and these same profit seekers want to allow profit insurance into this nation's long standing Social Security Entitlement Program, when the working class already knows that profit only adds to the cost to this nation's entitlement benefits. Isn't it strange that these plutocrats promote a Democracy in Iraq, while we're losing our freedoms in the United States? They propose standards and regulations for China when we can no longer maintain nonprofit entitlement standards for our Social Security Retirement Program. In fact, hasn't this NWO's wealthy aristocracy's insatiable appetite for profit from these human services totally overshadowed this nation's freedom and equality — clearly forcing the working class back into the same bondage of the thirties. Perhaps this is why these closely knit international investment bankers and corporations keep our nation in such a high state of fear and denial with all their unjust wars, lies, and deceit. Yes, the United States needs to protect its workforce, the backbone of this nation, and their Noncompetitive Entitlement Market, which involves the working classes' benefits and services. These benefits or services to humanity as well as this nation's infrastructure should never be used to earn a profit, and therefore these services require nonprofit standards and regulations under a centralized system that is managed efficiently and cost effectively without involving profit. Clearly this is meant to include such things as:

- This nation's Social Security benefit

- Any future single nonprofit prepayment healthcare service that treats our sick and disabled equally

- And all the services our citizens receive from a cost effective and well managed infrastructure.

And yes, all of these services and benefits are the property of the working class, which require they be efficiently managed under a centralized non competitive private nonprofit and/or government system or any combination thereof. These promised services should never again be cut or allowed to make such services and benefits fair game to the open market, where the working class can be taken advantage of. Nor should they ever be referred to as *"socialized"* or *"big government"* programs when these benefits are the sole property of the working class, thereby discouraging any further development of today's two level system — one for the have's and one for the have-not's. Social Security is not a retirement savings plan, but a universal nonprofit insurance program that helps protect workers, retirees, and their families from life's unknowns. Most of its benefits support retirees via old-age insurance, but some also provides insurance in case people become disabled, widowed, or orphaned. Social Security has been providing its citizens with old age, disability, and widow and orphan insurance for more than three quarters of a century, and it isn't going broke as most plutocrats suggest. It provides:

- Disability Insurance   16%
- Widowed and Orphaned Insurance   10%
- Old Age Insurance   73%

In that all Congressional Members are currently required to pay into the Social Security Entitlement Program without receiving any benefits — and since they have their own exclusive nonprofit federal programs (CSRS & FERS), it just may suggest why they say Social Security is going bankrupt and are so anxious to see Social Security be placed under a profit centered insurance program. The fact is that Social Security isn't going bankrupt, nor is bankruptcy even possible as the system is currently set up. Making no budgetary adjustments could mean Social Security won't be able to meet all its obligations in two decades from now, but the plan is definitely not going bankrupt. In fact, it currently is collecting more than it pays out, while its trust fund also is collecting interest. However, due to potential demographic and economic changes one can anticipate its insurance payments will begin to exceed income in the year 2021, and around the year 2033 the fund will be in trouble if no adjustments are made — but even then, the revenue Social Security collects each year would still be enough to pay out at least three-quarters of its current and scheduled benefits to well beyond the year 2090. For Social Security to go bankrupt, you'd have to totally ignore Social Security's revenue, and most profit oriented companies would go bankrupt in only a few years if they ignored all their revenues and sat back and watched their expenses drive their assets down to nothing. That's the same mistake numerous current politicians have openly made when they suggest they also want to adjust this country's budgetary expense downward without considering this country's income adjustments. That is why all successful businesses routinely adjust their budgeted income and expense annually. If one would look at the Social Security budget properly, they'd readily recognize they'd only have to adjust income for Social Security to about 0.9% of GDP in order to make Social Security's revenues match up with its expenses for the next 75 years — and that's an amount that is close to what the Bush tax cuts cost us. Under normal budgeting circumstances one solution would be to either exempt higher wage-earners from Social Security tax, like those that make more than $100,000, or we could raise the overall Social Security rate which current national poles support. There are many other options like cutting benefits or raising retirement age which the poles do not support — or we could go ahead and increase government expense by paying it out of the general fund. There are also many reasons for considering other projected Social Security shortfalls that must become a part of any plan and they would include such things as the fact that there have been about three workers for every Social Security beneficiary over the last three decades, and this will change to two workers by 2035. And yes, this could also put a strain on the system. Life expectancy at birth has also risen over the recent decades, as well as a declining birth rate and rising income inequality, which should all be considered in any future budgeting decisions. Therefore cutting benefits by increasing the retirement age and considering the fact that life expectancy is increasing must all be evaluated before they become any part of a Social Security master plan.

Although many think Social Security adds to the nation's deficit, it does not, since it has its own taxing source (Social Security Payroll Taxes) and therefore it cannot spend more than it earns. Under no circumstances should it be transferred to some profit insurance company to add profit to its cost. Much of this confusion stems from this country's very confusing federal accounting practices that list Social Security in the consolidated federal budget and the fact that the Social Security's trust fund invests in Treasury bonds that are debt investments. The payroll tax holiday was also established to lower payroll taxes in January 2011 to stimulate the economy and therefore the federal government made up the lost revenue to Social Security that would have been collected if the holiday had not been established. This holiday is expected to end next year. What is really needed, are politicians that have some understanding of budgeting and can make sensible business decisions.

Proposed Policy 3

The United States Government shall at all times protect the entitlement benefits, insurance and services for the disabled, the elderly and this nation's work force, which is the backbone of this nation. These entitlement benefits, insurance and services should never be used so someone can earn a profit, and therefore they require written government standards and regulations under a centralized structure that is managed both efficiently and cost effectively. This policy is meant to include such things as: Any God given natural product; our Social Security Benefits; our once very successful single nonprofit prepayment healthcare service that previously treated this nation's sick and disabled equally; as well as our entire infrastructure that should be designed to adequately service all of our humanity adequately under additional nonprofit entitlement programs. It should also be understood that these services, benefits and products are the "property" of the working class, the sick and disabled and the elderly, and therefore they should be efficiently managed and regulated under a single centralized noncompetitive private nonprofit and/or government entitlement structure or any combination thereof. Once this is accomplished, we should never again allow such entitlement services and benefits to become fair game to the open profit centered market, where the working class and this nation's citizens can be taken advantage of — nor should they negatively be politically classified as "Socialized" or "Big Government" programs when these benefits are the sole property of every qualified citizen of the United States, which embraces this outstanding "Democracy of We The People."

POLICY 4

Repeal the Federal Reserve Act

Prior to the 1907 Bankers' Panic or Knickerbocker Crisis, the United States had no central bank, which forced Congress to create a National Monetary Commission. As previously indicated, this was accomplished under the leadership of Senator Nelson Aldrich, who was the father-in-law of John D. Rockefeller, Jr. In 1913, this Commission recommended the creation of a Central Bank, and as a result, J.P. Morgan, John D. Rockefeller, Paul Warburg, Otto Kahn, and Jacob Schiff all played a major role in the establishment of the Federal Reserve System. You also need to remember that the Federal Reserve is privately owned and is not subject to oversight by either the Congress or the President — yet, Article I, Section 8, of the U.S. Constitution, grants the Congress the power to coin money and regulate this money's value. Because the Rockefellers; J.P. Morgan; Carnegie; Rothschild; Lazard; Seiff; Loeb; and Sachs families all together own controlling stock in this privately held Federal Reserve, their international investment banks are in a position to coin money and regulate its value, making huge profits by lending the Fed's fiat money (money without a gold standard), which they can create by the stroke of a pen. During the Great Depression, Franklin Delano Roosevelt was forced to take this country off the gold standard during the depression, and without the gold standard there is currently no way to protect the people's savings should any type of inflation occur. Other countries have also floated these unregulated currencies, since our global currency is no longer backed up by any type of standard. And now, since a large share of the international market is owned by these same powerful *Money Barons,* the dollar is totally regulated by the market this New World Order creates. Gold had previously served as one's protector of property rights, but today's out of control deficit spending has essentially opened the door to this powerful NWO's scheme of confiscating the vast majority of wealth — which they totally control. And since these banks establish their own policies, the government has essentially relinquished their tax dollars and their interest income to these privately held Federal and commercial banks. Once again it's important note, the Federal Reserve pays the Bureau of Engraving and Printing approximately $23 for each 1,000 notes printed. One million dollars in fiat money cost the Federal Reserve $230 for which this New World Order then secure a pledge of collateral equal to the face value from the U.S. government. This collateral is essentially our land, labor, and assets, which is conveniently collected for them by the government's IRS. By authorizing the Fed to regulate and create money, recessions, depressions and inflations, Congress has given these private international banks the power to create their huge profits at will. Prior to Woodrow Wilson's appointment as President, he'd been persuaded at the Democratic Party headquarters in 1912, on the importance of supporting the proposed Federal Reserve Act, and this country's first income tax back in 1913 — however he later admitted that this was a huge mistake. (See Appendix V Quotes, page 266) As previously indicated, establishing any national income tax was declared unconstitutional by the Supreme Court in 1885, so it required a constitutional amendment, which was proposed and later secretly and some think possibly illegally passed in Congress based on the efforts of Senator Nelson Aldrich. As presented to the American people it seemed reasonable enough, income tax on only one percent of income under $20,000, with the assurance that it would never increase, which of course never happened. What happened was John D. Rockefeller had found a way to be sure his loans would be paid by the Government, which started this corrupt scam that has now taken over the entire country. A total over throw of the Government was actually attempted in 1934, when many of these very same bankers and corporations attempted to unseat President Roosevelt in a plot that was publicly exposed by retired Marine Corps Major General Smedley Butler, when he uncovered their plot at the McCormack-Dickstein Congressional Committee meeting. In his testimony, Butler told this committee on July 17, 1932, he was approached by several wealthy businessmen who had asked him to help overthrow this nation's democracy in a military coup. In the Congressional Committee's report, Butler's allegations were later validated, but no prosecutions or further investigations ever followed, which is usually what happens when it involves this upper crust. In retrospect, the devastation of the Great Depression had caused many of these very rich families to actually question the foundation of our Democracy, considering Fascism, Socialism, or even Communism as an alternative that would give them greater control over their wealth. Yet even today, many of these same wealthy international investment bankers are still directly involved in this nation's current fiscal insolvency through their privately owned Federal Reserve. They have also achieved substantial control over much of this nation's gold since we went off our gold standard, and they of course still continue to aggressively seek total control over the World Market, the International Industrial Complex, and our Nation's Armed Services. In addition to all this, this international market has presented an enormous fiscal and political obligation for the United States, and by allowing this NWO to recklessly increase the size and cost of our government, it intentionally has now destroyed this nation's budget and our reputation. But what is so shocking today is only a handful of Americans can with any assurance explain what our real economic deficits are anymore, nor do they understand the size of the tax burden this wealthy cult has created for our children. Yet *"We the People"* blindly sat back and allowed a reduction in tax for this very wealthy top one percent of the wage earners at a time when this country's huge deficits were starting to spiral out of control. Isn't it foolish to believe our tax dollars support this nation, when so many of us know full well we are only paying the *Money Baron's* spiraling bank loan interest, while relinquishing our hard earned entitlement benefits that belong to the working class? For example:

We've obligated ourselves to more than a trillion dollars in un-audited loan expenditures for our unjust wars, and we can see no results that would even come close to justifying such exorbitant and uncontrolled spending. We're told we have to build and maintain the most powerful and expensive armed service in the world, when both the Congress and the Administration admit that terrorism can no longer be fought with conventional weapons. And with all this budget breaking spending, we find nothing meaningful being done to adequately protect our troops, our borders, our port authorities, or the implementation of our homeland security report — for which we've already received a second failing grade. In just six short years the neo-conservative kleptocratic administration took us from a $236 billion surplus to a deficit we've never experienced before; a deficit that currently exceeds sixteen and a half trillion dollars and is still rising — and yet our Congress does nothing! So just where has all this bank loan and interest money gone? And why did this country's debt increase some $8.146 trillion in just a short period of five years under this neo-conservative administration that openly and aggressively promoted wars and a one world government, which still continues to increase our debt at a rate of more than two billion dollars a day? That's an insurmountable figure by anyone's imagination — but here again, it's all a big secret, and unless we investigate the money trail, we'll never know. Should China call for the payment of their loans to us, or should we have to redeem the huge loans from our Social Security, which they deceitfully tell us is going bankrupt, this nation is doomed to bankruptcy if we're not bankrupt already by paying for these *Money Baron's* huge profits. In fact, we cannot even begin to find a just reason for the estimated two billion dollars a day we pay in interest to this NWO. Yet, our Congress votes to rebuild other countries, when far too many American paychecks are decreasing as favored executive benefits and international corporate profits are soaring to unheard of new levels. And yes, this country's work force is obligated to pay for all this while our representatives in Congress suggest we reduce our entitlement benefits as we're simultaneously being forced into lesser paying jobs while these international corporations hire illegal foreign cut rate help at the same time as some of our children are bringing home their school lunch to help feed their family.

You should also note that this country's trade deficits started to grow disproportionately as early as 1975, and over the years these deficits have been steadily climbing out of control, with no Congressional action.

For example:
- 1995 — $180 billion
- 1996 — $184 billion
- 1997 — $198 billion
- 1998 — $298 billion

- 1999 — $372 billion
- 2000 — $409 billion
- 2007 — $830 billion

Worse yet, these trade deficits are still growing while the off-shore tax fraud by this NWO has favored their totally controlled international corporations. Recently, the US has bought over 3 trillion dollars worth of foreign commodities with loans from these international bankers — which are designed to intentionally level this country to that of others through the following ineptly administered agreements:

- The General Agreement on Tariffs and Trade (GATT)
- The World Trade Organization (WTO)
- The North American Free Trade Agreement (NAFTA)
- The Central America Free Trade Agreement (CAFTA)
- The Free Trade Areas of the Americas (FTAA)

In fact, all these programs are currently stealing directly from our public treasury. And on top of all this, many of the international corporations are wildly and openly continuing to export our jobs from America — while they continue to intentionally and uncontrollably reduce average salaries across this nation. It's hard to believe God has sent this nation on any mission to free the entire world, while we as a nation acquiesce to this ridiculous NWO at our own destructive expense — spending their huge loans as if there's no tomorrow. Well let me assure you there will be no tomorrow if we continue to let these privately owned kleptocratic aristocracies take over our once sovereign nation under today's privately run International Monetary Fund — the privately held Federal Reserve — and their privately held World Bank. And if you look closely at all the facts, our nation is clearly on a direct path toward a Fascist Dictatorship, as these powerful bankers flatten the United States — making us easy prey for those countries that are now standing in the wings waiting to see this once great nation fail. Isn't this playing directly into Al Qaeda's hands? And all this is being done while our leaders maintain such a high level of terror and fear in the people that we've all become far less secure. Didn't the Napoleonic era in France, Caesar's Roman Empire, Russia, Spain, England, and more recently the Hitler Regime already try this? Emotion filled phrases like *"Weapons of Mass Destruction"* and terror alerts, shouldn't disorient us when our appointed leaders no longer do anything to protect us, or provide any hard evidence for solving this problem. Instead, they investigate the people who speak out against such terrorism, while declaring them the conspirator. This type of military science may perhaps blind some of the population for a period of time, but in the end, there will be a growing and dissenting population that can no longer be fooled by such ruthless tactics. Yes, it's common for almost everyone to want to rise to the top, but unless you are born into their cult, only a few will ever really be able to claim the power and wealth today's super rich (the upper 0.1%) possess. And because approximately eighty percent of the population tends to be followers, while only five percent or less are capable of assuming a position of leadership, these aggressive entrepreneurial leaders actually believe the general population can never provide the leadership required to manage this nation. And you know what? They just might be right — which doesn't speak well for our democracy. In fact, as many individuals seeks to rise to the top, they are also doomed to be cast aside when they eventually reach their zenith point, or try to reach too far. In fact, many of today's executives are used only temporarily by this extremely wealthy and tightly knit inner circle and will be cast aside when they are of no further use, or they offer a serious challenge to those that are currently in total control. It should also be understood that rules, laws, standards and regulations seldom if ever apply to this lofty upper crust; while deregulation and decentralization only applies to those businesses and governments that are not a part of their powerful monopoly. Therefore in studying this nation's financial dilemma, we also need to look very closely at the International Industrial Complex and all the crooked CEO's that have gotten into trouble because of today's reckless corporate deregulation. Currently, far too many corrupt executives, who have yet to be accepted into this inner circle, have been investigated by the Justice Department; the Security Exchange Commission (SEC); Congress; the National Association of Securities Dealers (NASD) and Self Regulating Organizations (SRO). In fact, as the deregulation of ethics and standards fired up hundreds of corporate scandals, which were previously referred to as *"The Great Cover-Up,"* we see only minimal evidence of justice for the working class who are always damaged by such illegal acts. In fact, almost all this rampant corporate deregulation has actually created a kind of malignant narcissism that has stimulated far too many ruthless corporate executives into a false type of self-adoration, all resulting in a host of grandiose implications.

Proposed Policy 4

The United States should repeal the Federal Reserve Act and the IRS code, taking back the ownership of our Federal Reserve and its banks, while establishing auditable internal controls for this country's future government owned Federal Banking System, which needs its monetary system to be based on a value standard such as gold. The Public Treasury should also become totally responsible for the creation of all money, which shall be kept both interest-free and debt-free – thereby establishing a solid pay as you go standard while aggressively repaying our current loans. The United States shall never again allow private banks or non government organizations to control this country's money, and this nation should never again borrow from privately owned profit centered banks.

POLICY 5

Control All Expenditures

The General Accounting Office (GAO) is the audit, evaluation, and investigative arm of the United States Congress legislative branch of our Government which was established as the General Accounting Office under the Budget and Accounting Act of 1921, which is to investigate all matters relating to the receipt, disbursement, and application of public funds. This office prepares reports to both the President and Congress and makes recommendations for greater economy or efficiency involving all public expenditures, thereby helping Congress meet its constitutional responsibilities to improve the performance and accountability of the federal government for the benefit of the American people. They accomplish this by conducting financial and performance audits, while serving as the congressional watchdog and the taxpayers' best friend to expose government waste and inefficiency.

The GAO is headed by the Comptroller General for a 15-year, non-renewable term and who is appointed by the President with the advice and consent of the Senate. There have been only seven Comptroller Generals in the past, giving the GAO a continuity of leadership that is seldom found in government. The Comptroller General may not be removed by the President, but can if necessary be removed by Congress through impeachment or a joint resolution for justified reasons.

The GAO also establishes standards for audits of government organizations, programs, activities, and functions, and of government assistance received by contractors, nonprofit organizations, and other nongovernmental organizations. These standards are called the Generally Accepted Government Auditing Standards (GAGAS), and are to be followed by auditors and audit organizations when required by law, regulation, agreement, contract, or policy.

All GAO reports are available on the GAO website (www.gao.gov), except for certain reports whose distribution is limited to official use to protect national and homeland security. The routine reports include:

- Federal Budget and Fiscal Issues to Financial Management
- Education; Retirement Issues
- Defense
- Homeland Security
- Administration of Justice
- Health Care
- Information Management and Technology
- Natural Resources
- Environment
- International Affairs
- Trade
- Financial Markets
- Housing
- Government Management and Human Capital

Each year the GAO also issues an audit report on the financial statements of the United States Government, outlining its public debt, while also providing a Federal Fiscal Outlook Report describing the deficit in cash, rather than an accrual basis, even though the accrual deficit would provide more information on the longer-term implications of the government's annual operations. The most recent GAO strategy plan, for 2010-2015, sets out four goals:

- Current and Emerging Challenges to the Well-being and Financial Security of the American People
- Changing Security Threats and the Challenges of Global Interdependence
- Transformation of the Federal Government to Address National Challenges
- Maximization of the Value of the GAO

The U.S. Treasury manages the day to day U.S. debt through its Bureau of the Public Debt under two main categories:

● Intra-governmental Holdings ($4.9 trillion debt)

● Debt Held by the Public ($11.6 trillion debt).

Intra-governmental Holdings — There are some 230 Federal agencies that buy U.S. Treasuries and as of September 2012 the Treasury Bulletin listed the following agencies:

<u>Agency</u>	<u>U.S. Treasuries</u>
• Social Security	$2.72 trillion
• Office of Personnel Management	$1.12 trillion
• Dept. of Health and Human Services	$69 billion
• Federal Deposit Insurance Corporation	$35 billion
• Department of Transportation	$20 billion
• Department of the Treasury	$23 billion
• Department of Labor	$21 billion
• Other Programs and Funds	$933 billion.

<u>Held by the Public</u> — The following public groups buy U.S. Treasuries, bills, notes, bonds, TIPS, Savings Bonds, and State and Local Government Series securities

<u>Organizations</u>	<u>Purchase Amount</u>
• Foreign	$5.311 trillion
• Federal Reserve	$166 trillion
• State and Local Government	$709.1 billion
• Mutual Funds	$864.9 billion
• Private Pension Funds	$605.2 billion
• Banks	$305.2 billion
• Insurance Companies	$259.1 billion
• U.S. Savings Bonds	$184.7 billion
• Other	$1.14 trillion

Note: The Office of Personnel Management includes Federal Employees Retirement, Life Insurance, Hospital Insurance Trust Funds, including Postal Service. Foreign governments and investors hold 48% of the nation's public debt, while 21% is held by U.S. government entities, such as the Federal Reserve and state and local governments. Mutual funds, private pension funds, savings bonds or individual treasury notes comprise 15 %, while the 16% is held by various businesses, banks, insurance companies, trusts and investors. Others includes: Individuals, government-sponsored enterprises, brokers and dealers, bank personal trusts and estates, corporate and non-corporate businesses, and other investors.

Thirty percent of the U.S. Treasury debt is held in trust for the people's retirement in Social Security, and retirement and pension funds and if the U.S. were to default, the greatest harm would be to its own U.S. citizen. The Federal Reserve really doesn't have a reason to own Treasury notes, but because of the many spiraling financial problems that started in 2007, the fed's and G.W. Bush needed to stimulate the economy by buying Treasury Notes, which would help to keep the interest rates low and help dispel the seriousness of the 2008 recession they were in. Because the Fed can create credit with fiat money out of thin air, if we ever expect to take the debt off the balance sheet, we need to resurrect the *Gold Standard* soon and stop this ridiculous creation of fiat money. According to the February 2006 U.S. Treasury report and Foreign Holding of U.S. Treasury Securities as of December 17, 2012 and a report for foreign countries as of October 2012, the following foreign countries hold U.S. Treasury Securities (debt) as follows:

Country	**Debt**
• China	$1.161 trillion
• Japan	$1.134 trillion
• Oil Exporting Countries	$266 billion
• Caribbean Banking Centers	$258 billion
• Brazil	$255 billion
• Luxembourg	$139 billion
• Belgium	$133 billion

Note: Taiwan, Switzerland, Russia, Hong Kong and the United Kingdom, were reported to each be holding U.S. Treasury Securities that range from $117 to $201 billion. China has been decreasing its holdings and if China

keeps the value of the dollar high and the Yuan relatively low, exports to the U.S. will appear more reasonable, which will in the long run help their economy.

Proposed Policy 5

The United States Government through the Government Accountability Office (GAO) should continue to responsibly audit, validate and control all capital and current expenditures, while recommending that this nation use only its own money for such expenditures, while responsibly planning and managing all capital improvements and infrastructure development.

POLICY 6

Enforce Ear Mark Transparency

The US does not have a spending problem so much as it has a corrupt financial system and a wealth and middle class inequality wage and earnings problem — a lack of a balanced free trade policies — and a profit seeking insurance (1945 McCarran Ferguson Act) and pharmaceutical healthcare service for the sick and disabled that has overwhelmed every family's day to day budget. In fact, our financial deregulation has destroyed our recent annual budget surplus and economy through the capitalist's desire to profit from all the nonprofit benefits we once provided to the middle class. The deregulation of trade standards for corporations, our ridiculous and unfair tax cuts for the wealthy ten percent, our corrupted political election system, as well as this nation's uncontrolled wars associated with the capitalist's profiteering have all added to today's dilemma. And on top of all this, we are now allowing these capitalists to create state controlled social systems that severely penalize the median wage earners, who are the backbone of this once great democracy. And this is all happening while the top one percent of these wage earners are making profits that are higher than anything ever experienced during the entire history of this nation. Yes, we have clearly opened the door to the robber baron's elite oligarchy of international investment banks, (NWO) that has been silently gaining greater world power and control during the entire twentieth century's out of control industrial advancements. And more recently we've even supported "The Troubled Asset Relief Program" (TARP) through our tax dollars, rather than let these mismanaged privately owned power structures feel the pain of their mismanaged and corrupt misuse of the people's savings to craft their dishonest profits. The problem is this nation is pouring their financial stimulus into an oligarchy of capitalist corruption, where our tax donations are being seized and misused under the guise of some intentionally created or natural crisis. As Milton Friedman in his book, *Capitalism and Freedom*, said, *"Only a crises — actual or perceived — produces real change,"* and so today's capitalist continues to create these crises that destroy the financial well being of our middle class. Although today's dysfunctional plutocrats in Washington may have recently been forced to delay their self-created disaster, by not sending this nation over the cliff in January 2013, it is now apparent that the entire Congress has been totally bought off and no longer represent *"We the People"* — as our voice has been entirely muted by campaign donations that have now far exceeded even the most shameful levels. Yes, our financial system is broken, based on an unsustainable US dollar and the uncontrollable Federal Reserve's excessive creation of fiat money. And now that the plutocrats in Washington have been totally corrupted, it will require the weeding out and incarceration of all the crooks that have benefited before we can eliminate this fraud that was created by this privately owned and totally controlled Federal Reserve and their sleazy partners in government. We all know the answer is transparency, reform, and equal justice for all under this nation's rule of law — and although this may never be fully achieved, it is at least worth pursuing if we ever expect to take back our democracy

Proposed Policy 6

The United States should legally enforce ear mark transparency prior to authorizing any related legislation and should require all public business and policy be opened to both public and legal scrutiny under this nation's Government of the People.

POLICY 7

Balance Foreign Trade

One of the world's long-term goals for deprived countries should be to replace foreign aid through self sustaining trade tax independence. In fact, the very act of trade taxation has already had an exceptionally beneficial effect on nurturing and developing the accountability of governments, and this suggests that nations need to be brought together to cooperate on trade tax policy, standards, rules and regulations — otherwise the policies of one country may seriously damage the policies of another. The current small-minded and biased national solutions to controlling the flow of money in and out of *"Tax havens,"* will only prevent the development of a comprehensive efficient cost effective plan, which requires some form of oversight and control between nations. Both Switzerland and the Cayman Islands were where these illicit *"Tax-havens,"* first got their start, and nations will have to universally take back total control under some form of international trade tax type regime if they ever expect to solve this exponentially growing problem. The reason this has become such an enormous concern for the United States is the unprecedented rise in wealth and control by the top one percent of worldwide income earners, while the U.S. trade tax deficits have been shifted to the working class. Yes, here again, by paying off this country's Congress or some off-shore *"Tax-haven,"* the elite one percent of income earners have once again escaped their responsibility with impunity. To solve this problem nations will need to band together to find an interim method of supplementing these offshore *"Tax-havens"* by replacing the current off shore profits involved, while the world economy restructures itself to an ethical and auditable trade tax system — that's if we can ever regain control over the wealthy one percent that currently have a strangle hold on the system. The United States also needs to stop the current lucrative campaign funds our plutocrats accept to turn their head from their Oath of Office. In any event, the continued theft of public assets must be brought to an end if this nation ever expects to regain its democracy and establish open and auditable transparency in the trade taxing system for these international corporations — so that they too are required to pay their fair share of the tax burden. Today's system only fosters criminal corruption through the theft of public funds by national and multinational corporations, individuals, lawyers, bankers and accountants that involve such legal concerns as:

- Tax-avoidance and tax-evasion
- Market manipulation and insider buying and selling
- The fraudulent misappropriation of funds
- The bribing of members of Congress
- The political theft and concealment of public assets off-shore

The current trade tax system provides a major competitive edge to the international wealth and their corporations, hedge funds and private equity companies — while ethical companies and individuals often find themselves at a serious disadvantage. In other words the haves should pay a higher income tax than the have-nots, and it should be based on an equal playing field that is fair and proportionate to one's income, which is the greatest political challenge facing the world today. In addition to one's income tax, the same ethical philosophy should include corporate tax, environmental taxes, inheritance taxes, customs duty fees and trade tax, as well as all other forms of tax that are paid by individuals, corporations, tax professionals, and governments. Yes, Americans need to promote a level playing field on our trade tax while opposing secrecy and tax regulation loopholes, problematic distortions, crimes and frauds, tax evasion, tax avoidance, and all the exploitation that presently exists. To accomplish this Americans need to have:

- Transparency
- International corporate cooperation on tax regulation and accountability
- Open competitive markets based on equitable taxation

● Progressive and equitable tax policy, standards, rules, regulations, and laws as well as current responsible leadership and enforcement

The NWO must also be blocked from continuing to set the political left against the right, so they can secretly implement their endless profit seeking goals, while destroying the working class's budget in the process. Therefore all Americans need to demand this nation's sovereignty be restored by our electorate before we can restore acceptable over-all international governance. International corporations and wealthy individuals (the top 1%) are currently the only real benefactors of today's corrupt *"Offshore Tax Loopholes"* that allow them to escape responsible trade tax payment, while the working class is left with the resulting tax burden. Today's *"Tax-havens"* allow the elite to pay very low, or sometimes no tax, thereby allowing them to hide from the policies, laws, rules, standards and regulations under their contrived cloak of secrecy. Not only does this distort markets, but it also destroys any form of democracy through the high level of fear they create by the poverty they generate amongst the working class, which is their ultimate aim. This nation's economic growth has been severely limited by this Shadow Government's secret desire for wealth at all costs, while their off-shore *"Tax-havens"* seem totally unconcerned as to the international impact and the resulting negative economics they create — and fighting and confronting this corruption will be one of the greatest tests this democracy has ever faced. Providing proper scrutiny, so these policies, laws, standards, rules and regulations are realistic and understandable to all corporations, has now become one of this nation's greatest concerns.

Holding what's been estimated to be more than eleven trillion dollars in offshore asset, so it cannot be taxed, potentially results in an annual loss in tax revenue close to 250 billion dollars. Just think of what this annual income could do to help fight climate change; the world's catastrophic water shortage; our nation's decaying infrastructure; our energy crisis; the world's exponentially growing population of seven billion human beings that is projected to grow to 26 billion by 2145; or the world's rapidly advancing poverty, which in this country has been recently estimated at 47 million people. It has also just been estimated that these assets, which are secretly held offshore beyond the access of taxation, are equal to about a third of our world's total assets. And the global annual cross-border flow of dollars from such criminal activity and other illegal tax evasion tricks have been estimated to be somewhere between $1 to 1.6 *trillion* per year. This offshore tax evasion not only occurs in small islands like the Caymans' and states like Switzerland but in international investment banks and financial centers in New York, London and Singapore, all providing and supporting secrecy and the related perks that only promote more tax evasion. And yes, this tax evasion is unconscionably and intentionally stripping the working class and our government of our public assets and investment capital for their own gain, which seriously deprives this once great country from ever reaching a balanced budget without these desperately needed tax revenues. Worse yet, globalization is being used as a front for this *Shadow Government's* (NWO's) insatiable appetite for profit — and Americans and all the other nations need to universally recognize this problem and aggressively fight such corrupt offshore tax tactics and everything they stand for.

In 1913, this nation's Congress, at the bequest of several very wealthy bankers and John D. Rockefeller, appointed the questionable National Monetary Commission, which it is often been said, *"illegally"* established the potential for their own NWO's scheme. However, it wasn't until after the Great Depression that things really began to seriously unravel as International Corporations began to open new world markets and exploit cross-border loopholes to avoid trade tax. And as a result, today's *"Tax-havens"* are seriously escalating competition in an effort to attract this huge amount of international capital. Therefore, the amount of wealth offshore is escalating by dimensions that have never before been seen in this new world market. Conversely, we know that taxation is the key to lifting hundreds of millions of people out of poverty, and that tax is the most fair and sustainable source of finance for any country's development. In fact, we've already determined that tax-revenues are the lifeblood of any countries social contract with their citizens. Therefore, a proper balance needs to be agreed upon and then enforced with corporations, governments and societies — and this will be no simple matter to accomplish. As we all know, the United States has been running consistent trade deficits for more than thirty years, largely because of the high imports of oil and other consumer products. The largest trade deficits have been with China, Japan, Germany, Mexico and Saudi Arabia, while the United States reached record surpluses with Hong Kong, Australia, Netherlands and Belgium in 2006. The U.S. balance of trade has averaged a negative -31,864 USD million from 1992 to 2012 — and in February of 1992, it reached an all time negative high of -83,100 USD million. The following describes 2011 and 2012:

2011 Month	USD Million	2012 Month	USD Million
Jan.	-40,454	Jan.	-50,421
Feb.	-47,521	Feb.	-52,209
March	-45,381	March	-44,507
April	-46,059	April	-51,647
May	-43,231	May	-49,647
June	-50,210	June	-46,930
July	-51,774	July	-40.846
Aug.	-45,613	Aug.	-41,630
Sept.	-45,091	Sept.	-42,581
Oct.	-44,009	Oct.	-40,277
Nov.	-43,121	Nov.	-42,240
Dec.	-47,524	Dec.	-48,730

Proposed Policy 7

The United States Government must balance its trade deficit, and tax foreign trade equally.

POLICY 8

Control No-bid Contracts

Competition in federal procurement contracting has become a major concern in the United States because of the sizable increases and the alleged misconduct involving the selection of noncompetitive contracts, which has been going on for far too long. Officials within the Department of Defense (DOD) actually have from time to time supported a reduction in the growing number of noncompetitive contracts, but it also should be noted that nothing has actually been done to correct this very serious problem, yet the DOD involves some 70% of the annual federal governments procurement spending.

The 1984 Competition in Contracting Act (CICA) was approved to oversee competition in federal procurement contracting, so any procurement contract not entered into through the use of proper procurement procedures, which are supported by statute, is subject to oversight by the CICA. Full and open competition through the use of competitive procedures is required unless certain circumstances exist that would permit agencies to use noncompetitive procedures. (Whatever that means) All contracts entered into without full and open competition are also considered noncompetitive, but the loophole is that noncompetitive contracts can still be in compliance when circumstances permitting other than full and open competition exists, such as:

- There is only a single source for goods or services

- There is an unusual and compelling urgency

- It involves products safeguarding the industrial base

- It must meet requirements of international agreements

- It involves legislative consent or purchase of brand-name items for resale

- It involves national security

- It involves contracts needed in the public interest

And so here again, there are far too many loopholes and the management is so decentralized it is almost impossible to provide adequate supervision or enforcement. Full and open competition usually involves the use of sealed bids that are considered competitive proposals, but loopholes are here again far too prevalent in what has now become a political nightmare.

And on top of all this, the CICA has far too many escape clauses that permit agencies to employ simplified product value procedures that confuse things even more, such as:

- When acquiring goods or services whose value is less than $150,000, or commercial goods or services whose expected value is less than $6.5 million, which can be increased to $12 million in case of some type of emergency, the procurement can vary from standard procedure.

Another confusion involves the issuance of orders under Task Order or Delivery Orders (TO/DO) is they are not considered under CICA supervision, even though the awarding of a TO/DO contract is under CICA supervision.

In 1994, the Federal Acquisition Streamlining Act (FASA) established a preference for multiple-award (TO/DO) contracts to include:

- The requirement that agencies are to provide contractors a fair opportunity to compete for orders (under multiple-award contracts) in excess of $3,000.

The Government Accountability Office (GAO) has also been authorized to:

● Oversee orders that increase the scope, period, or maximum value of an underlying contract.

And the National Defense Authorization Act (NDAA) for the fiscal year 2008 further limited the use of single-award (TO/DO) contracts that:

● Specify what constitutes a fair opportunity to be considered for orders in excess of $5.5 million under multiple-award contracts and also granted GAO jurisdiction to hear protests of orders valued in excess of $10 million.

Note: The provision authorizing GAO to hear such protests regarding the orders of civilian agencies is coming to an end in May 2011, however, the GAO recently found that it has jurisdiction over these protests because the NDAA for fiscal year 2008 amended FASA to provide that all limitations on GAO's jurisdiction over (TO/DO) order protests expired in May 2011, not just its authority over protests of (TO/DO) orders valued in excess of $10 million. Yet the 111th Congress enacted legislation extending the sunset date for GAO's jurisdiction over protests of orders valued in excess of $10 million issued by defense agencies until September 30, 2016 (P.L. 111-383, §825).

With all this sustained chaos and muddle-headedness is it any wonder why we need to urgently take action to protect our budget.

Public officials and politicians also present a growing problem. As previously stated in Chapter 5, Richard Cheney served as Secretary of the DOD from 1989 to 1993. During his Vice-Presidency, which began on January 1, 2001, he was referred to as the *"éminence grise,"* for good reason. Then from 1997 to 2001, while not in a government position, he served as the Chairman and CEO of the Dallas-based energy service company Halliburton, where it has been estimated he enriched his own wellbeing by some forty-million dollars during his four years at Halliburton. It should also be noted that while Cheney served as Vice-President, Halliburton was under investigation by the SEC for falsely reporting cost-overruns as revenues to the tune of $100 million, which had actually occurred during Cheney's watch when he served as Chairman and CEO at Halliburton and oversaw the implementation of this potentially serious accounting fraud in 1998. However, Cheney's more grievous and questionable example of potential conflict of interest related to the numerous noncompetitive and open ended bids that allowed $10.86 billion in tax dollars to flow to Halliburton while Cheney served as Vice-President. Here again his involvement and the open investigation of this potential abuse of awarding open ended contracts to favored corporations has seen only a very few CEO's or plutocrats ever go to jail. Senators and House Members that seek personal favors or who pursue string-pulling for the state they represent are also far too closely involved in this highly disputed bid process, and this abuse must also be openly faced up to and brought to an end along with a strict enforcement of ear mark transparency.

Proposed Policy 8

The United States should require all Federal and State Contracts universally utilize competitive bidding principles and all members of the Congress shall be restricted from either granting or influencing no-bid contracts to favored corporations, which constitutes a clear conflict of interest.

POLICY 9

Stop Policing Other Countries

The United States of America should maintain a strong military but we can no longer afford to police the world and continue to provide foreign aid at the rate we have in the past. With our national debt currently growing exponentially to more than sixteen and a half trillion, and the cost of maintaining U.S. military bases, which are currently seven times greater than any other nation, perhaps it's time to change direction. Yet we still continue to barrow almost two million dollars every hour as the Pentagon eats up well over 50% of our nation's annual discretionary spending budget. Our total military spending in the U.S. exceeds the military spending of China, Russia, Japan and India combined, currently constituting almost half of all military spending in the entire world. Do we even realize one F 22 Fighter jet cost this nation $360 million dollars, and we currently maintain military bases in more than 130 nations throughout the world — and worse yet, you can be assured that our policing other nations is no longer gaining friends. Our unjust wars with Iraq and Afghanistan alone have cost our working class more than a trillion dollars of their hard earned tax dollars, while costing every individual in the U.S. between three to four thousand dollars a year. The U.S. may be proud that they owe over one-third of all the debt in the world, but that's a label few families would like to see on our country.

On top of all that, our politicians continue to try and persuade us that foreign aid helps the giver more than the receiver, but we all know that is no longer true. Over the last five years we've watched our planes bomb Afghanistan, Iraq, Pakistan, Libya, Yemen and Somalia and it seems that the more we bomb the more these countries and the entire world hates us — in fact a growing number of them now openly say they want to destroy the United States. And to be honest about it, we are actually creating far more enemies than we're destroying, and with terrorists everywhere, don't you think it's time we find a different way to solve our terrorist problems — perhaps it is time we look to the UN for help. And if we do look to the UN, this needs to be accomplished very soon or the entire world will hate us even more for the amount of aggression, violence, injuries, and deaths our seventeen wars have created since World War II — when we said, "*No more wars unless we are attacked.*" On top of this, we can no longer afford the cost of war when our country is rapidly heading into an insurmountable depression. Yet we are currently on the verge of war with Iran, Syria and even North Korea, with an endless list of more to come if we continue this never-ending form of aggressive persuasion. Every American already knows that any conflict with terrorists requires something other than a powerful military force, and it's getting well past the time where we'll soon have to change the direction this nation has been heading.

After viewing several government reports on U.S. Foreign Aid, we can now fairly accurately determine that the United States has spent more than fifty-two billion on foreign aid in the fiscal year 2010, of which more than thirty-two billion was for economic aid and fifteen billion was for military aid. The top 25 countries that were the recipients of U.S Foreign Aid in Fiscal Year 2010 included:

Afghanistan, Pakistan, Israel, Iraq, Egypt, Haiti, Ethiopia, Sudan, Columbia, Kenya, Jordan, Mexico, Senegal, West Bank/ Gaza, South Africa, Tanzania, Russia, Nigeria, Georgia, Mozambique, Congo (Kinshasa), Indonesia, Zambia, Kazakhstan

Although the type of aid we provide is often referred to as "buying off," other countries, this needs to be reviewed in greater detail, because the implications of providing this human service are becoming overwhelmingly difficult. Since the type of Foreign Aid we currently provide is used as a tool to gain influence over developing countries, this subject also has enormous political implications. As a nation, we were the first to use this tool because of the 1913 bankers taking control of the Federal Reserve and other Multilateral Development Banks (MDB) who saw this as a tremendous advantage for themselves and their international corporations in gaining control over the developing country's businesses and their natural resources. And although the TLC was responsible for writing the By-Laws and Articles of Incorporation of the United Nations, this NWO only selfishly sought to control the business income and the natural resources of these developing countries. And since the TLC mistakenly did not elect to use the UN to provide a less entrepreneurial and more human foreign aid program, we now have a growing battle between China and the United States who unilaterally seek personal and financial gain through their bank loans from the Multilateral Development Banks (MDBs), such as the World Bank; the Asian Development Bank (ADB), and the Inter-American Development Banks. If this had originally been developed under a UN type organization, it may have had a better chance of providing this human service to the entire world without profit and control over natural resources being the primary goal of today's foreign aid program. So as a result we have a constant and growing conflict between China and the United States — a conflict that we are losing, as well as an ongoing battle between two super powers that will be very difficult to resolve peacefully. Chinese foreign aid has been growing rapidly in comparison to the United States, and we are already noticing that the Chinese government is able to wield considerable influence over a growing number of communist oriented developing nations, thereby rapidly advancing their own strategic and economic goals and objectives. This Chinese aid clearly undercuts the United States goals, such as our desire to promote democratic governance through developmental aid, while also advancing our global markets and economic reform. Some of the issues this duality of aid to other countries creates include:

- The resulting competition and alternative sources for country's to cost effectively fund their infrastructure and humanitarian services

- The Chinese failure to promote U.S. democratic governmental reform or human rights concepts, as they support regimes with poor human rights records

- It opens the door for China to focus their assistance on their own economic needs, such as expanding their access to oil, gas, and other natural resources that are already at serious shortage levels, as well as competitively marketing their Chinese products.

As a part of any Chinese aid contract, the recipient countries must adhere to diplomatic loyalty to China on political issue the United States has with them, such as on Taiwan, Tibet and many more controversial concerns between our countries. Both China and the U.S. seek greater influence in the Multilateral Development Banks (MDB's), such as the World Bank, since they use the MDB's to provide investment assistance to developing countries. Fortunately, the United States still holds the dominant shareholding power by controlling over 16 percent of the voting power in the World Bank's International Bank for Reconstruction and Development (IBRD), while China controls just under, 5 percent. In the Asian Development Bank (ADB) the U.S. again controls almost 16 percent of shareholder voting power while China controls a little more than 6 percent. And the United States also controls some 30 percent of the voting power in the Inter-American Development Bank, while China controls less than one percent, which gives the United States temporary advantage over the voting power of the multilateral development banks. However a very serious problem that is growing rapidly is these foreign aid countries are seeing this aid money going directly into the pockets of the power structure with less and less being used for the purpose it was intended, such as Pakistan. Therefore as our Congress determines its budget priorities, the effectiveness of funding for foreign aid requires far greater scrutiny regarding the fact that the current programs may not be accomplishing the goals originally intended. And how the Congress responds to this problem will influence U.S. foreign policy for years to come. In that foreign aid has been a huge financial and political drain on the United States, it appears we will eventually have no choice but to discontinue this program and let China pursue this role until they eventually reach that same conclusion. Although some of the programs are important human services the UN should assume, the U.S. can no longer expect its working class to add to its already budget breaking abyss that is well on its way to bankrupting our democracy. The human service of aiding the development of other countries must eventually fall to the UN.

Proposed Policy 9

The United States should stop policing and colonizing other countries and significantly reduce all international military bases, while only going to war or fighting terrorism when attacked by another country or terrorist as outlined under international law.

POLICY 10

Stop Exporting Jobs

According to the Bureau of Labor Statistics, (BLS) the unemployed remains at 12.3 million persons as of January 2013 and the unemployment rate was 7.9 percent, while the economy remains slow in its recovery, which has been the case for the last 43 months. The jobless for 27 weeks or more remains at 4.7 million, accounting for 38.1 percent of the 12.3 million unemployed — and the number of persons working part time because their hours were cut back or they were not able to find full time employment remains at 8 million. There is also a marginally attached work force of 804,000 that includes persons who are still looking for work, which are not included as unemployed. The 2012 employment growth averaged 181,000 per month in January 2013, while job gains occurred in Retail Trade, Construction, Health Care, and Wholesale Trade, despite the fact that jobs went down slightly in transportation and warehousing. Finding skilled workers has also become a serious problem in the U.S. as the demand for manufacturing jobs increased by some 25,000 in July 2012 — while the U.S. also found that foreign companies employ some 5 million Americans in jobs here in the U.S.

U.S. Est. Job Gains	Ave. Mo. 2012
Retail	+20,000
Construction	+24,666
Health Care	+26,666
Wholesale Trade	+24,250

The U.S. increase in debt to 16.5 trillion, while losing export capacity, has caused trade deficits to grow while displacing more than 2.7 million jobs during the period from 2001 to 2011. Most of these jobs were in manufacturing, which indicates international corporations are moving far too many of our manufacturing jobs overseas. CNN.Com — lists over 800 companies as "Exporting America," by sending American jobs overseas, or choosing to employ cheap overseas labor in place of American workers. Competition for low wage jobs with China and other underdeveloped countries has also driven down salaries in the U.S. for non-college degreed workers, which involves close to 70% (100 million) of the workers in the United States, according to the U.S. Census Bureau. Because of today's globalization trends, the average worker in the U.S. has experienced a drop in wages close to $1,500 per year. The trade deficit that has been with the U.S. for two decades increased substantially with the 2008 depression, which has also been a major factor in reducing wages, spending and jobs in the U.S. Isolationists would rather see the United States take care of its own, while the profit seeking NWO continues to distribute jobs across the globe while it supports costly wars, and gains greater control over other countries natural resources. Numerous articles that attempt to dispel the lost job fact as myth clearly demonstrates how the NWO controls the world news media. Of the - 2.7% (-2,742,200) jobs lost in all sectors between the years 2001 to 2011 — -76.9%, or some -2,109,700 million were from manufacturing type jobs caused by the growing trade deficits with China. More than half of the job losses attributed to China were computer and electronics type jobs, reaching some -38.8% (-1,064,800) of the manufacturing jobs related directly to this trade deficit and job loss to China:

Job Sector	Est. Annual Job Loss	2011-12
Computer and Peripheral Equipment	-620,700	22.6%
Semiconductors and Components	-235,000	8.6%
Communication/Audio/Video	-203,500	7.4%
Apparel/Accessories	-211,200	7.7%
Textile Mills/Product Mills	-106,200	3.9%
Fabricated Metal Products	-120,600	4.4%
Furniture/Fixtures	-80,700	2.9%
Plastic/Rubber Products	-57,600	2.1%
Motor Vehicle/Parts	-19,800	0.7%

Misc. Manufactured Goods	-111,800	4.1%
Administration Support Waste Mgt.	-160.600	5.9%
Prof. Scientific/Tech. Services	-145,000	5.3%
Other	<u>-157600</u>	<u>1.93%</u>
Total	**-2,109,700**	**76.9%**

As of June 2012, China owned $1.164 trillion in U.S. debt, some 25% of the total of 4.9 trillion held by foreign countries under what's called Intergovernmental Holdings, while Japan holds $1.134 trillion (23%). The Social Security (Social Security Trust Fund and Federal Disability Insurance Trust Fund) owns 2.72 trillion in U.S. Debt, some 25% of the total of 11.6 trillion held by the Public. The rest of the $16.5 trillion debt is owed by either the American people, or by the U.S. government. It's been long overdue that we stop profitable international corporations from avoiding taxes and sheltering income in the Cayman Islands or other tax havens, and it's been estimated this would generate just under $600 billion in revenue over the next ten years, while hopefully ending tax breaks for companies that ship jobs and/or factories overseas. Other things that would help the U.S. recover from the 2008 recession and help in balancing our budget include:

- A sharp reductions in defense spending
- Returning to the tax level before the Bush tax cuts
- End the international corporate offshore tax loopholes
- End the unjust religious wars

Proposed Policy 10

The United State's international corporations should be forced to stop exporting U.S. jobs, thereby protecting this country's sovereignty while discouraging any type of "New World Order" or any "International Industrial Monopoly." "Globalization of the open market" and the encouragement of worldwide "Humane Nonprofit Services" to all humankind should be diligently promoted. The United States shall protect the Open Market, which involves the selling of competitive and unregulated products in a

decentralized open and free market, where the consumer has a choice in what they receive for their dollar — while discouraging international corporate monopolies.

POLICY 11

Coordinate Elections

The way the United States conducts its election for both state and national candidates currently in office has become far too costly and politically controlled, requiring more than forty percent or more of the candidates time from the work they should be doing. The corruption of these salaried offices with all types and amounts of hidden and openly accounted for donations has also destroyed the ethics and morals that should be part of every public official's job. These donations have obligated the appointee to become beholding to those that offer monitory donations rather than the people they represent. Therefore a program that provides an equal and fair amount of campaign financing should be provided out of tax dollars rather than continuing this corrupting type of public offering that makes candidates constantly seek more money, making far too many of these public officials very wealthy and obligated to the donors.

Although existing debates allow the public an opportunity to see and evaluate the public official in person, the current debates have only proven to be detrimental and of no value when they become mud-slinging contests that only play the *"blame game,"* instead of discussions regarding what they as individuals propose to do if elected to that office. They are more concerned with shooting arrows than clearly stating why they are qualified to accomplish the written plan they should all provide for public review prior to election. Therefore it should be required that every candidate prepare their resume just as they do with and job search, for the public to read and evaluate. But more importantly, they should be required to present a written "Plan of Accomplishment" in writing, so the public can later measure their actual accomplishments once they have served in office. Their written plan of accomplishment should also be what each candidate intends to present and discuss at the debate. By doing this, there could be far fewer debates, which would result in far less cost and confusion. The public would also become more concerned about electing the most qualified candidate and the best professionally presented Plan of Accomplishment, rather than demeaning one another for an hour and a half over an endless number of debates. It would be acceptable for each candidate to point out problems with other candidate's plans, but at least they'd be discussing something that is tangible to the office they seek rather than every Democrat criticizing every Republican in every office and ever Republican damning every Democrat, which eventually leads to destroying any relationship that's required when they serve in office and need to jointly pass laws, rules and regulations, and policies. Based on today's debates (mud-slinging contests) between Republican and Democratic parties, is it any wonder why we have a totally dysfunctional House of Representatives and Senate, and so many confused state offices that remain in conflict because of their ridiculous lack of cooperation.

The United States Government's voting systems also need to become totally auditable using an approved single comprehensive computer based system that is standard throughout the entire country, and is based on the populous vote. It should also be efficiently managed by private citizens that sign a standard agreement that commits them to agree to act independent of either government or state appointed officials or parties and their members.

Proposed Policy 11

The United States should oversee and coordinate cost effective and efficiently run elections involving all state and national offices, while directing all philanthropic donations made to candidates to this nation's infrastructure which is currently in a hopeless and neglected state of disarray. The United States Government's voting systems needs to become totally auditable and be based on the populous vote, and it should be efficiently managed independent

of either government or state appointed officials or party members. This Government of the People should require that all candidates for public office be required to complete a formal application, which includes a comprehensive evaluation of the candidates past medical, family, and social history, as well as their qualifications, education, and experience - all openly available for public scrutiny prior to election. Each candidate for office should be required to prepare a statement outlining why they believe they are qualified to serve in the job they are seeking, while also requiring they outline in writing their primary goals and objectives in a written plan of accomplishment by date - as well as stating how they intend to pay for their proposals - rather than listen to them tediously damn their opponent in some pointless debate.

POLICY 12

Abide by the Geneva Convention

Stop wars and bring to justice the Iraq war criminals under the International World Court

In going to war with Iraq, America inadvertently chose to support George H. W. Bush's proposed NWO, the neoconservatives, and this country's alliance with Israel, the American Israel Public Affairs Committee (AIPAC) and their Likud-Zionist Prime Minister, Ariel Sharon — generating a new frontier of worldwide anti-Americanism and anti-Semitic bigotry of global proportions. It also suggests that many Republican conservatives and Democratic liberals were unknowingly forced into this predictably unsuccessful alliance with little or no understanding of the complex conflict that was raging between Judaism and Zionism; nor the religious, racial, and ethnic issues that are currently disrupting the entire Muslim and European cultures throughout the world. Here are some of the deceitful lies that were proposed:

- *Iraq is reconstituting its nuclear weapons. (10/07/02)*

- *Saddam Hussein is seeking quantities of uranium from Africa. (10/28/030)*

- *Saddam has reconstituted nuclear weapons. (03/16/03)*

- *The CIA has solid reporting of senior-level contacts between Iraq and al-Qaeda going back a decade. (10/07/02)*

- *Iraq has trained al-Qaeda members in bomb making and poisons and deadly gases, and their alliances with terrorists could allow Iraq to attack America. (10/07/02)*

- *Iraq has a growing fleet of manned and unmanned aerial vehicles that could disperse chemical or biological weapons. (10/07/02)*

- *We have seen intelligence over many months that Iraq has dispersed chemical and biological weapons, and that command control arrangements have been established. (02/08/03)*

- *Our conservative estimate is that Iraq has a stockpile of between 100 and 500 tons of chemical weapons agents to fill some 16,000 rockets. (02/05/02)*

- *We know where Iraq's WMD are, around Tikrit and Baghdad and east, south, and north somewhat. (03/30/03)*

- *We found a biological laboratory in Iraq, which the UN prohibited. (06/01/03)*

- *Blaming Iraq for the Trade Center destruction*

Although our national security interests relating to the destruction of the World Trade Center suggested some form of retaliation against terrorists, perhaps without having the facts it was irresponsible to add to the fear, anger, and resentment between Judaism and Zionism — thereby creating a problem which has been rapidly gaining more and more momentum in Iraq and its neighboring states of Iran, Afghanistan, Turkey, Libya, Syria, Lebanon, Jordan, Egypt, and Saudi Arabia, as well as Germany and France. And in that Iran now controls the Shiite population in both Iran and Iraq, they will inevitably blame the resulting religious war on America. A religious war called the "Rapture" or the "Apocalyptic Event" in which God will destroy the ruling powers of evil. In other words, they believe that all these suicidal bombings we see are acting in behalf of God — and that these protagonist will go to heaven in an unending war that culminates with the end of the earth.

Most of the world, outside of the United States, now recognizes the Iraqi war was not a matter of *"win or lose,"* and are just now realizing that it was a huge contrived mistake for the United States to ignore the real terrorist, Al Qaeda's Osama bin Laden. Even a few ethical politicians have been asking themselves — *"Just how could we have been so stupid as to authorize a unilateral act of aggression without a clear understanding of the facts?"* This decision was promoted based on Richard Pearl and co-author Douglas Feith's book, *"A Clean Break: A New Strategy for Securing the Realm,"* and based on this book the former Israeli Prime Minister, Netanyahu gave his approval, long before the Trade Center's destruction in New York. This book called for the elimination of Israel's enemy "Saddam Hussein," and the September 13, 1993 "Oslo Accord," which defined the interim self-government arrangements between the Palestinian Liberation Organization (PLO), and Israel. It proposed to install a Hashemite monarchy in Baghdad to destabilize the governments of Syria, Lebanon, Saudi Arabia, and Iran — recommending a regional dominance by Israel over that entire area, referred to as *"The Greater Israel,"* which was to become the sole power in the Middle East. In any event, this nation played a major role in this unilateral and potential criminal act of aggression in Iraq — which was approved without a clear and honest understanding and informed support of any of the neighboring countries, the United Nations, or the Muslims, estimated to be between 1.2 to 1.4 billion people throughout the world's almost seven billion population. Since the start of this war, the United States has spent far more than a trillion dollars instead of the originally projected $50 to $80 billion to fight this war that promoted *Greater Israel.* And more recently, Israel continues to defiantly and intentionally escalate its perpetual religious conflict with Lebanon and Jerusalem. As a result, no one is able to currently resolve this dangerous Zionist Israeli conflict with Judaism that the United States inadvertently created throughout the entire Islamic world — or the anti-Americanism and anti-Semitism that has been on the rise throughout the Middle East, Germany, France, as well as the entire world.

The complete disregard for President Ford's executive order banning assassinations by any US government (Formerly known as *Murder Incorporated*) must also be reestablished

Proposed Policy 12

If this nation is ever to regain the respect it once enjoyed, it needs to abide by the Geneva Convention this nation signed some five times. Therefore, the criminals that were responsible for the Iraq war and all its related atrocities need to be sought out and brought to justice under the International World Court in The Hague, just as the United States once demanded in the Nuremberg Trials that were held from 1995 to 1999. This country should also revoke all previous demands for absolute immunity for all U.S. Military personnel and civilian officials, as well as The Netherlands Invasion Act, which allows our U.S. Military to rescue any U.S. Personnel brought to trial in The Hague.

RECOMENDED INTERNATIONAL POLICY

Proposed Policy A

The United States should assist and support the UN in the very difficult task of developing a Comprehensive Master Plan for the human services of every nation, which then needs to be honestly and dynamically monitored and financed by each active and responsible participating sovereign state throughout the world, rather than just the United States and China.

Proposed Policy B

The United States should assist and support the UN in setting standards for a balanced and competitive industrial economic plan for all nations to follow as each nation seeks to profit fairly in an honest and open competitive market.

Proposed Policy C

The United States should assist and support the UN in fighting all forms of terrorism, demanding the World Court prosecute terrorists to the fullest extent, while the UN assumes full authority and responsibility to review; negotiate; and bring to a peaceful resolution all prospective wars before they start.

Proposed Policy D

The United States should assist and support the UN in coordinating an international peace keeping force comprised of a predetermined and equitably balanced military force from every participating nation, which shall be assigned to maintain World Peace while methodically investigating and destroying all weapons of mass destruction throughout the world.

And lastly, shouldn't the United States assist and support the UN in:

- *Enforcing the Non-proliferation Treaty involving Nuclear Weapons.*

- *Mediating and coordinating a fair and equitable plan for the use of the world's energy resources at the most cost effective and efficient level for all nations throughout the world.*

- *Resolving the world's dangerous and rapidly growing environmental problems.*

- *Seeking to prevent disease and disability by improving world-wide public health.*

- *Sanctioning nations that conduct genocide*

- *Coordinating standards regarding world trade policy.*

APPENDIX

APPENDIX I

TRILATERAL COMMISSION (TC)

<u>Membership List - May 2005</u>
<u>**EXECUTIVE COMMITTEE**</u>

David Rockefeller	Founder and Honorary Chairman
Thomas S. Foley	North American Chairman
Allan E. Gotlieb	North American Deputy Chairman
Lorenzo H. Zambrano	North American Deputy Chairman
Paul A. Volcker	North American Honorary Chairman
Michael J. O'Neil	North American Director
Peter Sutherland	European Chairman
Hervé De Carmoy	European Deputy Chairman
Andrzej Olechowski	European Deputy Chairman
Georges Berthoin	European Honorary Chairman
Otto Graf Lambsdorff	European Honorary Chairman
Paul Révay	European Director
Yotaro Kobayashi	Pacific Asia Chairman
Kim Kyung-Won	Pacific Asia Deputy Chairman
Shijuro Ogata	Pacific Asia Deputy Chairman
Tadashi Yamamoto	Pacific Asia Director

<u>EUROPEAN GROUP</u>

- Paul Adams, Chief Executive, British American Tobacco, London
- Urban Ahlin, Member of the Swedish Parliament and Chairman of the Committee on Foreign Affairs, Stockholm

- Krister Ahlström, Vice Chairman, Stora Enso and Fortum; former Chairman, Finnish Employers Confederation; former Chairman, Ahlström Corp., Helsinki
- Edmond Alphandéry, Chairman, Caisse Nationale de Prévoyance, Paris; former Chairman, Electricité de France (EDF); former *Minister of the Economy and Finance
- Bodil Nyboe Andersen, Chairperson of the Board of Governors, Danmarks Nationalbank, Copenhagen
- Jacques Andréani, Ambassadeur de France; former Ambassador to the United States
- *Stelios Argyros, Chairman and Managing Director, Preveza Mills, Athens; former Member of the European Parliament; Chairman of the Board, STET Hellas; former Vice President of UNICE, Brussels; former President and Chairman of the Board of the Federation of Greek Industries, Athens
- Jerzy Baczynski, Editor-in-Chief, Polityka, Warsaw
- Estela Barbot, Vice President, AGA, Porto; Vice President of the Board, AEP -- Portuguese Business Association; Consul of Guatemala, Lisbon
- François Bayrou, Member of the French National Assembly; President of the UDF Party; former Minister, Paris
- *Erik Belfrage, Senior Vice President, Skandinaviska Enskilda Banken; Director, Investor AB, Stockholm
- *Georges Berthoin, International Honorary Chairman, European Movement; Honorary Chairman, The Jean Monnet Association; Honorary European Chairman, The Trilateral Commission, Paris
- Nicolas Beytout, Editor, Le Figaro, Paris ; former Editor, Les Echos, Paris
- Carl Bildt, Chairman, Nordic Venture Network and Senior Adviser, IT Provider, Stockholm; former Member of the Swedish Parliament, Chairman of the Moderate Party and Prime Minister of Sweden; former European Union High Representative in Bosnia-Herzegovina & UN Special Envoy to the Balkans
- Lord Black of Crossharbour, Member of the House of Lords, London

- Ana Patricia Botin, Chairman, Banesto, Madrid; Member of the Board & of the Executive Committee, Banco Santander Central Hispano
- Jean-Louis Bourlanges, Member of the European Parliament (ALDE Group/UDF) and Chairman, Committee on Civil Liberties, Justice and Home Affairs, Brussels; former President of the European Movement in France, Paris
- *Jorge Braga de Macedo, President, Tropical Research Institute, Lisbon; Special Advisor to the Secretary General, Organisation for Economic Co-operation and Development (OECD), Paris; Professor of Economics, Nova University at Lisbon; Chairman, Forum Portugal Global; former Minister of Finance
- Rolf-E. Breuer, Chairman of the Supervisory Board, Deutsche Bank, Frankfurt-am-Main; President, Association of German Banks (BDB), Berlin
- Lord Brittan of Spennithorne, Vice Chairman, UBS Investment Bank, London; former Vice President, European Commission
- Robin Buchanan, Senior Partner, Bain & Company, London
- *François Bujon de l'Estang, Ambassadeur de France; Chairman, Citigroup France, Paris; former Ambassador to the United States
- Sven Burmester, Writer and Explorer, Denmark; former Representative, United Nations Population Fund (UNFPA), Beijing; former World Bank Deputy Secretary and Representative in Cairo
- Richard Burrows, Joint Managing Director, Pernod Ricard, Paris; Chairman and Chief Executive, Irish Distillers, Dublin; Deputy Governor of the Bank of Ireland; former President, IBEC (The Irish Business and Employers Confederation)
- *Hervé de Carmoy, Chairman, Almatis, Frankfurt-am-Main; former Partner, Rhône Group, New York & Paris; Honorary Chairman, Banque Industrielle et Mobilière Privée, Paris; former Chief Executive, Société Générale de Belgique
- Antonio Carrapatoso, Chairman of the Board of Directors, Vodafone Portugal, Lisbon; Member of the Board of Directors, Vodafone Spain & Vodacom
- Salvatore Carrubba, Culture Alderman, Municipality of Milan; former Managing Editor, Il Sole 24 Ore, Milan

- Henri de Castries, Chairman of the Management Board and Chief Executive Officer, AXA, Paris
- Luc Coene, Minister of State; Deputy Governor, National Bank of Belgium, Brussels
- Sir Ronald Cohen, Chairman, Apax Partners, London
- Vittorio Colao, Chief Executive Officer, RCS MediaGroup, Milan; former Managing Director, Vodafone Omnitel
- Bertrand Collomb, Chairman, Lafarge, Paris; Chairman, World Business Council for Sustainable Development
- *Richard Conroy, Chairman, Conroy Diamonds & Gold, Dublin; Member of Senate, Republic of Ireland
- Eckhard Cordes, Member of the Board, DaimlerChrysler, Stuttgart
- Alfonso Cortina, Chairman, Repsol-YPF Foundation & former Chairman and Chief Executive Officer, Repsol-YPF, Madrid
- Michel David-Weill, Chairman, Lazard LLC, worldwide; Managing Director and Président du Collège d'Associés-Gérants, Lazard Frères S.A.S., Paris; Deputy Chairman, Lazard Brothers & Co., Limited, London
- Baron Paul De Keersmaeker, Chairman of the Board of Domo, Corgo, Foundation Europalia International and the Canada Europe Round Table, Brussels; Honorary Chairman Interbrew, KBC, Nestlé Belgilux; former Member of the Belgian and European Parliaments and of the Belgian Government
- *Vladimir Dlouhy, Senior Advisor, ABB; International Advisor, Goldman Sachs; former Czechoslovak Minister of Economy; former Czech Minister of Industry & Trade, Prague
- Prince Edward, Duke of Kent, President of the All England Lawn Tennis and Croquet Club, Grand Master of the United Grand Lodge Freemasons, England and has served Grand Master of the Order of St Michael and St George
- *Bill Emmott, Editor, The Economist, London
- Thomas Enders, Executive Vice President, Member of the Board of Management & Head of the Defence and Security Systems Division, EADS, Munich

- Pedro Miguel Echenique, Professor of Physics, University of the Basque Country; former Basque Minister of Education, San Sebastian
- Laurent Fabius, Member of the French National Assembly and of the Foreign Affairs Committee; former Prime Minister & Minister of the Economy & Finance, Paris
- Oscar Fanjul, Honorary Chairman, Repsol YPF; Vice Chairman, Omega Capital, Madrid
- Grete Faremo, Former Executive Vice President, Storebrand; former Norwegian Minister of Development Cooperation, Minister of Justice and Minister of Oil and Energy, Oslo
- *Nemesio Fernandez-Cuesta, Executive Director of Upstream, Repsol-YPF; former Chairman, Prensa Española, Madrid
- *Nemesio Fernandez-Cuesta, Corporate Director of Shared Services, Repsol-YPF; former Chairman, Prensa Española, Madrid
- Jürgen Fitschen, Member of the Group Executive Committee, Deutsche Bank, Frankfurt-am-Main
- Klaus-Dieter Frankenberger, Foreign Editor, Frankfurter Allgemeine Zeitung, Frankfurt am Main
- Hugh Friel, Chief Executive, Kerry Group, Dublin
- Lykke Friis, Head of European Department, Federation of Danish Industries, Copenhagen
- *Michael Fuchs, Member of the German Bundestag, Berlin; former President, National Federation of German Wholesale & Export Traders
- Lord Garel-Jones, Managing Director, UBS Investment Bank, London; Member of the House of Lords; former Minister of State at the Foreign Office (European Affairs)
- Antonio Garrigues Walker, Chairman, Garrigues Abogados y Asesores Tributarios, Madrid
- Lord Gilbert, Member of the House of Lords; former Minister for Defence, London
- Prince Phillip of Greece, member, House of Lords, London
- Mario Greco, Managing Director, RAS, Milan

- General The Lord Guthrie, Director, N M Rothschild & Sons, London; Member of the House of Lords; former Chief of the Defence Staff, London
- Grand Duke William John Hagan II, Former Chairman, New Obelisk Press; Grand Master of the Order of Ormus, London
- Sirkka Hämäläinen, Former Member of the Executive Board, European Central Bank, Frankfurt-am-Main; former Governor, Bank of Finland
- Grand Duke Karl Habsburg, Member of European Parliament
- *Toomas Hendrik Ilves, Member of the European Parliament; former Estonian Foreign Minister and Member of the Parliament; former Ambassador to the United States, Canada and Mexico
- Alfonso Iozzo, Managing Director, San Paolo IMI Group, Turin
- *Mugur Isarescu, Governor, National Bank of Romania, Bucharest; former Prime Minister
- *Max Jakobson, Independent Consultant and Senior Columnist, Helsinki; former Finnish Ambassador to the United Nations; former Chairman of the Finnish Council of Economic Organizations
- *Baron Daniel Janssen, Chairman of the Board, Solvay, Brussels
- Zsigmond Jarai, President, National Bank of Hungary, Budapest
- Trinidad Jiménez, International Relations Secretary of the Socialist Party (PSOE) & Member of the Federal Executive Committee, Madrid
- *Béla Kadar, Member of the Hungarian Academy, Budapest; Member of the Monetary Council of the National Bank; President of the Hungarian Economic Association; Former Ambassador of Hungary to the O.E.C.D., Paris; former Hungarian Minister of International Economic Relations and Member of Parliament
- Karl Kaiser, Visiting Scholar, Weatherhead Center for International Studies, Harvard University, USA; Senior Scholar and former Otto-Wolff Director, Research Institute of the German Council on Foreign Relations (DGAP), Berlin; Professor Emeritus of Political Sciences, University of Bonn

- Robert Kassai, General Vice President, The National Association of Craftmen' s Corporations, Budapest
- *Lord Kerr, Member of the House of Lords; Director of Rio Tinto, Shell, and the Scottish American Investment Trust, London; former Secretary General, European Convention, Brussels; former Permanent Under-Secretary of State and Head of the Diplomatic Service, Foreign & Commonwealth Office, London; former British Ambassador to the United States
- Denis Kessler, Chairman and Chief Executive Officer, Scor, Paris; former Chairman, French Insurance Association (FFSA); Former Executive Vice-Chairman, MEDEF-Mouvement des Entreprises de France (French Employers' Confederation)
- Jiri Kunert, Chairman and Chief Executive Officer, Zivnostenska banka; President of the Czech Association of Banks, Prague
- *Count Otto Lambsdorff, Partner, Wessing Lawyers, Düsseldorf; Chairman, Friedrich Naumann Foundation, Berlin; former Member of German Bundestag; Honorary Chairman, Free Democratic Party; former Federal Minister of Economy; former President of the Liberal International; Honorary European Chairman, The Trilateral Commission, Paris
- Emilio Lamo de Espinosa, Director, Elcano Royal Institute of International and Strategic Studies; Professor of Sociology at the Universidad Complutense, Madrid
- Kurt Lauk, Member of the European Parliament (EPP Group-CDU); Chairman, Globe Capital Partners, Stuttgart; President, Economic Council of the CDU Party, Berlin; Former Member of the Board, DaimlerChrysler, Stuttgart
- Anne Lauvergeon, Chairperson of the Executive Board, Areva; Chairperson and Chief Executive Officer, Cogema, Paris
- Pierre Lellouche, Member of the French National Assembly and of the Foreign Affairs Committee, Paris; Chairman of the French Delegation to NATO's Parliamentary Assembly
- Enrico Letta, Member of the European Parliament (ALDE Group), Brussels; Secretary General, AREL; Vice President, Aspen Institute; former Minister of European Affairs, Industry, and of Industry and International Trade, Rome

- André Leysen, Honorary Chairman, Gevaert, Antwerp; Honorary Chairman, Agfa-Gevaert Group
- Marianne Lie, Director General, Norwegian Shipowner's Association, Oslo
- Count Maurice Lippens, Chairman, Fortis, Brussels
- Helge Lund, Chief Executive Officer of the Norwegian Oil Company, Statoil, Oslo
- *Cees Maas, Vice Chairman and Chief Financial Officer of the ING Group, Amsterdam; former Treasurer of the Dutch Government
- Peter Mandelson, Member of the European Commission (Trade), Brussels; former Member of the British Parliament; former Secretary of State to Northern Ireland and for Trade and Industry
- Abel Matutes, Chairman, Empresas Matutes, Ibiza; former Member of the European Commission, Brussels; former Minister of Foreign Affairs, Madrid
- Francis Maude, Member of the British Parliament; Director, Benfield Group; former Shadow Foreign Secretary, London
- Edgar Meister, Member of the Board, Deutsche Bundesbank, Frankfurt-am-Main; Chairman, the Banking Supervisory Subcommittee of the European Monetary Institute (EMI); Chairman, the Banking Supervision Committee of the European System of the Central Banks (ESCB)
- Vasco de Mello, Vice Chairman, José de Mello SGPS, Lisbon
- Joao de Menezes Ferreira, Chairman and Chief Executive Officer, ECO-SOROS, Lisbon; former Member of the Portuguese Parliament
- Peter Mitterbauer, Honorary President, The Federation of Austrian Industry, Vienna; President and Chief Executive Officer, MIBA, Laakirchen
- Mario Monti, President and Professor Emeritus, Bocconi University, Milan; Chairman of BRUEGEL and of ECAS, Brussels; former Member of the European Commission (Competition Policy)
- Dominique Moïsi, Special Advisor to the Director General of the French Institute for International Relations (IFRI), Paris

- Sir Mark Moody-Stuart, Chairman, Anglo American; former Chairman, Royal Dutch/Shell Group, London
- Klaus Murmann, Honorary Chairman, Confederation of German Employers' Associations (BDA), Berlin; Chairman, Sauer Holding, Neumünster
- Heinrich Neisser, President, Politische Akademie, Vienna; Professor of Political Studies at Innsbruck University; former Member of Austrian Parliament and Second President of the National Assembly
- Harald Norvik, Chairman and Partner, ECON Management; former President and Chief Executive, Statoil, Oslo
- Arend Oetker, Chairman, German Council on Foreign Relations (DGAP); Vice Chairman, Federation of German Industries; Chairman, Atlantik-Brücke (Atlantic Bridge); Managing Director, Dr. Arend Oetker Holding, Berlin
- *Andrzej Olechowski, Leader, Civic Platform; Former Chairman, Bank Handlowy; former Minister of Foreign Affairs and of Finance, Warsaw
- Richard Olver, Chairman, BAE Systems, London
- Janusz Palikot, Chairman of the Supervisory Board, Polmos Lublin; Vice President, Polish Confederation of Private Employers; Co-owner, Publishing House slowo/obraz terytoria; Member of the Board of Directors, Polish Business Council, Warsaw
- Dimitry Panitza, Founding Chairman, The Free and Democratic Bulgaria Foundation; Founder and Chairman, The Bulgarian School of Politics, Sofia
- Lucas Papademos, Vice President, European Central Bank, Frankfurt-am-Main; former Governor of the Bank of Greece
- Schelto Patijn, Member of the Supervisory Board of the Schiphol Group and Amsterdam RAI; former Mayor of the City of Amsterdam, The Netherlands
- Lord Patten of Barnes, Chancellor of the University of Oxford; Co-Chairman, International Crisis Group, Brussels; former Member of the European Commission (External Relations), Brussels; former Governor of Hong Kong; former Member of the British Cabinet, London

- Heinrich von Pierer, Chairman of the Board, Siemens, Munich
- Josep Piqué, Chairman of the Popular Party of Catalunya, Barcelona; Member of the Parliament of Catalunya; Member of the Spanish Senate; former Minister of Foreign Affairs
- Benoît Potier, Chairman of the Management Board, L'Air Liquide, Paris
- Alessandro Profumo, Chief Executive Officer, UniCredito Italiano, Milan
- Henri Proglio, Chairman, Veolia Environnement, Paris
- Luigi Ramponi, Member of Parliament; Chairman of the Defence Committee of the Chamber of Deputies, Rome; former Deputy Chief of the Defence Staff (Italian Army)
- Wanda Rapaczynska, President of the Management Board, Agora, Warsaw
- Heinz Riesenhuber, Member of the German Bundestag; former Federal Minister of Research and Technology, Berlin
- Gianfelice Rocca, Chairman, Techint Group of Companies, Milan; Vice President, Confindustria
- H. Onno Ruding, Chairman, Centre for European Policy Studies (CEPS), Brussels; Retired Vice Chairman, Citibank; former Dutch Minister of Finance
- Renato Ruggiero, Vice Chairman, Citigroup European Investment Bank, Zurich; former Italian Foreign Minister and Director General of WTO
- Anthony Ruys, Chairman of the Executive Board, Heineken, Amsterdam
- Jacques Santer, Former Member of the European Parliament; former President of the European Commission; former Prime Minister of Luxembourg
- Prince Rafael of Savoy, Business Person, Lisbon
- *Silvio Scaglia, Chairman and Founcer, e.Biscom, Milan; former Managing Director, Omnitel
- Paolo Scaroni, Chief Executive Officer, ENEL, Rome
- *Guido Schmidt-Chiari, Chairman, Constantia Group; former Chairman, Creditanstalt Bankverein, Vienna
- Henning Schulte-Noelle, Chairman of the Supervisory Board, Allianz, Munich

- Prince Charles of Schwarzenberg, Founder and Director, Nadace Bohemiae, Prague; former Chancellor to President Havel; former President of the International Helsinki Federation for Human Rights
- Miguel Sebastian, Chairman of the Economic Bureau of the Prime Minister of Spain; Professor of Economics at the Universidad Complutense, Madrid
- *Carlo Secchi, Professor of European Economic Policy, Bocconi University, Milan; former Member of the Italian Senate and of the European Parliament
- *Tøger Seidenfaden, Editor-in-Chief, Politiken, Copenhagen
- Maurizio Sella, Chairman, Banca Sella, Biella; Chairman, Association of Italian Banks (A.B.I.), Rome; Chairman, Finanziaria Bansel
- Stefano Silvestri, President, Institute for International Affairs (IAI), Rome; Commentator, Il Sole 24 Ore; former Under Secretary of State for Defence, Italy
- Lord Simon of Highbury, Member of the House of Lords; Advisory Director of Unilever, Morgan Stanley Europe and LEK; former Minister for Trade & Competitiveness in Europe; former Chairman of BP, London
- Nicholas Soames, Member of the British Parliament, London
- Hermann Otto Solms, Vice President of the German Bundestag, Berlin
- Sir Martin Sorrell, Chief Executive Officer, WPP Group, London
- Myles Staunton, Former Member of the Irish Senate & of the Dail; Consultant, Westport, Co. Mayo
- *Thorvald Stoltenberg, President, Norwegian Red Cross, Oslo; former Co-Chairman (UN) of the Steering Committee of the International Conference on Former Yugoslavia; former Foreign Minister of Norway; former UN High Commissioner for Refugees
- *Petar Stoyanov, President, Centre for Political Dialogue, Sofia; former President of Bulgaria
- Peter Straarup, Chairman of the Executive Board, Danske Bank, Copenhagen; Chairman, the Danish Bankers Association

- *Peter Sutherland, Chairman, BP p.l.c. ; Chairman, Goldman Sachs International; former Director General, GATT/WTO; former Member of the European Commission; former Attorney General of Ireland
- Björn Svedberg, Former Chairman and Chief Executive Officer, Ericsson, Stockholm; former President and Group Chief Executive, Skandinaviska Enskilda Banken
- Péter Székely, Chairman and Chief Executive Officer, Transelektro, Budapest; President, Confederation of Hungarian Employers' Organisations for International Co-operation (CEHIC); Vice President, Confederation of Hungarian Employers and Industrialists
- Pavel Telicka, Partner, BXL-Consulting, Prague
- Jean-Philippe Thierry, Chairman and Chief Executive Officer, AGF (Assurances Générales de France), Paris
- Marco Tronchetti Provera, Chairman, Telecom Italia; Chairman and Chief Executive Officer, Pirelli & C., Milan
- Elsbeth Tronstad, Director of Information, ABB, Oslo
- Loukas Tsoukalis, Jean Monnet Professor of European Integration, University of Athens; President of the Hellenic Foundation for European and Foreign Policy (ELIAMEP); Visiting Professor at the College of Europe
- Mario Vargas Llosa, Writer and Member of the Royal Spanish Academy, Madrid
- *George Vassiliou, Head of the Negotiating Team for the Accession of Cyprus to the European Union; former President of the Republic of Cyprus; Former Member of Parliament and Leader of United Democrats, Nicosia
- Franco Venturini, Foreign Correspondent, Corriere della Sera, Rome
- Friedrich Verzetnitsch, Member of Austrian Parliament; President, Austrian Federation of Trade Unions, Vienna; President, European Trade Union Confederation (ETUC)
- *Marko Voljc, General Manager of Central Europe Directorate, KBC Bank Insurance Holding, Brussels; former Chief Executive Officer, Nova Ljubljanska Banka, Ljubljana

- Alexandr Vondra, Managing Director of the Prague Office, Dutko Group Companies; former Czech Deputy Minister of Foreign Affairs
- Joris Voorhoeve, Member of the Council of State; former Member of the Dutch Parliament; former Minister of Defence, The Hague
- Panagis Vourloumis, Chairman and Chief Executive Officer, Hellenic Telecommunications Organization (O.T.E.), Athens
- Marcus Wallenberg, President and Chief Executive Officer, Investor AB, Stockholm
- Prince Charles of Wales, Duke of Cornwall of the House of Windsor, London
- *Serge Weinberg, Chairman and Chief Executive Officer, Weinberg Investissements; former Chairman of the Management Board, Pinault-Printemps-Redoute; former President, Institute of International and Strategic Studies (IRIS), Paris
- Heinrich Weiss, Chairman, SMS, Düsseldorf
- Nout Wellink, President, Dutch Central Bank, Amsterdam
- Arne Wessberg, Director General, YLE (Finnish Broadcasting Company) and Director General, YLE Group (YLE and Digits Oy), Helsinki; President, European Broadcasting Union (EBU)
- *Norbert Wieczorek, former Member of the German Bundestag & Deputy Chairman of the SPD Parliamentary Group, Berlin
- Hans Wijers, Chairman and Chief Executive Officer, Akzo Nobel, Arnhem
- Otto Wolff von Amerongen, Honorary Chairman, East Committee of the German Industry; Chairman and Chief Executive Officer, Otto Wolff Industrieberatung und Beteiligung, Cologne
- *Emilio Ybarra, former Chairman, Banco Bilbao-Vizcaya, Madrid

Former Members in Public Service

- Marek Belka, Prime Minister, Warsaw; former Ambassador-at-Large and Chairman, Council for International Coordination, Coalition Provisional Authority, Baghdad

- John Bruton, European Union Ambassador & Head, Delegation of the European Commission to the United States
- Patrick Devedjian, Minister for Industry, France
- Lene Espersen, Minister of Justice, Denmark
- Pedro Solbes, Deputy Prime Minister and Minister of the Economy and Finances, Spain
- Harri Tiido, Ambassador of Estonia and Head of the Estonian Mission to NATO, Brussels
- Karsten Voigt, Coordinator for German-American Cooperation, Federal Foreign Ministry, Germany

NORTH AMERICAN GROUP

- Madeleine K. Albright, Principal, The Albright Group LLC, Washington, DC; former U.S. Secretary of State
- Graham Allison, Director, Belfer Center for Science and International Affairs, Harvard University, Cambridge, MA
- Rona Ambrose, Member of Parliament, Ottawa, ON
- G. Allen Andreas, Chairman and Chief Executive, Archer Daniels Midland Company, Decatur, IL
- Michael H. Armacost, Shorenstein Distinguished Fellow, Asia/Pacific Research Center, Stanford University, Hillsborough, CA; former President, The Brookings Institution; former U.S. Ambassador to Japan; former U.S. Under Secretary of State for Political Affairs
- C. Michael Armstrong, Chairman, Comcast Corporation, Philadelphia, PA
- *Charlene Barshefsky, Senior International Partner, Wilmer, Cutler & Pickering, Washington, DC; former U.S. Trade Representative
- Alan R. Batkin, Vice Chairman, Kissinger Associates, New York, NY
- Maurizio Bevilacqua, Member of Parliament, Ottawa, ON
- Doug Bereuter, President, The Asia Foundation, San Francisco, CA; former Member, U.S. House of Representatives

- *C. Fred Bergsten, Director, Institute for International Economics, Washington, DC; former U.S. Assistant Secretary of the Treasury for International Affairs
- Catherine Bertini, Under-Secretary-General for Management, United Nations, New York, NY
- Dennis C. Blair, USN (Ret.), President, Institute for Defense Analyses, Alexandria, VA; former Commander in Chief, U.S. Pacific Command
- Herminio Blanco Mendoza, Private Office of Herminio Blanco, Mexico City, NL; former Mexican Secretary of Commerce and Industrial Development
- Geoffrey T. Boisi, former Vice Chairman, JPMorgan Chase, New York, NY
- Stephen W. Bosworth, Dean, Fletcher School of Law and Diplomacy, Tufts University, Medford, MA; former U.S. Ambassador to the Republic of Korea
- David G. Bradley, Chairman, Atlantic Media Company, Washington, DC
- Harold Brown, Counselor, Center for Strategic and International Studies, Washington, DC; General Partner, Warburg Pincus & Company, New York, NY; former U.S. Secretary of Defense
- *Zbigniew Brzezinski, Counselor, Center for Strategic and International Studies, Washington, DC; Robert Osgood Professor of American Foreign Affairs, Paul Nitze School of Advanced International Studies, Johns Hopkins University; former U.S. Assistant to the President for National Security Affairs
- George H.W. Bush, Former President, The United States of America, Texas
- Louis C. Camilleri, Chairman and Chief Executive Officer, Altria Group, Inc., New York, NY
- Gerhard Casper, President Emeritus, Stanford University, Stanford
- Lynne V. Cheney, Former Chairman, the National Endowment for the Humanities, Washington D.C.
- William Jefferson Clinton, Former President of the United States
- William T. Coleman III, Founder, Chairman, and Chief Executive Officer, Cassatt Corporation;

- Founder, former Chairman and CEO and Member, Board of Directors, BEA Systems, Inc., San Jose, CA
- William T. Coleman, Jr., Senior Partner and the Senior Counselor, O'Melveny & Myers, Washington, DC; former U.S. Secretary of Transportation
- Timothy C. Collins, Senior Managing Director and Chief Executive Officer, Ripplewood Holdings, New York, NY
- E. Gerald Corrigan, Managing Director, Goldman, Sachs & Co., New York, NY; former President, Federal Reserve Bank of New York
- Michael J. Critelli, Chairman and Chief Executive Officer, Pitney Bowes Inc., Stamford, CT
- Gerald L. Curtis, Burgess Professor of Politcial Science and Visiting Professor, Graduate Research Institute for Policy Studies, Tokyo
- Douglas Daft, former Chairman and Chief Executive Officer, The Coca Cola Company, Atlanta, GA
- Dennis D. Dammerman, Vice Chairman and Executive Officer, General Electric Company, Fairfield, CT
- Lynn Davis, Senior Political Scientist, The RAND Corporation, Arlington, VA; former U.S. Under Secretary of State for Arms Control and International Security
- Lodewijk J. R. de Vink, Chairman, Global Health Care Partners, Peapack, NJ; former Chairman, President, and Chief Executive Officer, Warner-Lambert Company
- Arthur A. DeFehr, President and Chief Executive Officer, Palliser Furniture, Winnipeg, MB
- André Desmarais, President and Co-Chief Executive Officer, Power Corporation of Canada, Montréal, QC; Deputy Chairman, Power Financial Corporation
- Jamie Dimon, President and Chief Operating Officer, JPMorgan Chase, New York, NY
- Peter C. Dobell, Founding Director, Parliamentary Centre, Ottawa, ON

- Wendy K. Dobson, Professor and Director, Institute for International Business, Rotman School of Management, University of Toronto, Toronto, ON; former Canadian Associate Deputy Minister of Finance
- Kenneth M. Duberstein, Chairman and Chief Executive Officer, The Duberstein Group, Washington, DC
- Robert Eckert, Chairman and Chief Executive Officer, Mattel, Inc., El Segundo, CA
- Jessica P. Einhorn, Dean, Paul Nitze School of Advanced International Studies, The Johns Hopkins University, Washington, DC; former Managing Director for Finance and Resource Mobilization, World Bank
- Jeffrey Epstein, President, J. Epstein & Company, Inc., New York, NY; President, N.A. Property, Inc.
- Dianne Feinstein, Member (D-CA), U.S. Senate
- Sandra Feldman, President Emeritus, American Federation of Teachers, Washington, DC
- Martin S. Feldstein, George F. Baker Professor of Economics, Harvard University, Cambridge, MA; President and Chief Executive Officer, National Bureau of Economic Research; former U.S.Chairman, President's Council of Economic Advisors
- Stanley Fischer, President, Citigroup International and Vice Chairman, Citgroup, New York, NY; former First Deputy Managing Director, International Monetary Fund, Washington, DC
- Richard W. Fisher, President and Chief Executive Officer, Federal Reserve Bank of Dallas, Dallas, TX; former U.S. Deputy Trade Representative
- *Thomas S. Foley, Partner, Akin Gump Strauss Hauer & Feld, Washington, DC; former U.S. Ambassador to Japan; former Speaker of the U.S. House of Representatives; North American Chairman, Trilateral Commission
- Francis Fukuyama, Bernard L. Schwartz Professor International Political Economy, Paul H. Nitze School of Advanced International Studies, The Johns Hopkins University, Washington, DC

- Dionisio Garza Medina, Chairman of the Board and Chief Executive Officer, ALFA, Garza Garcia, NL
- Richard A. Gephardt, former Member (D-MO), U.S. House of Representatives
- David Gergen, Professor of Public Service, John F. Kennedy School of Government, Harvard University, Cambridge, MA; Editor-at-Large, U.S. News and World Report
- Peter C. Godsoe, Chairman of Fairmont Hotels & Resorts; Retired Chairman and Chief Executive Officer of Scotiabank, Toronto, ON
- *Allan E. Gotlieb, Senior Advisor, Stikeman Elliott, Toronto, ON; Chairman, Sotheby's, Canada; former Canadian Ambassador to the United States; North American Deputy Chairman, Trilateral Commission
- Donald E. Graham, Chairman and Chief Executive Officer, The Washington Post Company, Washington, DC
- Jeffrey W. Greenberg, Private Investor, New York, NY; former Chairman and Chief Executive Officer, Marsh & McLennan Companies
- Maurice R. Greenberg, Chairman, American International Group, Inc., New York, NY
- Richard N. Haass, President, Council on Foreign Relations, New York, NY; former Director, Policy Planning, U. S. Department of State; former Director of Foreign Policy Studies, The Brookings Institution
- William A. Haseltine, Chairman and Chief Executive Officer, Haseltine Associates, Washington, DC;
- President, William A. Haseltine Foundation for Medical Sciences and the Arts; former Chairman and Chief Executive Officer, Human Genome Sciences, Inc., Rockville, MD
- Charles B. Heck, Senior Adviser and former North American Director, Trilateral Commission, New Canaan, CT
- *Carla A. Hills, Chairman and Chief Executive Officer, Hills & Company, International Consultants, Washington, DC; former U.S. Trade Representative; former U.S. Secretary of Housing and Urban Development

- Richard Holbrooke, Vice Chairman, Perseus LLC, New York, NY; Counselor, Council on Foreign Relations; former U.S. Ambassador to the United Nations; former Vice Chairman of Credit Suisse First Boston Corporation; former U.S. Assistant Secretary of State for European and Canadian Affairs; former U.S. Assistant Secretary of State for East Asian and Pacific Affairs; and former U.S. Ambassador to Germany
- Karen Elliott House, Senior Vice President, Dow Jones & Company, and Publisher, The Wall Street Journal, New York, NY
- James A. Johnson, Vice Chairman, Perseus LLC, Washington, DC; former Chairman and Chief Executive Officer, Federal National Mortgage Association (Fannie Mae)
- Alejandro Junco de la Vega, President and Director, Grupo Reforma, Monterrery, NL
- Robert Kagan, Senior Associate, Carnegie Endowment for International Peace, Washington, DC
- Charles R. Kaye, Co-President, Warburg Pincus LLC, New York, NY
- Henry A. Kissinger, Chairman, Kissinger Associates, Inc., New York, NY; former U.S. Secretary of State; former U.S. Assistant to the President for National Security Affairs
- Michael Klein, Chief Executive Officer, Global Banking, Citigroup Inc.; Vice Chairman, Citibank International PLC; New York, NY
- Enrique Krauze, General Director, Editorial Clio Libros y Videos, S.A. de C.V., Mexico City, DF
- Jim Leach, Member (R-IA), U.S. House of Representatives
- Gerald M. Levin, Chief Executive Officer Emeritus, AOL Time Warner, Inc., New York, NY
- Winston Lord, Co-Chairman of Overseeers and former Co-Chairman of the Board, International Rescue Committee, New York, NY; former U.S. Assistant Secretary of State for East Asian and Pacific Affairs; former U.S. Ambassador to China
- E. Peter Lougheed, Senior Partner, Bennett Jones, Barristers & Solicitors, Calgary, AB; former Premier of Alberta

- Roy MacLaren, former Canadian High Commissioner to the United Kingdom; former Canadian Minister of International Trade; Toronto, ON
- John A. MacNaughton, former President and Chief Executive Officer, Canada Pension Plan Investment Board, Toronto, ON
- Antonio Madero, Chairman of the Board and Chief Executive Officer, San Luis Corporacion, S.A. de C.V., Mexico City, DF
- *Sir Deryck C. Maughan, former Vice Chairman, Citigroup, New York, NY
- Jay Mazur, President Emeritus, UNITE (Union of Needletrades, Industrial and Textile Employees); Vice Chairman, Amalgamated Bank of New York; and President, ILGWU's 21st Century Heritage Foundation, New York, NY
- Hugh L. McColl, Jr., Chairman, McColl Brothers Lockwood, Charlotte, NC; former Chairman and Chief Executive Officer, Bank of America Corporation
- Henry A. McKinnell, President and Chief Executive Officer, Pfizer, Inc., New York, NY
- Marc H. Morial, President and Chief Executive Officer, National Urban League, New York, NY; former Mayor, New Orleans, LA
- Anne M. Mulcahy, Chairman and CEO, Xerox Corporation, Stamford, CT
- Brian Mulroney, Senior Partner, Ogilvy Renault, Barristers and Solicitors, Montréal, QC; former Prime Minister of Canada
- *Joseph S. Nye, Jr., Distinguished Service Professor at Harvard University, John F. Kennedy School of Government, Harvard University, Cambridge, MA; former Dean, John F. Kennedy School of Government; former U.S. Assistant Secretary of Defense for International Security Affairs
- David J. O'Reilly, Chairman and Chief Executive Officer, ChevronTexaco Corp., San Ramon, CA
- Richard N. Perle, Resident Fellow, American Enterprise Institute, Washington, DC; member and former Chairman, Defense Policy Board, U.S. Department of Defense; former U.S. Assistant Secretary of Defense for International Security Policy

- Thomas R. Pickering, Senior Vice President, International Relations, The Boeing Company, Vienna, VA; former U.S. Under Secretary of State for Political Affairs; former U.S. Ambassador to the Russian Federation, India, Israel, El Salvador, Nigeria, the Hashemite Kingdom of Jordan, and the United Nations
- Franklin D. Raines, former Chairman and Chief Executive Officer, Fannie Mae (Federal National Mortgage Association), Washington, DC; former Director, U.S. Office of Management and Budget, Office of the President
- Joseph W. Ralston, USAF (Ret)., Vice Chairman, The Cohen Group, Washington, DC; former Commander, U.S. European Command, and Supreme Allied Commander NATO; former Vice Chairman, Joint Chiefs of Staff, U.S. Department of Defense
- Charles B. Rangel, Member (D-NY), U.S. House of Representatives
- Hartley Richardson, President and Chief Executive Officer, James Richardson & Sons, Ltd., Winnipeg, MB
- Joseph E. Robert, Jr., Chairman and Chief Executive Office, J.E. Robert Companies, McLean, VA
- John D. Rockefeller IV, Member (D-WV), U.S. Senate
- Kenneth Rogoff, Professor of Economics and Director, Center for International Development, Harvard University, Cambridge, MA; former Chief Economist and Director, Research Department, International Monetary Fund, Washington, DC
- David M. Rubenstein, Co-founder and Managing Director, The Carlyle Group, Washington, DC
- Luis Rubio, President, Center of Research for Development (CIDAC), Mexico City, DF
- Arthur F. Ryan, Chairman and Chief Executive Officer, Prudential Financial, Inc., Newark, NJ
- Jaime Serra, Chairman, SAI Consulting, Mexico City, DF; former Mexican Minister of Trade and Industry
- Anne-Marie Slaughter, Dean, Woodrow Wilson School of Public and International Affairs, Princeton University, Princeton, NJ

- Gordon Smith, Director, Centre for Global Studies, University of Victoria, Victoria, BC; Chairman, Board of Governors, International Development Research Centre; former Canadian Deputy Minister of Foreign Affairs and Personal Representative of the Prime Minister to the Economic Summit
- Donald R. Sobey, Chairman Emeritus, Empire Company Ltd., Stellarton, NS
- George Soros, Chairman, Soros Fund Management LLC, New York, NY; Chairman, The Open Society Institute
- Ronald D. Southern, Chairman, ATCO Group, Calgary, AB
- James B. Steinberg, Vice President and Director of the Foreign Policy Studies Program, The Brookings Institution, Washington, DC; former U.S. Deputy National Security Advisor
- Barbara Stymiest, Chief Operating Officer, RBC Financial Group, Toronto, ON
- Lawrence H. Summers, President, Harvard University, Cambridge, MA; former U.S. Secretary of the Treasury
- John J. Sweeney, President, AFL-CIO, Washington, DC
- Strobe Talbott, President, The Brookings Institution, Washington, DC; former U.S. Deputy Secretary of State
- Luis Tellez, Managing Director, The Carlyle Group, Mexico City, DF; former Executive Vice President, Sociedad de Fomento Industrial (DESC); former Mexican Minister of Energy
- John Thain, Chief Executive Officer, New York Stock Exchange, Inc.; former President and Co-Chief Operating Officer, Goldman Sachs & Co., New York, NY
- G. Richard Thoman, Managing Partner, Corporate Perspectives and Adjunct Professor, Columbia University, New York, NY; formerly President and CEO, Xerox Corporation; formerly CFO and N° 2 officer, IBM Corporation
- *Paul A. Volcker, former Chairman, Wolfensohn & Co., Inc., New York; Frederick H. Schultz Professor Emeritus, International Economic Policy, Princeton University; former Chairman, Board of Governors, U.S. Federal Reserve System; Honorary North American Chairman and former North American Chairman, Trilateral Commission

- William H. Webster, Senior Partner, Milbank, Tweed, Hadley & McCloy LLP, Washington, DC; former U.S. Director of Central Intelligence; former Director, U.S. Federal Bureau of Investigation; former Judge of the U.S. Court of Appeals for the Eighth Circuit
- Fareed Zakaria, Editor, Newsweek International, New York, NY
- *Lorenzo H. Zambrano, Chairman of the Board and Chief Executive Officer, CEMEX, Monterrey, NL; North American Deputy Chairman, Trilateral Commission
- Ernesto Zedillo, Director, Yale Center for the Study of Globalization, Yale University, New Haven, CT; former President of Mexico
- Mortimer B. Zuckerman, Chairman and Editor-in-Chief, U.S. News & World Report, New York, NY
- Robert S. McNamara, Lifetime Trustee, Trilateral Commission, Washington, DC; former President, World Bank; former U.S. Secretary of Defense; former President, Ford Motor Company
- David Rockefeller, Founder, Honorary Chairman, and Lifetime Trustee, Trilateral Commission, New York, NY

Former Members In Public Service

- Richard B. Cheney, Vice President of the United States
- Paula J. Dobriansky, U.S. Under Secretary of State for Global Affairs
- Bill Graham, Canadian Minister of National Defence
- William J. McDonough, Chairman, Public Company Accounting Oversight Board
- Paul Wolfowitz, U.S. Deputy Secretary of Defense
- Robert B. Zoellick, U.S. Deputy Secretary of State

PACIFIC ASIAN GROUP

- Ali Alatas, Advisor and Special Envoy of the President of the Republic of Indonesia; former Indonesian Minister for Foreign Affairs; Jakarta

- Narongchai Akrasanee, Chairman, Seranee Holdings Co., Ltd., Bangkok
- Philip Burdon, former Chairman, Asia 2000 Foundation; New Zealand Chairman, APEC; former New Zealand Minister of Trade Negotiations; Wellington
- Fujio Cho, President, Toyota Motor Corporation
- Cho Suck-Rai, Chairman, Hyosung Corporation, Seoul
- Chung Mong-Joon, Member, Korean National Assembly; Vice President, Federation Internationale de Football Association (FIFA); Seoul
- Barry Desker, Director, Institute of Defence and Strategic Studies, Singapore
- Takashi Ejiri, Attorney at Law, Asahi Koma Law Office
- Jesus P. Estanislao, President and CEO, Institute of Corporate Directors/Institute of Solidarity in Asia; former Philippine Minister of Finance; Manila
- Hugh Fletcher, Director, Fletcher Building, Ltd.; former Chief Executive Officer, Fletcher Challenge; Auckland
- Hiroaki Fujii, Advisor and former President, The Japan Foundation; former Japanese Ambassador to the United Kingdom
- Shinji Fukukawa, Executive Advisor, Dentsu Inc.
- Yoichi Funabashi, Chief Diplomatic Correspondent and Columnist, The Asahi Shimbun
- Carrillo Gantner, Vice President, Myer Foundation; Melbourne
- Ross Garnaut, Head, Department of Economics, Research School of Pacific and Asian Studies, Australian National University, Canberra
- *Toyoo Gyohten, President, Institute for International Monetary Affairs; Senior Advisor, Bank of Tokyo-Mitsubishi, Ltd.
- Han Sung-Joo, President, Seoul Forum for International Affairs; former Korean Minister of Foreign Affairs; former Korean Ambassador to the United States; Seoul
- *Stuart Harris, Professor of International Relations, Research School of Pacific and Asian Studies, Australian National University; former Australian Vice Minister of Foreign Affairs, Canberra

- Tan Sri Dato' Azman Hashim, Chairman, AmBank Group, Kuala Lumpur
- John R. Hewson, Member, Advisory Council, ABN AMRO Australia
- Earnest M. Higa, President and CEO, Higa Industries
- Shintaro Hori, Managing Partner, Bain & Company Japan, Inc.
- Murray Horn, Managing Director, Institutional Banking, ANZ Banking Group, Ltd.; former Parliament Secretary, New Zealand Treasury; Auckland
- Hyun Hong-Choo, Senior Partner, Kim & Chang, Seoul; former Korean Ambassador to the United Nations and to the United States; Seoul
- Hyun Jae-Hyun, Chairman, Tong Yang Group, Seoul
- Shin'ichi Ichimura, Counselor, International Centre for the Study of East Asian Development, Kitakyushu
- Nobuyuki Idei, Chairman and Group CEO, Sony Corporation
- Takeo Inokuchi, Chairman and Chief Executive Officer, Mitsui Sumitomo Insurance Company, Ltd.
- Noriyuki Inoue, Chairman and CEO, Daikin Industries, Ltd.
- Rokuro Ishikawa, Chairman, Kajima Corporation
- Motoo Kaji, Professor Emeritus, University of Tokyo
- Koji Kakizawa, former Member, Japanese House of Representatives; former Minister for Foreign Affairs
- Kasem Kasemsri, Chairman, Natural Park Public Co., Ltd., Bangkok.; former Deputy Prime Minister of Thailand;
- Koichi Kato, Member, Japanese House of Representatives; former Secretary-General, Liberal Democratic Party
- Trevor Kennedy, Chairman, Oil Search, Ltd.; Chairman, Cypress Lakes Group, Ltd.; Sydney
- K. Kesavapany, Director, Institute of Southeast Asian Studies, Singapore
- Kim Kihwan, International Advisor, Goldman Sachs, Seoul; former Korean Ambassador-at-Large for Economic Affairs

- *Kim Kyung-Won, Adviser, Kim & Chang Law Office, Seoul; President Emeritus, Seoul Forum for International Affairs; former Korean Ambassador to the United States and the United Nations; Pacific Asia Deputy Chairman, Trilateral Commission; Seoul
- Kakutaro Kitashiro, Chairman of the Board, IBM Japan, Ltd.; Chairman, Japan Association of Corporate Executives
- Shoichiro Kobayashi, Advisor, Kansai Electric Power Company, Ltd.
- *Yotaro Kobayashi, Chairman of the Board, Fuji Xerox Co., Ltd.; Pacific Asia Chairman, Trilateral Commission
- Akira Kojima, Chairman, Japan Center for Economic Research (JCER)
- Koo John, Chairman, LS Cable Ltd.; Chairman, LS Industrial Systems Co.; Seoul
- Kenji Kosaka, Member, Japanese House of Representatives
- *Lee Hong-Koo, Chairman, Seoul Forum for International Affairs, Seoul; former Korean Prime Minister; former Korean Ambassador to the United Kingdom and the United States
- Lee In-ho, former President, Korea Foundation; former Korean Ambassador to Finland and Russia; Seoul
- Lee Jay Y., Vice President, Samsung Electronics, Seoul
- Lee Kyungsook Choi, President, Sookmyung Women's University, Seoul
- Adrianto Machribie, Chairman, PT Freeport Indonesia, Jakarta
- *Minoru Makihara, Senior Corporate Advisor, Mitsubishi Corporation
- Hiroshi Mikitani, Chairman, President and CEO, Rakuten, Inc.
- Yoshihiko Miyauchi, Chairman and Chief Executive Officer, ORIX Corporation
- Isamu Miyazaki, Special Advisor, Daiwa Institute of Research, Ltd.; former Director-General of the Japanese Economic Planning Agency
- *Kiichi Miyazawa, former Prime Minister of Japan; former Finance Minister; former Member, House of Representatives
- Yuzaburo Mogi, President and Chief Executive Officer, Kikkoman Corporation

- Mike Moore, former Director-General of the World Trade Organization; former Prime Minister of New Zealand; Member, Privy Council; Geneva
- Moriyuki Motono, President, Foreign Affairs Society; former Japanese Ambassador to France
- Jiro Murase, Managing Partner, Bingham McCutchen Murase, New York
- *Minoru Murofushi, Counselor, ITOCHU Corporation
- Masao Nakamura, President and Chief Executive Officer, NTT Docomo Inc.
- Masashi Nishihara, President, National Defense Academy
- Taizo Nishimuro, Chairman and Chief Executive Officer, Toshiba Corporation
- Roberto F. de Ocampo, President, Asian Institute of Management; Former Secretary of Finance, Manila
- Toshiaki Ogasawara, Chairman and Publisher, The Japan Times Ltd.; Chairman, Nifco Inc.
- Sadako Ogata, President, Japan International Cooperation Agency (JICA); former United Nations High Commissioner for Refugees
- *Shijuro Ogata, former Deputy Governor, Japan Development Bank; former Deputy Governor for International Relations, Bank of Japan; Pacific Asia Deputy Chairman, Trilateral Commission
- Sozaburo Okamatsu, Chairman, Research Institute of Economy, Trade & Industry (RIETI)
- *Yoshio Okawara, President, Institute for International Policy Studies; former Japanese Ambassador to the United States
- Yoichi Okita, Professor, National Graduate Institute for Policy Studies
- Ariyoshi Okumura, Chairman, Lotus Corporate Advisory, Inc.
- Anand Panyarachun, Chairman, Thailand Development Research Institute (TDRI); former Prime Minister of Thailand; Bangkok
- Ryu Jin Roy, Chairman and CEO, Poongsan Corp., Seoul
- Eisuke Sakakibara, Professor, Keio University; former Japanese Vice Minister of Finance for International Affairs
- Sakong Il, Chairman and Chief Executive Officer, Institute for Global Economics; former Korean Minister of Finance; Seoul

- Yukio Satoh, President, The Japan Institute of International Affairs; former Japanese Ambassador to the United Nations
- Sachio Semmoto, Chief Executive Officer, eAccess, Ltd.
- Masahide Shibusawa, President, Shibusawa Ei'ichi Memorial Foundation
- Seiichi Shimada, President and Chief Executive Officer, Nihon Unisys, Ltd.
- Yasuhisa Shiozaki, Member, Japanese House of Representatives; former Parliamentary Vice Minister for Finance
- Arifin Siregar, International Advisor, Goldman Sachs & Co.; former Ambassador of Indonesia to the United States; Jakarta
- Tan Sri Dr. Noordin Sopiee, Chairman and Chief Executive Officer, Institute of Strategic and International Studies, Kuala Lumpur
- Suh Kyung-Bae, President and CEO, Amore Pacific Corp., Seoul
- Tsuyoshi Takagi, President, The Japanese Foundation of Textile, Chemical, Food, Commercial, Service and General Workers' Unions (UI ZENSEN)
- Keizo Takemi, Member, Japanese House of Councillors; former State Secretary for Foreign Affairs
- Akihiko Tanaka, Director, Institute of Oriental Culture, University of Tokyo
- Naoki Tanaka, President, The 21st Century Public Policy Institute
- Sunjoto Tanudjaja, President and Chief Executive Officer, PT Great River International, Jakarta
- Teh Kok Peng, President, GIC Special Investments Private Ltd., Singapore
- Shuji Tomita, Senior Executive Vice President, NTT Communications Corporation
- Kiyoshi Tsugawa, Executive Advisor & Member of Japan Advisory Board, Lehman Brothers Japan, Inc.; Chairman, ARAMARK ASIA
- Junichi Ujiie, Chairman and CEO, Nomura Holdings, Inc.
- Sarasin Viraphol, Executive Vice President, Charoen Pokphand Co., Ltd.; former Deputy Permanent Secretary of Foreign Affairs of Thailand; Bangkok

- Cesar E. A. Virata, Director, Corporate Vice Chairman and Chief Executive Officer of Rizal Commercial Banking Corporation (RCBC); former Prime Minister of Philippines; Manila
- *Jusuf Wanandi, Co-founder and Member of the Board of Trustees, Centre for Strategic and International Studies, Jakarta
- Etsuya Washio, President, National Federation of Workers and Consumers Insurance Cooperatives (ZENROSAI): former President, Japanese Trade Union Confederation (RENGO)
- Koji Watanabe, Senior Fellow, Japan Center for International Exchange; former Japanese Ambassador to Russia
- Osamu Watanabe, Chairman, Japan External Trade Organization (JETRO)
- Taizo Yakushiji, Executive Member, Council for Science and Technology Policy of the Cabinet Office of Japan; Executive Research Director, Institute for International Policy Studies
- Tadashi Yamamoto, President, Japan Center for International Exchange; Pacific Asia Director, Trilateral Commission
- Noriyuki Yonemura, Counselor, Fuji Xerox Co., Ltd.

Note: Those without city names are Japanese Members. Korean names are shown with surname first.

Former Members in Public Service

- Hong Seok-Hyun, Korean Ambassador to the United States
- Masaharu Ikuta, Director General, Postal Services Corporation.
- Yoriko Kawaguchi, Special Advisor to the Prime Minister of Japan
- Hisashi Owada, Judge, International Court of Justice
- Takeshi Kondo, President, Japan Highway Public Corporation (Nihon Doro Kodan)
- Richard B. Cheney, Vice-President, the United States of America

PARTICIPANTS FROM OTHER AREAS:
"Triennium Participants"

- Abdlatif Al-Hamad, Director General and Chairman, Arab Fund for Economic and Social Development; former Kuwait Minister of Finance and Planning
- André Azoulay, Adviser to H.M. King Mohammed VI, Rabat, Morocco
- Domingo F. Cavallo, President, Accion por la Republica, Buenos Aires; former Economy Minister of Argentina
- Morris Chang, Chairman and Chief Executive Officer, Taiwan Semiconductor Manufacturing Co., Ltd., Taipei
- Hüsnü Dogan, General Coordinator, Nurol Holding, Ankara; former Chairman of the Board of Trustees, Development Foundation of Turkey; former Minister of Defence
- Jacob A. Frenkel, Vice Chairman, American International Group, Inc. and Chairman, AIG's Global Economic Strategies Group, New York, NY; Chairman and Chief Executive Officer, G-30; former Chairman, Merrill Lynch International; former Governor, Bank of Israel; former Economic Counselor and Director of Research, IMF; former Chairman, Board of Governors of the Inter-American Development Bank; former David Rockefeller Professor of Economics, University of Chicago
- Victor K. Fung, Chairman, Li & Fung, Hong Kong
- Frene Ginwala, Speaker of the National Assembly, Parliament of the Republic of South Africa, Cape Town
- H.R.H. Prince El Hassan bin Talal, President, The Club of Rome; Moderator of the World Conference on Religion and Peace; Chairman, Arab Thought Forum, Amman, Hashemite Kingdom of Jordan
- Serhiy Holovaty, Member of the Supreme Rada; President of the Ukrainian Legal Foundation; former Minister of Justice, Kiev, Ukraine
- Enrique V. Iglesias, President, Inter-American Development Bank; former Minister of Foreign Affairs of Uruguay
- Wang Jun, Chairman, China International Trust & Investment Corp., China

- Sergei Karaganov, Deputy Director, Institute of Europe, Russian Academy of Sciences; Chairman of the Presidium of the Council on Defense and Foreign Policy, Moscow, Russian Federation
- Jeffrey L.S. Koo, Chairman and Chief Executive Officer, Chinatrust Financial Holding Co., Taipei
- Richard Li, Chairman and Chief Executive Officer, Pacific Century Group Holdings Ltd., Hong Kong
- Itamar Rabinovich, President, Tel Aviv University, Israel; former Ambassador to the United States
- Rüsdü Saracoglu, President of the Finance Group, Koç Holding; Chairman, Makro Consulting, Istanbul; former State Minister and Member of the Turkish Parliament; former Governor of the Central Bank of Turkey
- Roberto Egydio Setubal, Director President, Banco Itaú S.A., Brazil
- Stan Shih, Chairman and Chief Executive Officer, The Acer Group, Taipei
- Gordon Wu, Chairman and Managing Director, Hopewell Holdings Ltd., Hong Kong
- Grigory A. Yavlinsky, former Member of the State Duma; Leader of the "Yabloko" Parliamentary Group; Chairman of the Center for Economic and Political Research, Moscow, Russian Federation
- Yu Xintian, President, Shanghai Institute for International Studies, Shanghai
- Yuan Ming, Director, Institute of International Relations, Peking University, Peking
- Zhang Yunling, Director, Institute of Asia-Pacific Studies, Chinese Academy of Social Sciences (CASS), Beijing
- Wang Jisi, Director, Institute for American Studies, Chinese Academy of Social Sciences (CASS), Beijing

APPENDIX II

THE COUNCIL ON FOREIGN RELATIONS (CFR)

http://en.wikipedia.org/wiki/Cpouncil_on_Foreign_Relations

The Board of Directors of the Council on Foreign Relations is composed in total of thirty-six officers. David Rockefeller is a Director Emeritus (Honorary Chairman). It also has an International Advisory Board consisting of thirty-five distinguished individuals from across the world. There are two types of membership: life, and term membership, which lasts for 5 years and is available to those between 30 and 36. Only US citizens (native born or naturalized) and permanent residents who have applied for U.S. citizenship are eligible. A candidate for life membership must be nominated in writing by one Council member and seconded by a minimum of three others (strongly encouraged to be other CFR members).

Corporate membership (250 in total) is divided into "Basic", "Premium" ($25,000+) and "President's Circle" ($50,000+). All corporate executive members have opportunities to hear distinguished speakers, such as overseas presidents and prime ministers, chairmen and CEOs of multinational corporations, and US officials and Congressmen. President and premium members are also entitled to other benefits, including attendance at small, private dinners or receptions with Senior American officials and world leaders.

Chairman of the Board:	Peter G. Peterson
Vice Chairman:	Carla A. Hills
Vice Chairman:	Robert E. Rubin
President:	Richard N. Haass

Our Puppet Government

Directors:
Peter Ackerman
Fouad Ajami
Madeleine K. Albright
Charlene Barshefsky
Henry S. Bienen
Stephen W. Bosworth
Tom Brokaw
Frank J. Caufield
Kenneth M. Duberstein
Martin S. Feldstein
Richard N. Foster
Ann M. Fudge
Helene D. Gayle
Maurice R. Greenberg
Richard C. Holbrooke
Karen Elliott House
Alberto Ibargüen
Henry R. Kravis
Michael H. Moskow
Joseph S. Nye, Jr
Ronald L. Olson.
James W. Owen
Thomas R. Pickering
Colin L. Powell
David M. Rubenstein
Richard E. Salomon
Anne-Marie Slaughter
Joan E. Spero
Laura D'Andrea
Tyson Vin Weber
Christine Todd Whitman
Fareed Zakaria

Some Corporate Members:

Alcoa	American International Group
Bank of America	Bloomberg

Boeing	BP
Chevron	Citigroup
ExxonMobil	Ford Motor
General Electric	Goldman Sachs
Halliburton	IBM
JP Morgan Chase	Kohlberg Kravis Roberts & Co.
Lehman Brothers	Lockheed Martin
McGraw-Hill	McKinsey
Merck	Merrill Lynch
News Corporation	Shell Oil
Time Warner	Toyota (North America Inc.)

Notable Current Council Members 1988

Dick Cheney   Fred Thompson

Jonothan S. Bush (G. W. Bush's First Cousin)

Condoleezza Rice	Paul Wolfowitz	Robert M. Gates
John D. Negroponte	Richard Perle	Leslie Gelb
Colin Powell	Alice Rivlin	Madeleine Albright
Zbigniew Brzezinski	Henry Kissinger	Jack Welch
Alan Greenspan	Paul Volcker	Vernon Jordan
John C. Whitehead	George Soros	Brent Scowcroft
George Shultz	James Woolsey	Jimmy Carter
Warren Christopher	James D. Wolfensohn	Steven Weinberg
Edgar Bronfman	Barbara Walters	Paul R. Krugman
Lawrence Eagleburger	Thomas Friedman	Peggy Dulany
David Rockefeller, Jr.	John D. Rockefeller, IV	
Ethan Bronner	Warren Hoge	

More Recent Members:

Steve Brock (U.S. navy)
Tom Brokaw (media)
Bill Clinton (past President)
John Edwards (politics)
Roger W. Ferguson, Jr.
Chris Heinz politics, banking
John Kerry (politics)
Stanley O'Neal (banking)

Henry Paulson
Charles Prince (banking)
Karenna Gore Schiff
Ron Silver (actor)
Jonathan Soro
Lesley Stahl (media)
Adam Wolfensohn
Robert Zoellick
Angelina Jolie (actress), "under consideration"

Notable historical members:

Charles Peter McColough	George Kennan
John J. McCloy	Paul Nitze
Strobe Talbott	Caspar Weinberger
Robert Lovett	John Foster Dulles
Allen Dulles	Dean Rusk
Nelson Rockefeller	John D. Rockefeller 3rd
Robert McNamara	Felix Rohatyn
Paul Warburg	C. Douglas Dillon
Eugene Rostow	Walt Rostow
Albert Wohlstetter	Roberta Wohlstetter
Arthur Schlesinger	McGeorge Bundy
William Bundy	Gerald Ford

List of Chairmen:
Russell Cornell Leffingwell 1946-53
John J. McCloy 1953-70
David Rockefeller 1970-85
Peter George Peterson 1985-

List of Presidents:
John W. Davis 1921-33
George W. Wickersham 1933-36
Norman H. Davis 1936-44
Russell Cornell Leffingwell 1944-46
Allen Welsh Dulles 1946-50
Henry Merritt Wriston 1951-64

Grayson L. Kirk 1964-71
Bayless Manning 1971-77
Winston Lord 1977-85
John Temple Swing 1985-86 (Pro tempore)
Peter Tarnoff 1986-93
Alton Frye 1993
Leslie Gelb 1993-2003
Richard N. Haass 2003-

Source: The Council on Foreign Relations from 1921 to 1996: Historical
Roster of Directors and Officer
http://en.wikipedia.org/aiki/Council_on_Foreign_Relations
A more detailed list of some 4426 members can be obtained on the
internet by requesting a "List of CFR Members."

APPENDIX III

THE AMERICAN LEGISLATIVE EXCHANG COUNCIL (ALEC)

ALEC ALUMNI IN CONGRESS
U.S. SENATE

- Sen. Mike Enzi (R-WY)
- Sen. Lindsey Graham (R-SC)
- Sen. James Inhofe (R-OK)
- Sen. Jon Kyl (R-AZ)
- Sen. Joe Manchin (D-WV)
- Sen. Jerry Moran (R-KS)
- Sen. Jim Risch (R-ID)
- Sen. Marco Rubio (R-FL)
- Sen. Richard Shelby (R-AL)
- Sen. Roger Wicker (R-MS)
- Former Sen. George Allen (R-VA) (RAN for U.S. Senate against former VA Gov. Tim Kaine (D)) recipient of ALEC's Thomas Jefferson Freedom Award in 1996, former co-chair of ALEC Federal Forum

U.S. HOUSE OF REPRESENTATIVES

- Rep. John Boehner (R-OH)
- Rep. Eric Cantor (R-VA)
- Rep. Sandy Adams (R-FL)
- Rep. Rodney Alexander (R-LA)
- Rep. Justin Amash (R-MI)
- Rep. Steve Austria (R-OH)
- Rep. Spencer Bachus (R-AL)
- Rep. Rick Berg (R-ND)

- Rep. Jaime Herrera Beutler (R-WA)
- Rep. Diane Black (R-TN)
- Rep. Marsha Blackburn (R-TN)
- Rep. Dan Boren (D-OK)
- Rep. Leonard Boswell (D-IA)
- Rep. Kevin Brady (R-TX)
- Rep. Dan Burton (R-IN)
- Rep. David Camp (R-MI)
- Rep. John Campbell (R-CA)
- Rep. Howard Coble (R-NC)
- Rep. Mike Coffman (R-CO)
- Rep. Tom Cole (R-OK)
- Rep. John Culberson (R-TX)
- Rep. Jeff Denham (R-CA)
- Rep. Charlie Dent (R-PA)
- Rep. Mario Diaz Balart (R-FL)
- Rep. Jeff Duncan (R-SC)
- Rep. Michael G. Fitzpatrick (R-PA)
- Rep. John Randy Forbes (R-VA)
- Rep. Rodney Frelinghuysen (R-NJ)
- Rep. Cory Gardner (R-CO)
- Rep. Scott Garrett (R-NJ)
- Rep. James Gerlach (R-PA)
- Rep. Bob Gibbs (R-OH)
- Rep. Phil Gingrey (R-GA)
- Rep. Sam Graves (R-MO)
- Rep. Tom Graves (R-GA), former ALEC Tax and Fiscal Policy Task Force member
- Rep. Morgan Griffith (R-VA)
- Rep. Brett Guthrie (R-KY)
- Rep. Andy Harris (R-MD)
- Rep. Vicky Hartzler (R-MO)
- Rep. Richard Norman "Doc" Hastings (R-WA)
- Rep. Bill Huizenga (R-MI)
- Rep. Lynn Jenkins (R-KS)
- Rep. Sam Johnson (R-TX)
- Rep. Walter Jones (R-NC)

- Rep. James "Jim" Jordan (R-OH)
- Rep. Steve King (R-IA)
- Rep. Jack Kingston (R-GA)
- Rep. Raul Labrador (R-ID)
- Rep. Doug Lamborn (R-CO)
- Rep. Robert Latta (R-OH)
- Rep. Jerry Lewis (R-CA)
- Rep. Frank LoBiondo (R-NJ)
- Rep. Frank Lucas (R-OK)
- Rep. Blaine Luetkemeyer (R-MO)
- Rep. Kenny Marchant (R-TX)
- Rep. Thomas McClintock (R-CA)
- Rep. Cathy McMorris Rodgers (R-WA)
- Rep. John Mica (R-FL)
- Rep. Jeff Miller (R-FL)
- Rep. Kristi Noem (R-SD)
- Rep. Alan Nunnelee (R-MS)
- Rep. Steven Palazzo (R-MS)
- Rep. Erik Paulsen (R-MN)
- Rep. Ed Perlmutter (D-CO) - Rep. Perlmutter is no longer listed as an ALEC alumnus in Congress by ALEC.
- Rep. Joseph Pitts (R-PA)
- Rep. Todd Platts (R-PA)
- Rep. Bill Posey (R-FL)
- Rep. Thomas Price (R-GA)
- Rep. David Rivera (R-FL)
- Rep. Mike D. Rogers (R-AL)
- Rep. Mike J. Rogers (R-MI)
- Rep. Ileana Ros-Lehtinen (R-FL)
- Rep. Dennis Ross (R-FL)
- Rep. Lucille Roybal-Allard (D-CA)
- Rep. Edward Royce (R-CA)
- Rep. Jean Schmidt (R-OH)
- Rep. Kurt Schrader (D-OR)
- Rep. David Schweikert (R-AZ)
- Rep. Austin Scott (R-GA)
- Rep. Tim Scott (R-SC)

- Rep. Michael Simpson (R-ID)
- Rep. Adrian Smith (R-NE)
- Rep. Steve Southerland (R-FL)
- Rep. Steve Stivers (R-OH)
- Rep. Marlin Stutzman (R-IN)
- Rep. John Sullivan (R-OK)
- Rep. Pat Tiberi (R-OH)
- Rep. Scott Tipton (R-CO)
- Rep. Daniel Webster (R-FL)
- Rep. Lynn Westmoreland (R-GA)
- Rep. Joe Wilson (R-SC)
- Rep. Kevin Yoder (R-KS)
- Rep. Don Young (R-AK)

Former ALEC Alumni in Congress include Former Assistant Minority Leader Don Nickles, Former Speaker of the House Dennis Hastert, Former House Majority Leader Tom DeLay and Former Deputy Majority Whip and subject of the 2006 page scandal, Mark Foley.

APPENDIX IV

THE SHRUB DYNASTY

Richard B. Cheney, who served as George W's Vice-President, first started his career in politics when he served on Gerald Ford's transition team and then as Deputy Assistant to President Ford in 1974 — before becoming Secretary of Defense for George Sr. from 1989 to 1993. He was often referred to as the *"éminence grise"* of George W's administration. Prior to becoming the Vice-President, he served as the Chairman and CEO of the Dallas-based energy service company Halliburton, which was once under investigation by the SEC for falsely reporting cost-overruns as revenues to the tune of $100 million when Cheney oversaw the implementation of this serious accounting fraud back in 1998. Cheney's more grievous and questionable examples of potential corruption relate to the numerous non competitive and open ended bids that allowed $10.86 billion in tax dollars to flow to Halliburton — but here, once again, nothing has actually been done to openly investigate this potential abuse of awarding contracts to favored corporations.

Donald H. Rumsfield, who recently served as George W's Secretary of Defense, first got his start in politics as far back as 1960 as a legislator and former friend of Richard Nixon, serving as President Ford's Secretary of Defense before failing in his attempt to become the vice-presidential nomination in 1980 and the presidential nomination in 1988.

Karl Rove, George W's political adviser and the most controversial architect of such fear phrases as *Axis of Evil; Shock and Awe; and Stay the Course* — regularly accused the Shrub opponents of being *conspirators, fascists,* or a *supporters of totalitarianism.* The professionals who questioned the destruction of the Twin Towers were immediately labeled as conspirators — using the consistent Rove strategy of attacking the messenger.

Richard N. Pearl, the Zionist, also known as *The Prince of Darkness*, and co-author of *"A Clean Break: A New Strategy for Securing the Realm,"* served as George W's Assistant Secretary of Defense for International Policy. He was also closely identified with Conrad Black, the former chairman of Hollinger International Incorporated, which owns some 400 worldwide newspapers that trumpeted Pearl's anti-Saddam sentiments well before the war with Iraq — a news-media that controls almost everything this powerful political inner circle wants us to read.

Douglas J. Feith, a Zionist who served as George W's Under-Secretary of Defense for Policy before the Iraqi war, and co-authored with Mr. Pearl *"A Clean Break: A New Strategy for Securing the Realm."*

Paul Dundes Wolfowitz, who served some 30 years under six Presidents before accepting his third tour of duty at the Defense Department as George W's Deputy Secretary of Defense before being rewarded with a key appointment as CEO of the World Bank, where he could play a major role in the international industrial take-over of the world-market. Wolfowitz had also been a strong proponent of Israel ruling the Middle East as described in his many speeches, testimonials and articles that deal with the West and the Muslim world.

Lewis "Scooter" Libby, who resigned as Chief of Staff to the Vice-President after being found guilty of perjuring himself before a Grand Jury. Later he received a Presidential pardon from serving time in jail.

George Tenet, the CIA Director, who counseled George "W" saying: ". . . only an all-out US military assault can realize American aims," in Iraq. He also received the President's Medal of Freedom.

Bill Kristol, Editor of *The Weekly Standard,* who was very influential in Washington politics during George W's presidency. He is one of the dual authors of, *The War Over Iraq.*

Other less prominent supporters that have played a role in supporting the *"Shrub Dynasty"* include:

Richard Doty: Who served as George W's personal attorney when George sold his failing Arbusto and Spectrum 7 oil companies to Harken Energy, and became a member of the Harken board of directors as well as a member of the Harken auditing committee. Harken paid a substantial amount for that acquisition at a time when George W's father was President. Since George "W" served on the auditing committee, it was highly unlikely for him not to know the Harken Company was in a financial crisis before he questionably dumped his stock.

On July 12, 2002 the *Washington Post* published *"The Harken Energy Distraction,"* in an effort to defend George W. when the failing Harken Company was being investigated by the SEC, where Richard Doty also served as General Counsel. The article said, most of the questions surrounding W's millions -

> *"have been aired over the years and one has been the subject of government investigation. Congress shouldn't let the temptation to play politics with this issue distract from corporate reform."*

Bush also quickly attacked the messenger saying:

> *"All the questions are old 'stuff,' and any further investigation was an unjustified attempt to win petty political advantage."*

And then the *Post* added:

> *"The Security Exchange Commission investigated the case and did not take action, apparently because it could not find firm evidence of wrong doing."*

However, the SEC was not really looking very hard since the case involved the President's son and the SEC, which was headed by a *Shrub* appointee. Richard Doty, the SEC's General Counsel was responsible for making the decisions concerning any legal action by the SEC. Doty also happened to be George W's personal lawyer when he assisted him with the Texas Rangers deal that netted George W. millions of dollars and helped propel him into the presidency. The money Bush made was essentially taken from the Harken investors who all lost money when the company's stock value fell, after this accounting fraud was revealed. It was also highly unlikely that George W., a key owner and board audit committee member was not aware that a restatement of the stock was coming. George W. was also notified by memo, right after he sold his stock that a company shutdown was coming on June 30. A federal report of W's sale of stock was required when any insider sells shares in his own company because such a large sell-off of company stock by its directors or executives is generally a sign that something is amiss within the company, as was the case with Harken. George W's "*late*" filing of his report, by some 34 weeks, was clearly valid circumstantial evidence of such a potential fraudulent act.

John Negroponte: Served as US ambassador to Honduras during the illegal CIA-backed war against Nicaragua, overseeing the Contra operation in that country. Nicaragua succeeded in winning a ruling from the World Court at The Hague, finding the US guilty of criminal aggression, which prompted the US to withdraw from the World Court. In explaining his veto, Negroponte said:

> *"With our global responsibilities, we are and will remain a special target, and cannot have our decisions second-guessed by a court whose jurisdiction we do not recognize."*

This type of veto provoked outrage in Europe as President Ramano Prodi, the European Commissioner tried to settle things down by saying:

> *"It's another movement of division between Europe and the US that we have to avoid at all cost,"*

Clare Short, Brittan's International Development Secretary said the US position constituted:

> *"an enormous disappointment to everyone in the world who wants some basic rules of decency that apply to all rulers everywhere at all times,"*

Negroponte had served as the first United States Director of National Intelligence from April 21, 2005 to February 13, 2007 — and later as the fifteenth United States Deputy Secretary of State.

George Soros: Billionaire who rescued George W's Harken Energy Corporation with Harvard's help.

Bill De Witt: Part owner of Spectrum 7, who had acquired George W's failed oil business, Arbusto, and later sold out for a profit to Harken. He also came to George W's rescue by offering him a chance to bid for the Rangers, while his father was serving as President.

James R. Bath: Salem bin Laden's business rep in Texas and neighbor to George W. Bush who obtained Laden financing for George W's Arbusto Company.

The Salem bin Laden Family: Osam bin Laden's oldest brother also financed George W's Arbusto Company. He later died in an unexplained freak flying accident outside of San Antonio, Texas on May 29, 1988. After Salem's death, the Saudi relationship with the Bush family came to an end. Then after the 9/11 attack on the Trade Center, while a national ban on all flights was in place, the bin Laden family was immediately flown out of the country.

Osama bin Laden: President Reagan and George H. W. Bush Sr. funded the covert and military Al Qaeda *"Afgan"* operation through the CIA and BCCI.

Sadam Husien: Both Rumsfield and Reagan supported the *"Kerd"* war.

Khalid bin Mahfouz: One of the richest men in the World was the controlling shareholder of Bank of Credit and Commerce International (BCCI), which was secretly financed by the Bush CIA.

Aga Hasop Abedi: Founder of BCCI, who dealt directly with the CIA Director George H. W. Bush Sr. and then William Casey, the next head of CIA.

Herbert "Pug" Winokur: One of the seven members of the Harvard Corporation's governing body, who also served as the director of the Harvard Management Corporation (HMC) that invested in Harken, and was a long time member of the Enron board of directors. He approved the many fraudulent financial arrangements engineered by George "W" at Harken, and Enron's former CEO, Jeffry Skillings.

Note: *Jeffrey Skillings was the architect of the fraudulent financial arrangements engineered at Enron, and was one of the few that was actually sent to jail. And although Ken Lay, Board Chairman and former CEO died, this country still needs to investigate Lay's close ties to the Shrub Dynasty.*

Robert Stone: While George "W" was at *Harken Energy* — HMC was controlled by Robert Stone, an oil man and long-time supporter of Bush senior.

Lawrence Lindsey: Received a Doctorate from Harvard, and served as Bush's Chief Economic Adviser and on Enron's Advisory Board.

Robert Zoellick: Received a degree from Harvard, and served as Bush's US Trade Representative and also on Enron's Advisory Board.

Lawrence Summers: The previous Treasury Secretary and a President at Harvard who made the following promise to Ken Lay, saying:

"I'll keep an eye on power deregulation and energy-market infrastructure issues."

Note: Kenneth Lay, Chairman and CEO of Enron, was also one of the *Shrub Dynasty's* biggest financial backers.

Richard Rainwater: A wealthy Texas financier joined George "W" and several other investors that bought the Texas Rangers in 1989.

Thomas Hicks: A rich financier, and one of the wealthiest buyout specialists in Texas, served as the Chairman and CEO of Hicks, Muse, Tate & Furst, and bought the Texas Rangers team in 1998 for $250 million. It was estimated that George "W" was to receive a $2 million return on his investment, but mysteriously his return actually netted him some $13 million on the deal. After George "W" won the Texas gubernatorial election, Hicks transferred his allegiance from Ann Richards, the previous Democratic Governor, to George "W" . . . giving him a $25,000 campaign contribution one month after his election. George W. Bush then appointed Hicks to the University Of Texas Board of Regents, giving Hicks considerable latitude to use the University's public funds to invest in ventures of his own choosing. George W. then established the University of Texas Investment Management Company (UTIMCO) ... similar to what he'd worked at with Harvard under the HMC. Nine billion of the Texas school's assets were then handed over to UTIMCO for investment. Unlike the Texas Board of Regents, UTIMCO was not required to open its meetings or publish its activities. They were then and are still free of public oversight, becoming the first external investment corporation formed by a public university — making this public fund available to these wealthy power brokers, tax free. In 2008, UTIMCO controlled the General Endowment Fund and extensive land and oil holdings that are valued at more than seven billion dollars.

Frank Carlucci: In 1995, $10 million went from UTIMCO to the Carlyle investment group, which also has close ties to the Shrub Dynasty. Frank Carlucci, the former Secretary of Defense under Reagan, was then the Chairman of Carlyle.

James Baker III: The former Secretary of State under George H. W. Bush Sr. is also closely linked to Carlyle. George senior also previously worked for Carlyle, and in the 1990's, George "W" served on the Board of Directors of Caterair, a company that was acquired by Carlyle in 1989.

Henry Kravis: UTIMCO also invested $50 million in the KKK 1996 Fund, a subsidiary of Kohlberg Kravis Roberts, a leveraged buyout firm that left targeted companies nearly bankrupt during the 1980's. Henry Kravis, the company's founding partner was a Financial Co-Chairman for George H. W. Bush senior's campaign in 1992, and this firm was listed in 2005 as a corporate member of the Council on Foreign Relations.

The Bass Family: UTIMCO also invested $20 million in a deal involving the Bass family, a family that was financially helped by Richard

Rainwater. The Bass family financed the preliminary exploration oil-drilling rights off the coast of Barhain, for Harken Energy. Harken Energy, who had never drilled off coast before, obtained a very questionable and extraordinary contract that shocked the entire professional oil drilling community, when many very qualified and experienced companies submitted competitive bids on this project. It should also be noted that the Bass family organization has been one of George W's largest career patrons.

Thomas White: Bush's Army Secretary, who was Vice Chairman of Enron Energy Services concealed hundreds of millions of dollars in losses, which eventually plunged California into a devastating energy crisis by manipulating the electricity market.

Harvey Pitt: Who Bush appointed to head the Security and Exchange Commission (SEC), was an attorney who previously represented the big accounting firms, including the convicted Arthur Anderson, and the major investment houses which were all under investigation. Pitt actually met with Xerox and KPMG executives while their firms were under investigation by his Security and Exchange Commission (SEC). George W's former personal lawyer, James R. Doty, was also the SEC general counsel. Moreover, the lawyer who represented George W. during the Harken investigation, Robert Jordan, was a former law partner of Doty at the Baker Botts firm. Pitt held many private meetings with Cheney prior to his becoming Vice President, where it has been reported that Cheney assured him of his prospective appointment as the future head of the energy commission.

Robert Jordan: Who served as the attorney for George W. Bush during the Harken investigation, was a former law partner of Doty at the Baker Botts firm.

APPENDIX V

QUOTES

Some Interesting Quotes: From James Alexander "The Hidden History of Money"

William Jennings Bryan:

> *"Money power denounces, as public enemies, all who question its methods or throw light upon its crimes."*

Don't be intimidated by the agents of the Money Powers!

George Soros:

> *"Instability is cumulative, so that eventual breakdown of freely floating exchanges is virtually assured."*

Rep. Louis McFadden, Chairman of the House Committee on Banking and Currency, quoted in the New York Times June 1930:

> *"The Federal Reserve Bank of New York is eager to enter into close relationship with the Bank for International Settlements [B.I.S.]....The conclusion is impossible to escape that the State and Treasury Departments are willing to pool the banking system of Europe and America, setting up a world financial power independent of and above the Government of the United States....The United States under present conditions will be transformed from the most active of manufacturing nations into a consuming and importing nation with a balance of trade against it."*

Keith Bradsher of the New York Times, August 5, 1995:

> *"In a small Swiss city sits an international organization so obscure and secretive....Control of the institution, the Bank for International Settlements, [B.I.S.] lies with some of the world's most powerful and least visible men: the heads of 32 central banks, officials able to shift billions of dollars and alter the course of economies at the stroke of a pen."*

Dr. Malcolm Knight, BIS Managing Director went on record when he said:

> *"We are not a central bank. We are the bank for the central bankers."*

Rothschild once said:

> *"Who controls the issuance of money controls the government!"*

> **Note:** Mayer Amschel Bauer was the son of Moses Amschel Bauer, a money lender and goldsmith. Mayer was born in Frankfurt, Germany in 1743, and he later opened a counting shop, placing a large Red Shield (called "Roth Schild" in German) with a Roman Eagle and Hexagram displayed on a flag. His shop was later called "Rothschild" signifying great wealth, and influence, and being identified as the first international bank. This Rothschild Dynasty eventually grew to dominate trans-Atlantic banking. The Rockefellers and the Rothschilds' were the first of the *Money Barons* to enter this country.

President James A. Garfield:

> *"Whoever controls the volume of money in any country is absolute master of all industry and commerce."*

Sir. Reginald Mckenna, former President of the Midland Bank of England:

> *"Those who create and issue money and credit direct the policies of government and hold in the hollow of their hands the destiny of the people."*

John C. Calhoun:

> *"A power has risen up in the government greater than the people themselves, consisting of many and various powerful interests combined in one mass, and held together by the cohesive power of the vast surplus in the banks."*

William Patterson:

> *"The bank hath benefit of interest on all moneys which it creates out of nothing."*

John Maynard Keynes, chief architect of our current fiat-paper money system:

> *"By a continuing process of inflation, governments can confiscate, secretly and unobserved, an important part of the wealth of their citizens".*

President Woodrow Wilson: Just before his death, he is reported to have stated to friends that he had been *"deceived"* and that *"I have betrayed my Country"* referring to the Federal Reserve Act, passed during his Presidency in 1913. He went on to say:

> *"A great industrial nation is controlled by its system of credit. Our system of credit is concentrated. The growth of the Nation and all our activities are in the hands of a few men. We have come to be one of the worst ruled, one of the most completely controlled and dominated governments in the world--no longer a government of free opinion, no longer a government of conviction, and vote of the majority, but a government by the opinion and duress, of small groups of dominant men."*

Robert H. Hemphill, Credit Manager of Federal Reserve Bank, Atlanta, Georgia:

> *"This is a staggering thought. We are completely dependent, on the Commercial Banks. Someone has to borrow every dollar, we have in circulation, cash or credit. If the Banks create ample synthetic money, we are prosperous; if not, we starve. We are, absolutely, without a permanent money system. When one gets a complete grasp of the picture, the tragic absurdity, of our hopeless position, is almost incredible, but there it is. It is the most important subject intelligent persons can investigate and reflect upon. It is so important that our present civilization may collapse, unless it becomes widely understood, and the defects remedied very soon."*

David Rockefeller addressed a re-union of the Association of the Bilderberg Group, The Council on Foreign Relations, and the Trilateral Commission in Sand, Baden Baden, Germany, in June 1991.

> *"We are grateful to the Washington Post, the New York Times, Time magazine and other great publications whose directors have attended our union and have respected their promises of discretion for almost four decades... it would not have been possible to develop our world project if we had been subjected to the full fire of publicity all these years [that's "We the People"] The supranational sovereignty of an intellectual élite and of world Bankers is surely preferable to the self-determination which has been practised for centuries past."*

Gore Vidal said:

> *"The United States is always at war; perpetual war for perpetual peace."*

Karl Grossman, professor of journalism at the State University of New York College said:

> *"In the past 30 years the US has bombed or attacked Syria, Lebanon, Nicaragua, Sudan, Korea, Vietnam, Cambodia, Laos, Iraq, Guatemala, Japan, East Timor, Nicaragua, El Salvador, Colombia, Dominican Republic, Somalia, Haiti, Yugoslavia, Panama, Afghanistan, etc.. What do these*

countries have in common? They are all non-members of the World Trade Organization."

Alan Greenspan, 17 February 2000 Congressional testimony said:

"... We have a problem trying to define exactly what money is...the current definition of money is not sufficient to give us a good means for controlling the money supply..."

CONGRESSIONAL RECORD, MAY 11, 1972:

"Some people think the Federal Reserve Banks are United States government institutions, they are not government institutions, they are private credit monopolies."

CONGRESSIONAL RECORD, JUNE 10, 1932, p. 12595:

"The Federal Reserve Board, and the Federal Reserve Banks are private Corporations."

APPENDIX VI

WALT SPEECH TO CONGRESS
(CONGRESSIONAL RECORD, MARCH 15, 1978)

"Ladies and gentlemen, I am here today, not as a member of the Armed Forces but as a common citizen, an average American. As one who is deeply and alarmingly concerned about the security of our freedoms, I am here today to speak to you because I feel it is my duty and obligation to my country. More deeply, I feel an obligation to those Americans whom I have seen sacrifice their lives on the field of battle to preserve freedoms, I believe our freedoms are in greater jeopardy today then ever before in the history of our nation. We are joined now in a most critical battle to preserve our freedoms. To me it is a continuation of the battles in which our heroic Americans have sacrificed their lives. There is not booming guns or dropping bombs but the enemy is real, many faced, insidious and clever, and the results can be just as deadly to our freedoms.

In a democratic Republic, military leaders do not commit their countries to wars. Political leaders initiate the wars and order the military to fight them. The leaders who start the war are never active participants on the field of battle . . . For those who maneuver us into war, war is a game in which our young men are pitted against a designated enemy in deadly combat.

More important, no longer can the internationalist political leaders hope not to be personally involved in a major conflict because intercontinental nuclear weapons are boundless in death and destruction effects. For this reason, I do not believe international political leaders will ever allow a nuclear conflict. But, I also believe that these same boundless weapons of death and destruction will be used to blackmail nations into submission, submission to a new international order, a "one world" government where the Government will be the master and the people will be the slaves.

I believe that our country, the United States of America, will be the first target. I believe that the stage is now being set for the blackmail action. How else can we explain:

Why we were not allowed to win the war in Korea or Vietnam?

Why we have given the USSR money, food, materials, and technology to allow them to build up the greatest military power in the world in some respects-

Why we are destroying our friends in Taiwan, South Korea, and South Africa, and at the same time, extending a friendly and helping hand to Cuba, Red China, and other Communist dominated countries-

Why we are trying to give away the Panama Canal when its loss would divide our Naval Forces into two parts - and be a severe blow to the economy of our country-

Why have we deliberately cut back the effectiveness and capability of our Armed Forces by denying them the B-1 and other critically needed weapons systems without even requiring a reciprocal reduction of Russian Backfire Bombers-

Why have we denied our nation an anti-aircraft defense and a civil defense while the Soviet Union, in direct violation of the intent and spirit of SALT I agreement, has built a civil defense to protect its people and industries and an anti-aircraft and missile defense of enormous proportions?

The Soviet Union has six times more nuclear explosive power in their intercontinental missile warheads than we have. They have nearly four times the number of submarines and twice the number of combat surface ships than we have. For more than ten years, they have had, in their operating forces, several hundred cruise missiles of two hundred miles range.

As a result of my military training, I have learned to consider only the enemy's capabilities and not his intentions. His intentions can change over night, his capabilities cannot.

This then could be a time for nuclear blackmail. And our nation naked for the lack of defenses, the blackmail could force some political leaders to capitulate.

These national and international political leaders have made other preparations for the opportune hour. They have prepared a "Declaration of INTERdependence" and a "New State of America" Constitution which would subordinate our Constitution, our Armed Forces and our economy to that of the "One World Government" (The United Nations).

Our freedoms as guaranteed by our Constitution would no longer exist. No longer would our people be the power and our Government the servant. The Government would be the master and our people would be the slaves.

Is our position hopeless?

No! Not if our people can be awakened to the military, economic and political threat facing us . . . However, time is running out! I predict, that before too long, those who signed or endorsed the "Declaration of INTERdependence," will be telling us that the only way we can save ourselves and other nations from a nuclear holocaust, is to form into a "New World Order" with a one world government. If the average American continues to be misinformed or uninformed or unaware of the blackmail maneuver and the majority of the members of Congress refuse to stand up against such a threat then our case will be hopeless and the middle class, free enterprise and all other freedoms, we have mistakenly taken for granted, will be only memories."

APPENDIX VII

INTERVIEWS

Explosions
http://911research.wtc7.net/sept11/analysis/interviews.html
<u>Reports of Sights and Sounds of Explosions in the Oral Histories</u>
[The witnesses consistently describe loud bangs at the onsets of the events, and explosive features characteristic of controlled demolition.]

Rich Banaciski -- Firefighter (F.D.N.Y.) [Ladder 22] ... and then I just remember there was just an explosion. It seemed like on television they blow up these buildings. It seemed like it was going all the way around like a belt, all these explosions.

Brian Becker -- Firefighter (F.D.N.Y.) [Engine 28] The collapse hadn't begun, but it was not a fire any more up there. It was like -- it was like that -- like smoke explosion on a tremendous scale going on up there.

Greg Brady -- E.M.T. (E.M.S.) [Battalion 6] We were standing underneath and Captain Stone was speaking again. We heard -- I heard 3 loud explosions. I look up and the north tower is coming.

Timothy Burke -- Firefigter (F.D.N.Y.) [Engine 202] ---But it seemed like I was going oh, my god, there is a secondary device because the way the building popped. I thought it was an explosion.

Frank Campagna -- Firefighter (F.D.N.Y.) [Ladder 11] --- You see three explosions and then the whole thing coming down.

Craig Carlsen -- Firefighter (F.D.N.Y.) [Ladder 8] ... you just heard explosions coming from building two, the south tower. It seemed like it took forever, but there were about ten explosions. At the time I didn't realize what it was.

Jason Charles -- E.M.T. (E.M.S.) ... and then I heard an explosion from up, from up above, and I froze and I was like, oh, s___, I'm dead because I thought the debris was going to hit me in the head and that was it.

Frank Cruthers -- Chief (F.D.N.Y.) [Citywide Tour Commander] ... there was what appeared to be at first an explosion. It appeared at the very top, simultaneously from all four sides, materials shot out horizontally. And then there seemed to be a momentary delay before you could see the beginning of the collapse.

Kevin Darnowski -- Paramedic (E.M.S.) I heard three explosions, and then we heard like groaning and grinding, and tower two started to come down.

Dominick Derubbio -- Battalion Chief (F.D.N.Y.) [Division 8] It was weird how it started to come down. It looked like it was a timed explosion ...

Karin Deshore -- Captain (E.M.S.) Somewhere around the middle of the World Trade Center, there was this orange and red flash coming out. Initially it was just one flash. Then this flash just kept popping all the way around the building and that building had started to explode.

Brian Dixon -- Battalion Chief (F.D.N.Y.) ... the lowest floor of fire in the south tower actually looked like someone had planted explosives around it because the whole bottom I could see -- I could see two sides of it and the other side -- it just looked like that floor blew out. I looked up and you could actually see everything blew out on the one floor. I thought, geez, this looks like an explosion up there, it blew out.

Michael Donovan -- Captain (F.D.N.Y.) I thought there had been an explosion or a bomb that they had blown up there.

James Drury -- Assistant Commissioner (F.D.N.Y.) I should say that people in the street and myself included thought that the roar was so loud that the explosive - bombs were going off inside the building.

Thomas Fitzpatrick -- Deputy Commissioner for Administration (F.D.N.Y.) Some people thought it was an explosion. I don't think I remember that. I remember seeing it, it looked like sparkling around one specific layer of the building.

My initial reaction was that this was exactly the way it looks when they show you those implosions on TV.

Gary Gates -- Lieutenant (F.D.N.Y.) So the explosion, what I realized later, had to be the start of the collapse. It was the way the building appeared to blowout from both sides. I'm looking at the face of it, and all we see is the two sides of the building just blowing out and coming apart like this, as I said, like the top of a volcano.

Kevin Gorman -- Firefighter (F.D.N.Y.) [Ladder 22] ... I thought that when I looked in the direction of the Trade Center before it came down, before No. 2 came down, that I saw low-level flashes.

Gregg Hansson -- Lieutenant (F.D.N.Y.) Then a large explosion took place. In my estimation that was the tower coming down, but at that time I did not know what that was. I thought some type of bomb had gone off.

Timothy Julian -- Firefighter (F.D.N.Y.) [Ladder 118] You know, and I just heard like an explosion and then cracking type of noise, and then it sounded like a freight train, rumbling and picking up speed, and I remember I looked up, and I saw it coming down.

John Malley -- Firefighter (F.D.N.Y.) [Ladder 22] I felt the rumbling, and then I felt the force coming at me. I was like, what the hell is that? In my mind it was a bomb going off.

James McKinley -- E.M.T. (E.M.S.) After that I heard this huge explosion, I thought it was a boiler exploding or something. Next thing you know this huge cloud of smoke is coming at us, so we're running.

Joseph Meola -- Firefighter (F.D.N.Y.) [Engine 91] As we are looking up at the building, what I saw was, it looked like the building was blowing out on all four sides. We actually heard the pops. Didn't realize it was the falling -- you know, you heard the pops of the building. You thought it was just blowing out.

Kevin Murray -- Firefighter (F.D.N.Y.) [Ladder 18] When the tower started -- there was a big explosion that I heard and someone screamed that it was coming down and I looked away and I saw all the windows domino.

Janice Olszewski -- Captain (E.M.S.) I thought it was an explosion or a secondary device, a bomb, the jet -- plane exploding, whatever.

Daniel Rivera -- Paramedic (E.M.S.) [Battalion 31] At first I thought it was -- do you ever see professional demolition where they set the charges on certain floors and then you hear "Pop, pop, pop, pop, pop"? That's exactly what -- because I thought it was that.

Angel Rivera -- Firefighter (F.D.N.Y.) That's when hell came down. It was like a huge, enormous explosion. I still can hear it. Everything shook.

Kennith Rogers -- Firefighter (F.D.N.Y.) I figured it was a bomb, because it looked like a synchronized deliberate kind of thing. I was there in '93.

Patrick Scaringello -- Lieutenant (E.M.S.) I started to treat patients on my own when I heard the explosion from up above.

Mark Steffens -- Division Chief (E.M.S.) Then there was another it sounded like an explosion and heavy white powder ...

John Sudnik -- Battalion Chief (F.D.N.Y.) Then we heard a loud explosion or what sounded like a loud explosion and looked up and I saw tower two start coming down. Crazy.

Jay Swithers -- Captain (E.M.S.) I took a quick glance at the building and while I didn't see it falling, I saw a large section of it blasting out, which led me to believe it was just an explosion. I thought it was a secondary device, but I knew that we had to go.

David Timothy -- E.M.T. (E.M.S.) The next thing I knew, you started hearing more explosions. I guess this is when the second tower started coming down.

Albert Turi -- Deputy Assistant Chief (F.D.N.Y.) And as my eyes traveled up the building, and I was looking at the south tower, somewhere about halfway up, my initial reaction was there was a secondary explosion, and the entire floor area, a ring right around the building blew out.

Thomas Turilli -- Firefighter (F.D.N.Y.) ... it almost actually that day sounded like bombs going off, like boom, boom, boom, like seven or eight, and then just a huge wind gust just came.

Stephen Viola -- Firefighter (F.D.N.Y.) ... that's when the south tower callapsed, and it sounded like a bunch of explosions.

William Wall -- Lieutenant (F.D.N.Y.) [Engine 47] At that time, we heard an explosion. We looked up and the building was coming down right on top of us ... (1)
References
1. The Sept. 11 Records, *New York Times*, the witnesses consistently describe loud bangs at the onsets of the events, and explosive features characteristic of controlled demolition.

Dust Clouds
http://911research.wtc7.net/wtc/evidence/oralhistories/dustcloud.html
Description of Dust Clouds in Oral Histories

Glenn Asaeda -- Civilian (E.M.S.) [M.D., Deputy Medical Director]
and the next thing I noticed, that jet engine sound and then a loud crash
and then pitch black.

After I realized that we actually made it through this initial whatever it
was, it was so dark that I actually thought they had closed the loading bay
doors as a security measure for us, but it turns out it was just the debris
and the smoke and whatnot that made it pitch black.

But really, it was so dark, you couldn't see the hand in front of your face.
... So we turned around and ran north, at which point the plume of the
smoke, again, kind of a warm feeling came by us, luckily no debris,
almost kind of lifting us and then kind of surrounding us again.

Glenn Asaeda -- Civilian (E.M.S.) [M.D., Deputy Medical Director]
and the next thing I noticed, that jet engine sound and then a loud crash
and then pitch black.

After I realized that we actually made it through this initial whatever it
was, it was so dark that I actually thought they had closed the loading bay
doors as a security measure for us, but it turns out it was just the debris
and the smoke and whatnot that made it pitch black.

But really, it was so dark, you couldn't see the hand in front of your face.

So we turned around and ran north, at which point the plume of the
smoke, again, kind of a warm feeling came by us, luckily no debris,
almost kind of lifting us and then kind of surrounding us again

Christopher Attanasio -- E.M.T. (E.M.S.)
So we proceeded to the ambulance, put on our turnout gear, helmet and
turnout coat, and as we were taking the equipment out of the ambulance,
the second tower -- the second tower, started to come down. As the
tower was coming down, we ran. I ran, I guess it was west to the West
Side Highway. The tower came down. I grabbed my partner, we ran.
When the tower finally came down, there was a white cloud of smoke
that hit us, knocked us to our feet. It was very hard to breathe. We

inhaled a lot of white powder, whatever it was, dust, concrete, whatever it was

Anthony Bartolomey -- E.M.T. (E.M.S.) [Battalion 4]
So I'm not sure if I was still in the church when the second tower came down because we were in there for quite a while before you could see outside enough to step out because the soot and the dust, the black in the sky to the point where it looked like it was nighttime outside

James Bastile -- Division Commander (E.M.S.) [Division 2]
We were operating in the lobby, and all of a sudden we heard the roar of a jet engine, is what it sounded like. We thought that there was another plane coming into the building. We went from the lobby area into an elevator bank area -- escalators that led into the concourse area. So essentially a wall that we went around from the command post area to the escalator area. Not two seconds later debris and dust started to come in, and essentially we were just shut down. Everything was dark, pitch-black.... It went down, got filled with this dust and dirt, debris, again, this cloud. I opened up my eyes. It was total darkness I guess for about two, three minutes. I thought I guess this is what it's like to be dead.

Richard Battista -- Firefighter (F.D.N.Y.) [Engine 76]
When I saw that, Lieutenant Farrington told us to move back so we were sort of underneath a garage area when we first heard reports or guys yelling that one of the towers was coming down. I was able to stick my head out and look up a bit and once I saw that I just immediately turned around and ran into the building. Within seconds everything was pitch dark

Thomas J. Bendick -- Civilian (E.M.S.) [Division 1]
Then in a couple of seconds, the roar stopped and I guess like in a split second it was just pure black.

Eric Berntsen -- Firefighter (F.D.N.Y.)
Then I looked up and I saw a dark cloud and I grabbed my helmet. The force knocked me down, blew me. I don't know how far I went, but I went forward pretty far. It knocked the wind out of me. I got covered

with debris and just kept my hands on my helmet. Something pretty big hit me and knocked my helmet off. I felt a blast and just a lot of pressure when it hit me. So I had no helmet. I put my hands back on top of my head and I felt debris hit me. I felt weight piling up on my back, and I figured I was going to be under what I thought was about 10 feet of rubble.

David Blacksberg -- E.M.T. (E.M.S.)
I looked -- I ran, and a whole lot of people, we were all running together. I looked back, and it was like it was this cloud of smoke, but it was like an avalanche, because you could see the smoke and everything tumbling right at you. You couldn't see up, you couldn't see back, and no matter how fast you ran, you couldn't out run it, and it overtook us, and finally I found my partner.

Robert Browne -- Deputy Chief (E.M.S.)

At that point, it was like -- it got totally pitch black. I couldn't see anything. I couldn't breathe. There was a wave that was -- I don't know if you're a beach person, but if you're a beach person and you ever been in the ocean, and you have a large wave come over you, and you can just feel it keep coming and coming. It's like the debris just kept coming and piling up and piling up, and when it finally did stop, I wasn't sure if I was alive or if I was dead. It was pitch black.

I can remember reaching for my radio and calling out a Mayday for the corner of Liberty and West, and nobody answered. There was no answer. It was just dead quiet, and I just assumed at that point that everybody was gone, and I wasn't -- I couldn't -- you know, I didn't call out any more. Then as the thick black, black smoke and blackness around me started to clear a little bit, and it started to get a little bit grayer, kind of like got to a dark gray, and then it got like a lighter gray, I could hear -- as it started to get lighter, I could hear people from the distance yelling for help.

Timothy Burke -- Firefighter (F.D.N.Y.)
All of a sudden the noises stopped, the sound of the building falling stopped. We all turned around and it was dark now. We really couldn't

see. We got back to there -- we went back to the garage as far in it as we were, we were all full of the cloud. The cloud was in [the garage]. All eating the cloud, whatever it was like, very thick. I kept saying it was like a 3 dimensional object. It wasn't smoke. It was like everything. It was like a sand storm. .. but it was very silent after the building fell. Then all the Maydays started happening, the guys were screaming

Ed Cachia -- Firefighter (F.D.N.Y.) [Engine 53]
We were just kind of blown into the garage with all the dust and the debris material from the building. It came up rapidly right up the street. As I remember turning, if you were out in the street somewhat, a good amount out in the street, you were kind of blown down the street, where we were kind of forced into the garage.

We were encapsulated in this garage for quite some time, maybe 15 minutes or so. You couldn't see. You couldn't breathe. You couldn't even hear because all the residue and material was in your ears and your nose and your mouth. Then as a few minutes went by, you heard some voices. It was dead silence at first. Just different emotions: How are we going to get out of here? I can't see. I can't breathe. My chest. It was still completely black. You couldn't see an inch in front of your face.

Peter Cachia -- E.M.T. (E.M.S.) [Battalion 4]
I went under the truck while the tower came down and the ground was shaking and the truck was shaking and I thought that was it for me. I thought I was done. I stayed under there until I guess everything was over. I remember opening my eyes and looking out and it was just pitch black.

Frank Cruthers -- Chief (F.D.N.Y.) [Citywide Tour Commander]
Following the North Tower collapse:
So I took a look around in that lobby, grade level lobby to see if there was access to continue more directly to get through the building and out the north side to get to the command post. While I was doing that, I heard more rumbling. I took refuge on the west side of the escalator corner. Once again there was a tremendous cloud. It was pitch black. I waited again until the cloud began to lift.

Timothy Julian -- Firefighter (F.D.N.Y.) [Ladder 118]
I made it right to the corner, and there's a column right there, and I was with my guys. We all made it to like the column, and I remember it was plate glass behind me, and I'm thinking I'm going to get hit by this glass and like a porcupine. I'm going to get it, you know, but nonetheless, it rumbled.

It was the loudest rumbling I ever heard. The ground shook, and I got thrown down, and I remember it just got black, and I got knocked down. I remember getting buried. I think I ducked more or less, you know, pieces of metal -- something hit me, not that heavy, though. Wasn't an I beam or else I wouldn't be talking to you, and I remember that being on me, and I kind of -- I was able to stand up and push everything off me, but now I felt like I was in the street or the sidewalk, and it was hot, smoky. I felt like I was in a fire, and I remember digging my way out. A lot of cementation, powdery insulation, whatever you want to call it. Almost like being in a blizzard with some metal debris right on me. Fortunately nothing heavy hit me.

Ground Shaking
http://911research.wtc7.net/wtc/evidence/oralhistories/shaking.html
<u>Reports of Ground Shaking in the Oral History</u>
The oral histories released on August 12, 2005 contain many recollections of ground shaking occurring during the collapses.

Brian Becker -- Lieutenant (F.D.N.Y.) [Engine 28]
We felt -- our whole building that we were in, when World Trade Center 2 collapsed, that was the first one to collapse. We were in World Trade Center 1. It was a tremendous explosion and tremendous shaking of our building. We thought it was our building maybe collapsed, there was a collapse above us occurring. It was tremendous shaking and like everybody dove into this stairwell and waited for, I guess, 20, 30 seconds until it settled, and that was our experience of the other building collapsing.

Michael Beehler -- Firefighter (F.D.N.Y.) [Ladder 110]
I was by I guess the outer part of the building and I just remember feeling the building starting to shake and this tremendous tremendous like roar and I just -- I kind of didn't even notice it, but like out of the corner of my eye, I saw out of the building, I saw a shadow coming down. At that point I thought it was the upper part of the north tower that had just basically like toppled over, fell off. I didn't actually see the building part go by me, because I think I was on the opposite side. But I just remember feeling this tremendous tremendous shake and hearing this, like, noise. Again I can't describe. What I did was I ended up running out.

Jody Bell -- E.M.T. (E.M.S.)
I lost track of time. You start to hear this rumble. You hear this rumble. Everything is shaking. Now I'm like, what the hell could that be. I'm thinking we're going to get bombed. This is an air raid. You hear this thunder, this rumbling. Then you see the building start to come down. Everybody's like, "Run for your lives! The building is coming down!" At that moment when that building was coming down, I was strapping a patient onto a stair chair.

Eric Berntsen -- Firefighter (F.D.N.Y.)
That's when we heard the building start shaking. I looked up into the Marriott, because you could see up into it from where we were standing, and just saw black, like dust. I saw stuff falling off the ceiling and I saw just black dust coming down. I turned and I ran a couple of steps west, a couple of steps east, and then we turned up north, up into the concourse, because I didn't see anything falling in that area at that time. So I felt that was the safest direction to go. I jumped into a corner. The lights went out. I jumped into a corner under an archway. I thought maybe that might provide some better support. I just held my helmet. I figured we were going to get like a pancake collapse on top of us. After the building stopped shaking and there was no rumbling noise any more, Vinny Picciano of 212 regrouped the company by saying 212, regroup, get back.

David Blacksberg -- E.M.T. (E.M.S.)
I lost track of time of when the second building was coming down. It sounded like one big rumble, and then it just sounded like it just continued, and I was -- I wasn't really paying attention. I was looking at the sound.

Robert Bohack -- Lieutenant (F.D.N.Y.)
from inside the North Tower:
We began, with the Port Authority cops, to come down the stairs. As soon as we got into the stairway, the building started shaking like an earthquake. I thought the building was coming down.

Nicholas Borrillo -- Firefighter (F.D.N.Y.)
on 23rd floor of North Tower:
Then we heard a rumble. We heard it and we felt the whole building shake. It was like being on a train, being in an earthquake. A train is more like it, because with the train you hear the rumbling, and it kind of like moved you around in the hall. Then it just stopped after eight or ten seconds, about the time it took for the building to come down.

Peter Cachia -- (E.M.S.) [Battalion 4]
I was like a little too close to the tower when it started coming down, because when I started running, I knew I was too close and I really didn't think I was going to get out of there. So about halfway up Liberty Street I saw a truck, I guess an SUV. It wasn't a police or a fire vehicle. It was just a car that was parked there. I went under the truck while the tower came down and the ground was shaking and the truck was shaking and I thought that was it for me. I thought I was done. I stayed under there until I guess everything was over.

Louis Cook -- Paramedic (E.M.S.
I made it up onto the -- I guess you call it the concourse level, the mezzanine level, and onto the foot bridge when I started to hear -- I thought I heard an explosion of some sort, but I kind of dismissed it. I figured, ah, it's just something burning upstairs. I really didn't think of what was going on. Okay. I start going across this pedestrian bridge. I'm the only one on this bridge. I'm walking across it, and then I just

remember feeling a rumble and hearing this rumbling sound that was really intense. It actually shook my bones.

Paul Curran -- Fire Patrolman (F.D.N.Y.)
North Tower.
I went back and stood right in front of Eight World Trade Center right by the customs house, and the north tower was set right next to it. Not that much time went by, and all of a sudden the ground just started shaking. It felt like a train was running under my feet.

The next thing we know, we look up and the tower is collapsing.

Joseph Fortis -- E.M.T. (E.M.S.)
The ground started shaking like a train was coming. You looked up, and I guess -- I don't know, it was one that came down first or two? Which one? ... We were standing on West Street, and the ground started to shake. You looked up, and it looked like a ticker tape parade off the back of the building, because all this stuff started coming down.

Timothy Julian -- Firefighter (F.D.N.Y.) [Ladder 118]
You know, and I just heard like an explosion and then cracking type of noise, and then it sounded like a freight train, rumbling and picking up speed, and I remember I looked up, and I saw it coming down.
I made it right to the corner, and there's a column right there, and I was with my guys. We all made it to like the column, and I remember it was plate glass behind me, and I'm thinking I'm going to get hit by this glass and like a porcupine. I'm going to get it, you know, but nonetheless, it rumbled.

It was the loudest rumbling I ever heard. The ground shook, and I got thrown down, and I remember it just got black, and I got knocked down. I remember getting buried.

Bradley Mann -- Lieutenant (E.M.S.)
Shortly before the first tower came down, I remember feeling the ground shaking. I heard a terrible noise, and then debris just started flying everywhere. People started running.

Keith Murphy -- (F.D.N.Y.) [Engine 47]
At the time, I would have said they sounded like bombs, but it was boom boom boom and then the lights all go out. I hear someone say oh, s___, that was just for the lights out. I would say about 3, 4 seconds, all of a sudden this tremendous roar. It sounded like being in a tunnel with the train coming at you. It sounded like nothing I had ever heard in my life, but it didn't sound good. All of a sudden I could feel the floor started to shake and sway. We were being thrown like literally off our feet, side to side, getting banged around and then a tremendous wind starting to happen. It probably lasted maybe 15 seconds, 10 to 15 seconds. It seemed like a hurricane force wind. It would blow you off your feet and smoke and debris and more things started falling.

WTC 7 Collapse Foreknowledge
http://911research.wtc7.net/wtc/evidence/oralhistories/b7foreknowledge.html
Reports of foreknowledge of the Collapse of Building 7 in the Oral Histories
The oral histories released on August 12, 2005 contain many reports of warnings of the collapse of WTC Building 7 at various times during the day. Most of the warnings were from after about 4 PM.

Joseph Cahill -- Paramedic (E.M.S.)
The reason we were given for why we were moving was that 7 World Trade Center was going to collapse or was at risk of collapsing. So we must have been somewhere in this area where we would have had a problem with that. But I honestly don't remember.

They wanted us to move the treatment sector because of 7 World Trade Center was imminently to collapse, which, of course, it did.

Tiernach Cassidy -- Firefighter (F.D.N.Y.), Engine 3
Then, like I said, building seven was in eminent collapse. They blew the horns. They said everyone clear the area until we got that last civilian out. We tried to give another quick search while we could, but then they wouldn't let us stay anymore. So we cleared the area. ... So yeah, then we just stayed on Vesey until building seven came down.

287

Pete Castellano -- Firefighter (F.D.N.Y.), Ladder 149
We were ordered down from the tower ladder because of a possible collapse at Tower 7.

Jason Charles -- E.M.T. (E.M.S.), Battalion 13
So we started heading over to where Building 7 was at and they were like Building 7 is going to collapse, you can't go over there, this and that, and there was another building that they thought was going to collapse that was like right behind the triage center, the building that we were in.

Frank Congiusta -- Battalion Fire Chief (F.D.N.Y.)
While we were searching the subbasements, they decided that Seven World Trade Center, which was across the street, was going to collapse. So they called us out.

When I came out, they were calling us on the radio to tell us to get out. Then I reported that the search was negative, and then they wouldn't let anybody near the site pretty much, because Seven World Trade Center was going to come down.

Louis Cook -- Paramedic (E.M.S.)
We got to Chambers and Greenwich, and the chief turns around and says, 'There's number Seven World Trade. That's the OEM bunker.' We had a snicker about that. We looked over, and it's engulfed in flames and starting to collapse.

We hear over the fire portable, 'Everybody evacuate the site. It's going to collapse.' Mark Steffens starts yelling, 'Get out of here! Get out of here! Get out of here! We've got to go! We've got to go! It's going to collapse.'

We pulled the car over, turned around and just watched it pancake.

Frank Cruthers -- Fire Chief (F.D.N.Y.)
Early on, there was concern that 7 World Trade Center might have been both impacted by the collapsing tower and had several fires in it and there was a concern that it might collapse. So we instructed that a collapse area –

-- be set up and maintained so that when the expected collapse of 7 happened, we wouldn't have people working in it. There was considerable discussion with Con Ed regarding the substation in that building and the feeders and the oil coolands and so on. And their concern was of the type of fire we might have when it collapsed.

Roy David -- Fire Lieutenant (F.D.N.Y.), Battalion 8
At Pace University we had -- we set up -- I'm sorry, we set up in that lobby of that building, the lobby and the actual whole first floor. There was a threat of collapse of building number seven, so 225, we had to evacuate it.

Frank Fellini -- Fire Chief (F.D.N.Y.)
The major concern at that time at that particular location was number Seven, building number seven, which had taken a big hit from the north tower. When it fell, it ripped steel out from between the third and sixth floors across the facade on Vesey Street. We were concerned that the fires on several floors and the missing steel would result in the building collapsing.

So for the next five or six hours we kept firefighters from working anywhere near that building, which included the whole north side of the World Trade Center complex. Eventually around 5:00 or a little after, building number seven came down.

Brian Fitzpatrick -- Firefighter (F.D.N.Y.), Ladder 22
We were then positioned on Vesey Street between North End and the West Side Highway because there was an imminent collapse on 7 World Trade, and it did collapse.

Joseph Fortis -- E.M.T (E.M.S.), Battalion 13
When the third building came down, we were on that corner in front of the school, and everybody just stood back. They pulled us all back at the time, almost about an hour before it, because they were sure -- they knew it was going to come down, but they weren't sure. So they pulled everyone back, and everybody stood there and we actually just waited and just waited and waited until it went down, because it was unsafe.

Ray Goldbach -- Fire Captain (F.D.N.Y.), Executive Assistant to the Fire Commissioner
There was a big discussion going on at that point about pulling all of our units out of 7 World Trade Center. Chief Nigro didn't feel it was worth taking the slightest chance of somebody else getting injured. So at that point we made a decision to take all of our units out of 7 World Trade Center because there was a potential for collapse.

Made the decision to back everybody away, took all the units and moved them all the way back toward North End Avenue, which is as far I guess west as you could get on Vesey Street, to keep them out of the way.

George Holzman -- Firefighter (F.D.N.Y.), Ladder 47
We stayed there for quite sometime when I don't even know who, I think it was someone, Lieutenant Lowney spoke to, asked us to leave the area, they were concerned about 7 World Trade Center collapsing.

Edward Kennedy -- Firefighter (F.D.N.Y.), Engine 44
That was the only Mayday that I remember, and to tell you the truth, the only guy that really stands out in my mind that I remember being on the radio was Chief Visconti.

I remember him screaming about 7, No. 7, that they wanted everybody away from 7 because 7 was definitely going to collapse, they don't know when, but it's definitely going to come down, just get the hell out of the way, everybody get away from it, make sure you're away from it, that's an order, you know, stuff like that.

Matthew Long -- Firefighter (F.D.N.Y.), Ladder 43
And at that point they were worried that 7 was coming down so they were calling for everyone to back out.
So I waited for -- we waied for the boss, Lieutenant Rohan, in the middle of the rubble and we all walked out together back to the West Side Highway and pretty much hung out by the marina when 7 came down.

Because they were just adamant about 7 coming down immediately. I think we probably got out of that rubble and 18 minutes later is when 7 came down.

Thomas McCarthy -- Fire Chief (F.D.N.Y.)
So when I get to the command post, they just had a flood of guys standing there. They were just waiting for 7 to come down.

I made it down Vesey Street to just in front of the overpass of 7 World Trade. People were saying don't stand under there, it's going to come down.

So at that point we were a little leery about how the bridge was tied in, so no one was really going onto it, and then they were also saying 7 was going to come down. They chased everyone off the block.

Kevin McGovern -- Firefighter (F.D.N.Y.), Engine 53
At that time Seven World Trade Center was burning and was in danger of collapsing. After a while the lieutentant said, "Let's move, let's get out of here, let's take a break."

Actually I think at that point just as we were leaving, guys -- I don't know who it was. I guess it was a chief was saying clear the area, because they were worried about number Seven World Trade Center coming down and burying guys who were digging.

So we basically went back to the rig, because they were clearing that area out. It took about three hours for Seven World Trade Center to actually come down. So we were off to the side.

Vincent Massa -- Firefighter (F.D.N.Y.), Engine 64
At this point Seven World Trade Center was going heavy, and they weren't letting anybody get too close. Everybody was expecting that to come down.

I remember later on in the day as we were waiting for seven to come down, they kept backing us up Vesey, almost like a full block. They were concerned about seven coming down, and they kept changing us, establishing a collapse zone and backing us up.

Daniel Nigro -- Department Cheif (F.D.N.Y.)
The most important operational decision to be made that afternoon was the collapse had damaged 7 World Trade Center, which is about a 50 story building, at Vesey between West Broadway and Washington Street. It had very heavy fire on many floors and I ordered the evacuation of an area sufficient around to protect our members, so we had to give up some rescue operations that were going on at the time and back the people away far enough so that if 7 World Trade did collapse, we wouldn't lose any more people.

We continued to operate on what we could from that distance and approximately an hour and a half after that order was given, at 5:30 in the afternoon, 7 World Trade Center collapsed completely.

Christopher Patrick Murray -- Firefighter (F.D.N.Y.), Engine 205
Probably about 4:00 o'clock, 5:00 o'clock, our radios went dead, because we heard reports all day long of 7 World Trade possibly coming down and I think at 5:30 that came down.

William Ryan -- Fire Lieutenant (F.D.N.Y.)
Then we found out, I guess around 3:00 o'clock, that they thought 7 was going to collapse. So, of course, we've got guys all in this pile over here and the main concern was get everybody out, and I guess it took us over an hour and a half, two hours to get everybody out of there.

So it took us a while and we ended up backing everybody out, and that's when 7 collapsed.

Thomas Smith -- Firefighter (F.D.N.Y.)
They backed me off the rig because seven was in dead jeopardy, so they backed everybody off and moved us to the rear end of Vesey Street. We just stood there for a half hour, 40 minutes, because seven was in imminent collapse and finally did come down.

Robert Sohmer -- Fire Captain (F.D.N.Y.)
As the day went on they started worrying about 7 World Trade Center collapsing and they ordered an evacuation from that area so at that time,

we left the area with the other companies, went back to the command post on Broadway

We were about to proceed our operation there and this was in the afternoon, I would say approximately maybe 2:00 roughly, where we started to operate and then they asked us to fall back again due to the potential of 7 World Trade Center collapsing.

James Wallace -- Firefighter (F.D.N.Y.)
They were saying building seven was going to collapse, so we regrouped and went back to our rig. We went to building four or three; I don't know. We were going to set up our tower ladder there. They said no good because building seven is coming down.

Rudolf Weindler -- Fire Lieutenant (F.D.N.Y.)
I ran into Chief Coloe from the 1st Division, Captain Varriale, Engine 24, and Captain Varriale told Chief Coloe and myself that 7 World Trade Center was badly damaged on the south side and definitely in danger of collapse. Chief Coloe said we were going to evacuate the collapse zone around 7 World Trade Center, which we did.

Decosta Wright -- E.M.T. (E.M.S.)
They said -- we were like, are you guys going to put that fire out? I was like, you know, they are going to wait for it to burn down and it collapsed.

Yes, so basically they measured out how far the building was going to come, so we knew exactly where we could stand.

5 blocks. 5 blocks away. We still could see. Exactly right on point, the cloud just stopped right there. Then when that building was coming down, the same thing, that same rumbling.

APPENDIX VIII

RESURRECTED HIJACKERS

Of the 19 hijackers allegedly identified by the FBI as dead, the following were later found to be alive:

Abdulaziz Alomari was identified by the FBI as the hijacker who accompanied Mohamed Atta from the connecting flight from Portland and helped him hijack and pilot Flight 11 into the North Tower. Abdulaziz told the London-based *Asharq Al-Awsat* newspaper: "The name [listed by the FBI] is my name and the birth date is the same as mine, but I am not the one who bombed the World Trade Center in New York." Saudi Embassy officials in Washington defended the innocence of Alomari, saying that his passport was stolen in 1996 and that he had reported the theft to the police.

Saeed Alghamdi, a Saudi Airlines pilot, was identified by the FBI of being a hijacker of Flight 93, which crashed in Pennsylvania. Alghamdi was "shocked and furious" to learn this three days after the attack, noting that his name, place of residence, date of birth, and occupation matched those described by the FBI. "You cannot imagine what it is like to be described as a terrorist - and a dead man - when you are innocent and alive," said Alghamdi, who considered legal action against the FBI.

Salem Al-Hamzi was identified by the FBI as one of the hijackers of Flight 77, thought to have crashed into the Pentagon. Al-Hamzi said: "I have never been to the United States and have not been out of Saudi Arabia in the past two years."

Ahmed Al-Nami was identified by the FBI as one of the hijackers of Flight 93. Al-Nami said: "I'm still alive, as you can see. I was shocked to see my name mentioned by the American Justice Department. I had never even heard of Pennsylvania where the plane I was supposed to have hijacked."

Waleed Alshehri a Saudi Arabian pilot, was identified by the FBI as one of the hijackers of Flight 11. Alshehri turned up in Morocco after the attack where he contacted both the Saudi and American authorities to tell them he was not involved in the attack.

Abdulrahman al-Omari a Saudi Airlines pilot, was identified by the FBI as one of the hijackers of Flight 11. After learning this, he visited the US consulate in Jeddah to demand an explanation.

Ameer and Adnan Bukhari were named by *CNN* as suspected hijackers of Flight 175, the jetliner which crashed into the South Tower, in an article dated 9/13/01. In a correction, *CNN* stated that Ameer Bukhari died in a small plane crash in Florida, and that Adnan was still alive in Florida, having passed a polygraph test to confirm his innocence."

APPENDIX IX

THE DAVIS DRUG MARK-UP STUDY

Celebrex: 100 mg – Consumer price (100 tablets): $130.27 – Cost of general active ingredients: $0.60-Percent markup: **21,712%**

Claritin: 10 mg – Consumer Price (100 tablets): $215.17 – Cost of general active ingredients: $0.71-Percent – markup: **30,306%**

Keflex: 250 mg – Consumer Price (100 tablets): $157.39 – Cost of general active ingredients: $1.88-Percent markup: **8,372%**

Lipitor: 20 mg – Consumer Price (100 tablets): $272.37 – Cost of general active ingredients: $5.80 – Percent markup: **4,696%**

Norvasc: 10 mg – Consumer price (100 tablets): $188.29 – Cost of general active ingredients: $0.14 – Percent markup: **134,493%**

Paxil: 20 mg – Consumer price (100 tablets): $220.27 – Cost of general active ingredients: $7.60 – Percent markup: **2,898%**

Prevacid: 30 mg – Consumer price (100 tablets): $44.77 – Cost of general active ingredients: $1.01 – Percent markup: **34,136%**

Prilosec: 20 mg – Consumer price (100 tablets): $360.97 – Cost of general active ingredients $0.52 – Percent markup: **69,417%**

Prozac: 20 mg – Consumer price (100 tablets): $247.47 – Cost of general active ingredients: $0.11 – Percent markup: **224,973%**

Tenormin: 50 mg – Consumer price (100 tablets): $104.47 – Cost of general active ingredients: $0.13 – Percent markup: **80,362%**

Vasotec: 10 mg – Consumer price (100 tablets): $102.37 – Cost of general active ingredients: $0.20 – Percent markup: **51,185%**

Xanax: 1 mg – Consumer price (100 tablets) : $136.79 – Cost of general active ingredients: $0.024 – Percent markup: **569,958%**

Zestril: 20 mg – Consumer price (100 tablets) $89.89 – Cost of general active ingredients $3.20 – Percent markup: **2,809%**

Zithromax: 600 mg – Consumer price (100 tablets): $1,482.19 – Cost of general active ingredients: $18.78 – Percent markup: **7,892%**

Zocor: 40 mg – Consumer price (100 tablets): $350.27 – Cost of general active ingredients: $8.63 – Percent markup: **4,059%**

Zoloft: 50 mg – Consumer price: $206.87 – Cost of general active ingredients: $1.75 –Percent markup: **11,821%** *(11)*

APPENDIX X

PSRO's

The Provider Sponsored Organization–PSO– which is composed of a group of physicians and other providers who contracted directly with Medicare and other buyers of healthcare services. They don't work with insurance companies.

The Health Maintenance Organization–HMO– which is a group of doctors, hospitals and other healthcare providers that market what is referred to as a comprehensive range of healthcare services. They propose to market these services to an enrolled population that pays a fixed amount of money for a defined period of time.

The Preferred Provider Organization–PPO– which is a group of physicians, a group of hospitals, or a group of physicians and hospitals that contracted with an employer to provide services to their employees.

*The Independent Practice Association–IPA–*which is a group of physicians and other providers that contract with health plans.

The Point of Service organization–POS– which allows HMO members to obtain services from providers that are not within their network.

The Physician Hospital Organization–PHO– which is a group of physicians' practices that are owned by a hospital or a hospital system.

The Physician Practice Management Company – PPM – which provides administrative services such as billing and contracting with health plans for large groups of physicians.

APPENDIX XI

DEATHS, ACCIDENTS, RESIGNATIONS AND FIRINGS

General Policy: After a Senate investigation exposed the many attempted assassination of Fidel Castro, the Cuban President, and numerous other criminal activities in the 1960s and 1970s, President Gerald Ford issued an executive order banning assassinations by any US government agency. Prior to that time, the CIA had become notorious for engineering many successful assassinations, including the following:

> **Patrice Lamumba,** the Congolese Prime Minister
> **Salvador Allende,** the Chilean President
> **Rafael Trujillo,** the Dominican President
> **Che Guevara,** Agentine–born Marxist revolutionary and Cuban Guerrilla leader

In June 2002, the *Washington Post* and many other dailies reported the administration plan calls for the "possible use of CIA and US Special Forces teams, similar to those deployed in Afghanistan since the September 11 terrorist attacks. Such teams would be authorized to kill Sadam Hussein if they were acting in self defense." From this, "it would appear that the administration is publicly reviving the criminal and reviled methods employed by the CIA previously, when the agency ran what amounted to Murder Incorporated." It appears the Bush administration has made no attempt to conceal its intentions, since this plan for more assassinations has been featured by the *Washington Post* and other national dailies.

In 1998, Iraq expelled United Nations weapons inspectors after escalating provocations and growing suspicions that the inspection operation was a Trojan horse for US attempts to kill Hussein. Scott Ritter, a former US Marine, headed the concealment Investigation Unit from the United Nations Special Commission Unit (UNSCOM) that operated in Iraq. He had testified that Iraq's weapons program had been destroyed and the country had effectively been disarmed. The Los Angeles Times quoted Ritter in June of 2002 as saying: "I recall during my time in Iraq the dozens of extremely fit 'missiles experts' and 'logistic specialists' who frequented my inspection teams and others," ... These "experts," he said, were "drawn from such US units as Delta Force or from CIA paramilitary teams such as the Special Activities Staff." [in other words, they were trained assassins] According to Ritter, the Iraqi regime had long suspected that the inspections "were nothing more than a front for a larger effort to eliminate their leader." With the Bush administration's release of its "Covert" action plan, [in the Washington Post article and other national dailies] he added, "The Iraqis will never trust an inspection regime that has already shown itself susceptible to infiltration and manipulation by intelligence services to Iraq ... The true target of the supposed CIA plan may not be Hussein but rather the weapons inspection program itself." He'd said. While the United Nations officials were trying to negotiate an agreement with Baghdad to allow a resumption of the inspections. Iraq's foreign minister and the UN secretary general met in July. The Bush administration is [was] determined to block such an agreement. And halt any multinational operation that could call into question its unsubstantiated allegations about an Iraq threat. This is [was] the principle purpose of the administrations leaking [to the Washington Post] details of its plans for a covert war and the assassination of the Iraqi president, according to someone intimately familiar with US machinations in the region. In other words the Bush regime was intent on going to war, and were not happy when the inspections were once again resumed ... therefore they next seized upon the Anthrax attacks.

Five People Died from Anthrax: Barbara Hatch Rosenberg, who chairs the Federation of American Scientists Working Group on Biological Weapons, suggested a cover up in a June 19 statement on the probe: "Either the FBI is under pressure from DOD [Department of

Defense] or CIA not to proceed because the Suspect knows too much and must be controlled forever from the moment of arrest; (For the good of the country, is it really more important to hide what he knows than to let justice be served?)," wrote Ms. Rosenberg, "or the FBI is sympathetic to the views of the bio-defense clique; or the FBI really is as incompetent as it seems." The suspect is [was] believed to be a current or recent scientific employee at the US Army Medical Research Institute of Infectious Diseases (USAMRIID), located at Fort Detrick, Maryland. Those familiar with the investigation have suggested that the FBI has refused to make an arrest because the individual who carried out the attack "knows too much" about Washington's own secret biological weapons program. This article went on to say : "There is another, more sinister possibility—that the anthrax attacks were carried out by elements within the government with the aim of terrorizing the population into unquestioning support for the Bush administration's "war of terrorism." Col. David Franz, the former commander of the USAMRIID program, said: **"five people died"** all due to this highly questionable anthrax act of terror.

In an article by Patrick Martin, on May 15, 2002, *"Anthrax attacks: FBI cover-up and New York Times whitewash,"* he states, biological warfare expert Steven Block of Stanford University told the Dallas Morning News in an interview published April 1, that the perpetrators of the attack "either had to have information from the United States or maybe they were the United States." The FBI also might be holding back, "because the person that's involved with it may have secret information that the United States government would not like divulged."

Persian Gulf War: Another article indicated that the destruction of the Persian Gulf War in 1991, not merely destroyed military targets, but ... electricity, water purification and healthcare facilities, resulting in an appalling loss of life. According to some estimates, the death toll from disease and malnutrition directly attributable to the US war—most of it consisting of **young Iraqi children—stands at over 1.5 million.** The almost continual fly-over's, bombings, sanctions and the potential assassination of their leader would suggest that perhaps, the aim of any attack on Iraq will be [was] not the elimination of biological, chemical or nuclear weapons programs, but the furtherance of Washington's hegemonic control over the oilfields of the Persian Gulf. While there is little doubt that such killings have once again surfaced … until recently every subsequent administration has at least paid lip service to the Ford ban.

Note: In reviewing the many mysterious incidents under the George W. Bush administration, it's frightening to find so many deaths, accidents, resignations, and firings that have involved victims who might have spoken out in opposition to today's corruption, while in every walk of life people live in fear and terror today. Those who have died, and those who still live in fear of retaliation if they speak out, are of such a number that it's time for an unbiased investigation of these so-called incidents, which can no longer be passed off as circumstantial by Karl Rove. Fortunately, with the President's current low pole ratings, it's been indicated that several CIA agents are seriously rethinking their confidential commitment to the CIA, and may soon risk exposing more detail on this important issue if placed under oath. It should also be noted that there are no accurate records of the number of prisoners who have been tortured to death in the current Iraqi war, but estimates are set at 666,000 Iraqi deaths and we need to determine the accurate number in that this was clearly an unjust attack without provocation.

Plane Crashes have frequently been involved in the death of numerous politicians that were in conflict with this Aristocracy and the CIA. One of the more controversial deaths, was described by VOXNEWS on 10/25/02 in an article entitled *"Senator Paul Wellstone Assassinated by group linked to Bush Sr."* Ironically, VOXNEWS had previously predicted this assassination in an article entitled "Democratic Senator to be Assassinated Soon," saying the death would appear to be either a plane "accident" or by "natural causes," whichever is most easily accomplished … to "rebalance the scale". The article goes on to say, "The private covert intelligence groups behind George Bush Sr. are extraordinarily well funded with petrochemical billions. They are deadly, work completely autonomously, in a terrorist formation identical to a terrorist organization, and are absolutely religiously dedicated to accomplishing objectives … They will not rest until the Senate is under [Republican control]… the darkest force ever to seize control of the American Empire – The clandestine industrial / military / intelligence triad who is currently represented by George Bush Jr."

Sam Smith of the *Progressive Review* on Oct. 25 published a story titled, "Politicians Killed in Plane Crashes." This story identifies some 22 air crashes involving state and federal officials, and one ambassador **(Arnold Raphael)** and one cabinet official **(Ron Brown)**. … Six of the fatalities occurred during election campaigns and include:

> **Rep. Hale Boggs,** D-La., was an outspoken member of the Warren Commission investigating the assassination of JFK.

> **Rep. Jerry Litton,** D-Mo., was killed while campaigning for a U.S. Senate seat in Missouri, two months before the election.

> **Rep. Larry McDonald**, D-GA, national chairman of the John Birch Society and creator of a private intelligence operation called Western Goals. At that time he was linked to a scandal involving massive domestic spying, and CIA and covert operatives like Gen. John Singlaub.

> **Rep. Larkin Smith,** D-Miss, was investigating the deaths of five Green Beret colonels who were connected to a covert CIA drug operation known as Watchtower.

> **Secretary of Commerce Ron Brown**, a Democrat killed in a plane crash with many unresolved mysteries including a post mortem photo showing a bullet wound in his skull.

> **Mel Carnahan,** who was running for a Senate seat, was also killed in a plane crash just day before the 2000 election in Missouri, where his wife Jean held on to the seat by filling in for her husband until a new election was held. He was running against John Ashcroft.

Senator Paul Wellstone ranked high as a Bush Administration enemy. The Nov. 4, 2002 issue of *Time* recounts an open encounter with the elder Bush. Wellstone had voted against Homeland Security, the Iraqi use of force resolution and many of Bush's judicial nominees under a Senate controlled 50-49 by the Democrats. So what happened? Just three days after the crash, the FBI and some 50 of the worlds leading newspapers indicated the crash had been caused by "freezing rain and snow," limited visibility, and likely icing of the wings. Yet, none of these conditions as described existed or had anything to do with the crash. The Wellstone plane had notified the Federal Aviation Administration just 60 seconds prior to the crash, when everything was normal, that it was on approach to the airport and had activated the runway lights. A witness told authorities that the plane passed just 100 feet over his house crabbing to the right. He felt and heard the crash about two miles away and heard a loud shot, which he thought was a rifle. Many unanswered question remain but this tragedy, not like the Carnahan's crash, killed the entire family instead of leaving anyone alive like Jean Carnahan. In another article from *Wilderness Publications*, Michael C. Ruppert writes, "Was Paul Wellstone Murdered?" saying – "History Suggests It – Crash Inconsistencies Suggest It – Many, Including Some Members of Congress, Believe It." The article itself describes, "The air crash deaths of Senator Paul Wellstone, his wife, daughter, three staff members and two pilots at approximately 10:25 a.m. on Oct. 25 in Eveleth, Minnesota has given rise to the widespread belief – shared by two members of the House of Representatives who spoke on condition of anonymity – that the crash was a murder."

Others Deaths and Accidents of Concern:

Anson Ng, a reporter for the Financial Times, and **Danny Casolaro**, a freelance reporter were both mysteriously killed while attempting to expose the BCCI corruption. In September 1991, *Time* magazine carried an article describing BCCI as "a vast, stateless, multinational corporation that deploys its own intelligence agency, complete with a paramilitary wing and enforcement units, known collectively as the Black Network." The BCCI's "Black Network," created under the direction of Bush senior, then the Director of the CIA, was apparently connected to at least 16 suspicious deaths, (not listed here) including these two reporters who had been working on the BCCI story.

Barry Seal In a report by Daniel Hopsicker and Michael Ruppert entitled *"Why Does George W. Bush Fly in Drug Smuggler Barry Seal's Airplane?"* it tells of the notorious drug smuggler, who once flew C-123 military cargo planes filled with cocaine into Mena, Arkansas on behalf of the contras; and Terry Reed, author of *"Compromised,"* who were both sent on a drug sting for the CIA as undercover agents (uc) to entrap some wealthy Texans. It turns out that the Texans were George W. and Jeb Bush, who flew into a Florida airport on the Governor's aircraft, which was a Beechcraft King Air 200 with FAA registration number N6308F – Serial Number BB-1014, to pick up kilos of cocaine themselves. This plane was previously owned by Barry Seal. A hidden DEA camera filmed the tail number of the aircraft and both Bush's participation, which was quickly covered up. Journalist Sandra Hicks describes how Seals kept the names, dates, places, tape recordings and videos as his "insurance policy." However, Seals was gunned down in 1986 by a hit team of drug traffickers under the National Security Council staffer Lt. Colonel Oliver North. Terry Reed's book *"Compromised,"* also disappeared from bookshelves after finally being published in Canada. As a result, Daniel Hopsicker, a former producer at NBC, wrote a book called *"Berry and the Boys."*

Raymond Lemme, a Florida state government inspector, who in June 2003 investigated claims that Tom Feeny, a running mate of Jeb Bush who was rewarded with a plum congressional seat, had asked Clint Curtis with Yang Enterprises, and a Florida programmer, to developed vote-rigging software that could control the touch terminal computer vote and suppress the black vote. Later, experts using these machines validated the ability to significantly skew the precinct's results by millions of votes without leaving a trace in any of the 30 states the system was used in. Lemme informed Curtis, "he'd successfully tracked this corruption all the way to the top" and that "the story would break in a few weeks; but on

July 1, 2003, Lemme was found dead. Lemme was a happily married man, eagerly planning his daughters wedding, but the police ignored the facts and listed the death as a suicide. The police said there were no photos, but then pictures turned up on the inter-net and were later confirmed as authentic by the police, presenting evidence that Lemme was beaten. Curtis testified to this before a state congressional committee, but after the police spoke with a high Florida state government official, the state congressional investigation was abruptly shut down. James Baker, the notorious Bush family fixer, spearheaded the investigation of the 2000 vote in Florida. The close Diebold relationship to George senior, the company that developed the touch terminal software, had previously assured the former president that they would not provide an audit trail, while a simple printing of the confirmation vote could have easily provided a very acceptable audit trail. Nothing has been done to clarify this convenient death of Lemme, nor has any action been taken to rectify the degradation of the American electoral process other than appointing another blue ribbon panel of the establishment, with James Baker appointed to co-chair the effort.

J.H. Hatfield, the man who wrote the controversial biography, *"Fortunate Son: George W. Bush and the Making of an American President."* Hatfield, 43, was found dead of an apparent prescription drug overdose in a hotel room in Springdale, Arkansas on July 18, 2001. Once again, police declined to investigate.

Salem bin Laden, Osam bin Laden's oldest brother, died in an unexplained freak flying accident outside of San Antonio, Texas on May 29, 1988. His death brought to an abrupt end, an intriguing eleven year personal and business relationship between President George "W" and Salem, who was "W's" first business partner, as well as the head of the bin Laden family fortune. Salem and George "W" were founders of the Arbusto Energy oil company in Texas. "Arbustro" actually means "shrub" in Spanish, but the Bush family interpreted it as a "bush". Shortly after Bush's father was appointed director of the CIA, James R. Bath, a friend, neighbor, and a pilot in the International Guard with George W; signed a trust agreement with Salem in 1976, as his Houston representative for one of the largest construction company's in the world, the Bin Laden Brother's Construction, where he funneled "Laden" money into W's start up oil company. Although Bush told The Houston Post in 1990, he'd "never done any business" with Bath, Bath received a 5 percent interest in two of W's Arbustro-related limited partnerships. Bill White, a real estate partner with Bath, said: George Bush senior, then the head of the CIA, wanted Bath involved with the Arabs, and The Houston Chronicle of June 4, 1992 indicated that the Saudis were using Bath and their huge financial resources to influence U.S. Policy during the Reagan and Bush administrations. Salem was an excellent pilot, with more than 15,000 hours of flight experience, who perhaps was directed to fly right instead of left after take-off, striking and becoming entangled in power lines that were only 150 feet high. Since that time, the Saudi relationship with the Bush family has cooled considerably, removing our air base and military from that country. Did George W's personal involvement with Salem and the Black Network of the BCCI Outlaw Bank scandal somehow bring this story to a dead end by design? Here again, the police attempted to explain it as a freak accident, but we'll never know. Did we really know that our President had such close personal ties with the Saudis? Did any of us know that the world now associates that same "bin Laden" name with Salem's brother Osama bin Laden, the prime suspect behind the terror atrocities of Sept. 11, as well as the secret flights of so many "bin Laden" family members from this country following the destruction of the Trade Center?

Darlene Novinger In Rodney Stitch's book, *"Defrauding America,"* he writes that "Darlene Novinger, and FBI investigator, told him that during an investigation she discovered that George Bush and two of his sons were using drugs and prostitutes in a Florida hotel while Bush was vice president. She said that when she reported these findings to her FBI supervisors they warned her not to reveal what she discovered. Novinger had been requested to infiltrate drug trafficking operations in South America and the United States. Later she was pressured to quit the FBI position; her husband was beaten to death; and four hours after she appeared on a July 1993 talk show describing her findings (after she was warned not to appear), her father mysteriously died. A dead white canary was left on his grave as a warning to her. After receiving death threats she went into hiding, from where she occasionally appeared as a guest on talk shows, and called Stitch from undisclosed locations." She'd worked on Operations Nimbus, investigating large scale drug smuggling on the Eastern seaboard — involving a Lebanese family by the name of William Smatt. The operation was tied to the Lebaneses fascist Phalange and implicated VP Bush and son Jeb. Before Operation Nimbus was shut down, veteran US Customs investigator Joe Price filed corroborating reports implicating Bush. In 1983, FBI agents arrested him on a narcotics trafficking charge.

Margie Schoendinger claimed she was raped by George 43 and several CIA men. Later, she was shot in the head

Major Ambarak S. Alghamdl Victim of a mysterious, unexplained, and largely uncommented-upon plane crash on May 8, 2004, which occurred in clear weather, including two Raytheon Corporation victims from the E-Systems division, capable of taking down or disrupting airplanes ... with advance guiding systems. Alghamdl worked as an instructor at Pensacola Naval Air Station where reports suggested that two 9/11 terrorist hijackers Saeed Alghamdl and Ahmed Alghamdl received flight training at this secure military base. Ambarack remained as an instructor at this base after 9/11.

Rudi Dekkers, (attempts to kill that failed) a Dutch citizen who was President of Huffman Aviation in Florida survived a crash in Cancun on Christmas 2002, and then a second helicopter crash in the Caloosahatchee river on January 24, 2003, just prior to his scheduled meeting to testify at a congressional hearing. Federal agents seized all the records from Huffman Aviation, the flight school of terrorist Mohammed Atta, and other 9/11 hijackers within hours of the attacks of September 11th and loaded them onto a C-130 cargo plane. Whatever secrets Dekkers possessed about the terrorists must have suddenly been deemed sensitive enough to be escorted from Sarasota, Fl. to Washington by Florida Governor Jeb Bush.

Reporter Kristen Breitweiser, grilled a senior FBI agent, asking, "With all the warnings about the possibilities of Al Qaeda using planes as weapons, and the Phoenix Memo ... that Osama bin Laden was sending operatives ... for flight training, why didn't you check out flight schools before Sept. 11?" The agent replied, "Do you know how many flight schools there are in the U.S.? ... We couldn't have investigated them all and found these few guys." But the question that remains today is how the federal authorities knew within hours of the attack, that Huffman Aviation was the flight school to obtain and secure the records from.

Daniel Hopsicker, a reporter and author of *"Welcome to Terrorland,"* reports from an article in *The Mad Cow Morning News,* that the I.N.S. was seeking to place the Huffman records and the 9/11 conspiracy investigation out of reach from any independent investigation. Wally Hilliard, the owner of Hilliard's, and his associate Du Bain, had a cozy relationship with Jeb Bush where they would charter his flights at virtually no cost. They also were well known for their illegal cargo from Venezuela, and both Bush and Secretary of State Katherine Harris were providing celebrity endorsements well after the company was busted by DEA agents. Hilliard's operation was called at various times Florida Air, Sunrise Airlines, with Bush posing with the family when it was called Discover Airlines. Whatever their name was, it was an operation that trained murderous terrorists and brought heroin into America.
Charges on Dekkers were later dropped.

Arnie Kruithof (another attempt to kill that failed) On June 26, 2002, Arnie Kruithof, the owner of the flight school that trained Ziad Jarrah, narrowly survived still another plane crash in Venice, Florida.

John O'Neil- Further light on Bush's contacts for oil with the Taliban was presented in a book released in November 2001, entitled *"Bin Laden, the Forbidden Truth,"* written by Jean-Charles Brisard and Guillaume Dasquie. Brisard ... a former French secret service agent, and Dasquie ... a former investigative journalist, write that "the Bush administration was willing to accept the Taliban regime, despite the charges of sponsoring terrorism, if it cooperated with plans for the development of the oil resources of Central Asia." Until August, they claim, the US government saw the Taliban "as a source of stability in Central Asia that would enable the construction of an oil pipeline across Central Asia." In fact, Brisard said, "Talks between the Bush administration and the

Taliban began in February2001, shortly after Bush's inauguration. A Taliban emissary arrived in Washington in March with presents for the new chief executive, including an expensive carpet. But the talks themselves were less than cordial. At one moment during the negotiations, the US representatives told the Taliban, *'either you accept our offer of a carpet of gold, or we bury you under a carpet of bombs'.*" As a result, "John O'Neil, deputy director of the FBI, resigned in July in protest over this obstruction." O'Neil told Brisard and Dasquie in their interview with him, "the main obstacles to investigate Islamic terrorism were US oil corporate interests and the role played by Saudi Arabia in it." And like so many other strange coincidence, O'Neil was killed on September 11.

Abdul Haq- Robert C. (Bud) McFarlane, the National Security Adviser said he'd previously "held meetings with Abdul Haq [the former mujahedin leader] and other former mujahedin in the course of the fall and winter of 2000." Then after the Bush administration took office, "McFarlane parlayed his Republican connections into a series of meetings with the State Department, Pentigon and even White House Officials. All encouraged the preparation of an anti-Taliban military campaign." According to McFarlane, Abdul Haq "decided in mid-August to go ahead and launch operations in Afghanistan. In other words this phase of the anti-Taliban war was under way well before September 11. McFarlane's revelations come in the course of a bitter diatribe against the CIA for 'betraying' Abdul Haq, failing to back his operations in the Toro Bora Mountains in Afghanistan, and leaving him to die at the hands of the Taliban."

Note: These are only a few of the numerous reports of suspicious deaths that have not been investigated by an unbiased authority. Needless to say, the Bush ties with the CIA and the BCCI prevent an unbiased review.

Terminations:
Paul H. O'Neill, former Treasury Secretary, in and article by Joseph Kay on 28 June 2002, entitled, *"Threatened collapse of WorldCom sends political establishment into crisis,"* said O'Neill resigned stating, "I think we've got to prosecute people to the full extent of the law. In some cases we

need to strengthen the law, so the government can go after executives. O'Neill recently called for corporate criminals to be 'hanged from the highest branch.' He should be careful. If taken seriously, his words could be interpreted as a threat against the life of the president and his entire cabinet." In Paul O'Neill's new book, the ex-Treasury secretary criticized the administration by saying, "Bush planned Iraq invasion before 9/11." On CBS News' 60 Minutes he also said, "The Bush administration began planning to use U.S. troops to invade Iraq within days after the former Texas governor entered the White House three years ago. From the very beginning, there was a conviction that Saddam Hussein was a bad person and that he needed to go," O'Neill told CBS, according to excerpts released by the network. "For me, the notion of pre-emption, that the U.S. has the unilateral right to do whatever we decide to do, is a really huge leap." No wonder he suddenly resigned.

Kitty Kelly, author of *"The Family, The real story of the Bush Dynasty,"* who wrote a fully documented book that was not entirely complementary of the Bush family, was terminated summarily after publication. Clearly this action was prompted at the request of the powerful Bush Regime.

There have been numerous resignations that all relate to some conflict with the Bush dynasty, which should receive further investigation by an unbiased outside organization. I have only listed three resignations (terminations) that include John O'Neil, Paul O'Neill and Kitty Kelly, but there are many more.

Dan Rather, the CBS newscaster, and his staff were essentially fired after years of honest and ethical reporting when an attempt to expose the truth about the Bush nepotism, which was being openly presented to the public. Their firing was a direct result of undue influence by both the government and large corporations over newsrooms, which spurred Mr. Rather's decision to file a $70 million lawsuit against CBS and its former parent company. On September 20, 2007 Mr. Rather said on CNN's *Larry King Live*:

> *"Somebody, sometime has got to take a stand and say democracy cannot survive, much less thrive with the level of big corporate and big government*

311

interference and intimidation in news,"

Dr. Steven E. Jones, a noted Physicist and Archaeometrist at BYU — calls for a serious investigation of the study committee's hypothesis that WTC 7 and the Twin Towers were brought down by impact damage and fires, rather than the use of pre-positioned cutter-charges. He's been placed on paid leave pending further investigation.

APPENDIX XII

LETTER TO CONGRESS

1. All members of the United State's House of Representatives and Senate and this government's Administration should be restricted by an unbiased administrative committee of *"We the People"* from accepting any corporate employment or position, stock, or direct or indirect donations, campaign donations, subsidies, gifts, outside benefits or membership during their tenure in office and for a period of five years following their term in office, thereby utilizing their substantial retirement programs, which were designed to protect them from this type of conflict of interest or outside influence. As a result, the United States Government will therefore be required to grant adequate public campaign subsidy for all approved government candidates running for public office.

2. The United States shall develop and implement a single Tax Standard, which is adequate to meet all of this country's financial needs, and which is proportionate to every citizen's earnings and purchases in the open market. All other Federal tax, including tax-exempt foundations that serve as repositories for divested interests that make one's assets non-taxable to avoid estate and gift taxes, should also be brought to an end.

3. The United States Government shall at all times protect the entitlement benefits, insurance and services for the disabled, the elderly and this nation's work force, which is the backbone of this nation. These entitlement benefits and services should never be used so someone can earn a profit, and therefore they require written government standards and regulations under a centralized structure

that is managed both efficiently and cost effectively. This is also meant to include such things as: Any God given natural product; our Social Security Benefits; our once very successful single nonprofit prepayment healthcare service that previously treated this nation's sick and disabled equally; as well as our entire infrastructure that should be designed to adequately service all of our humanity adequately under additional nonprofit entitlement programs. It should also be understood that these services, benefits, insurance and products are the "property" of the working class, the sick and disabled and the elderly, and therefore they should be efficiently managed and regulated under a single centralized noncompetitive private nonprofit and/or government entitlement structure or any combination thereof. Once this is accomplished, we should never again allow such entitlement services and benefits to become fair game to the open profit centered market, where the working class and this nation's citizens can be taken advantage of — nor should they negatively be politically classified as "Socialized" or "Big Government" programs when these benefits are the sole property of every qualified citizen of the United States, which comprises this outstanding "Democracy of We The People."

4. The United States should repeal the Federal Reserve Act and the IRS code, taking back the ownership of our Federal Reserve and its banks, while establishing auditable internal controls for this country's future government owned Federal Banking System, which needs its monetary system to be based on a value standard such as gold. The Public Treasury should also become totally responsible for the creation of all money, which shall be kept both interest-free and debt-free – thereby establishing a solid pay as you go standard while aggressively repaying our current loans. The United States shall never again allow private banks or non government organizations to control this country's money, and this nation should never again borrow from privately owned profit centered banks.

5. The United States Government through the Government Accountability Office (GAO) should continue to responsibly audit, validate and control all capital and current expenditures, while

recommending that this nation use only its own money for such expenditures, while responsibly planning and managing all capital improvements and infrastructure development.

6. The United States should legally enforce ear mark transparency prior to authorizing any related legislation and should require all public business and policy be opened to both public and legal scrutiny under this nation's Government of the People.

7. The United States Government must balance its trade deficit, and tax foreign trade equally.

8. The United States should require all Federal and State Contracts universally utilize competitive bidding principles and all members of the Congress shall be restricted from either granting or influencing no-bid contracts to favored corporations, which is a clear conflict of interest.

9. The United States should stop policing and colonizing other countries and significantly reduce all international military bases, while only going to war or fight terrorism when attacked by another country or terrorist as outlined under international law.

10. The United State's international corporations should be forced to stop exporting U.S. jobs, thereby protecting this country's sovereignty while discouraging any type of "New World Order" or any "International Industrial Monopoly." "Globalization of the open market" and the encouragement of worldwide "Humane Nonprofit Services" to all humankind should be diligently promoted. The United States shall protect the Open Market, which involves the selling of competitive and unregulated products in a decentralized open and free market, where the consumer has a choice in what they receive for their dollar — while discouraging international corporate monopolies.

11. The United States should oversee and coordinate cost effective and efficiently run elections involving all state and national offices, while directing all philanthropic donations made to candidates to this nation's infrastructure which is currently in a hopeless and neglected state of disarray. The United States Government's voting systems needs to become totally auditable and be based on the populous vote, and it should be efficiently managed independent of either government or state appointed officials or party members. This Government of the People should require that all candidates for public office be required to complete a formal application, which includes a comprehensive evaluation of the candidates past medical, family, and social history, as well as their qualifications, education, and experience - all openly available for public scrutiny prior to election. Each candidate for office should be required to prepare a statement outlining why they believe they are qualified to serve in the job they are seeking, while also requiring they outline in writing their primary goals and objectives in a written plan of accomplishment by date - as well as stating how they intend to pay for their proposals - rather than listen to them tediously damn their opponent in some pointless debate.

12. If this nation is ever to regain the respect it once enjoyed, it needs to abide by the Geneva Convention this nation signed some five times. Therefore, the criminals that were responsible for the Iraq war and all its related atrocities need to be sought out and brought to justice under the International World Court in The Hague, just as the United States once demanded in the Nuremberg Trials that were held from 1995 to 1999. This country should also revoke all previous demands for absolute immunity for all U.S. Military personnel and civilian officials, as well as The Netherlands Invasion Act, which allows our U.S. Military to rescue any U.S. Personnel brought to trial in The Hague.

RECOMENDED INTERNATIONAL POLICY

Proposed Policy A

The United States should assist and support the UN in the very difficult task of developing a Comprehensive Master Plan for the human services of every nation, which then needs to be honestly and dynamically monitored and financed by each active and responsible participating sovereign state throughout the world, rather than just the United States and China.

Proposed Policy B

The United States should assist and support the UN in setting standards for a balanced and competitive industrial economic plan for all nations to follow as each nation seeks to profit fairly in an honest and open competitive market.

Proposed Policy C

The United States should assist and support the UN in fighting all forms of terrorism, demanding the World Court prosecute terrorists to the fullest extent, while the UN assumes full authority and responsibility to review; negotiate; and bring to a peaceful resolution all prospective wars before they start.

Proposed Policy D

The United States should assist and support the UN in coordinating an international peace keeping force comprised of a predetermined and equitably balanced military force from every participating nation, which shall be assigned to maintain World Peace while methodically investigating and destroying all weapons of mass destruction throughout the world.

And lastly, shouldn't the United States assist and support the UN in:

- *Enforcing the Non-proliferation Treaty involving Nuclear Weapons.*

- *Mediating and coordinating a fair and equitable plan for the use of the world's energy resources at the most cost effective and efficient level for all nations throughout the world.*

- *Resolving the world's dangerous and rapidly growing environmental problems.*

- *Seeking to prevent disease and disability by improving world-wide public health.*

- *Sanctioning nations that conduct genocide*

- *Coordinating standards regarding world trade policy.*

POSTSCRIPT

On July 4, 2013, our country will be celebrating its 237th Birthday, and in 2016, we will have survived some 240 years as a Democracy. History suggests that the length of life for a Democracy is usually 200 years, and if we look closely at this country's current state of affairs it is highly unlikely we can remain a Democracy much beyond this 237th birthday if we do not make some immediate changes.

Alexis de Tocqueville, sometimes referred to as Alexander Frazer Tytler, or Alexander Tyler, a Scottish history professor from the University of Edinburgh, and his controversial statement in, *The Fall of a Republic,* which is also referred to as *The Fall of a Democracy,* back in the early days of the industrial revolution said:

> *"A democracy is always temporary in nature. A democracy cannot exist as a permanent form of government. It can only exist until the voters discover that they can vote themselves money from the public treasure. From that moment on the majority always votes for the candidates who promise the most money from the public treasury, with the result that a democracy always collapses over loose fiscal policy followed by a dictatorship."*

Tyler, went on to explain how this democracy cycle moves from bondage to faith, to courage, to liberty, to abundance, to complacency, to apathy, and then dependence before returning all the way back to bondage. And yes, our Democracy has experienced the most revolutionary twentieth-century of abundance any nation could possibly hope for, but it's now becoming obvious that the United States is once again moving into the apathy, dependence and then bondage stages because of our politician's irresponsible and loose fiscal policies. It's also hard to believe our nation has become totally dependent on some powerful self serving *"New World Order"* that will inevitably force the working class back into bondage by taking away their freedoms, while we foolishly languish in some sort of perpetual state of fear and indifference at what our elected politicians are doing to destroy our country. But one thing for sure, this *New World Order* will eventually collapse just as the middle class is now doing.

Simon Kuznets, an economist Belarusian immigrant to the United States developed the upside down Kuznet's U curve, which even more clearly traces this Alexis de Tocqueville phenomenon of today's unusual movements in society — describing how as the economy becomes more sophisticated and productive society moves from low inequality to high inequality, just as we have previously experienced, and then back to low inequality as society collapses. And that's where we are now heading. Worse yet, surging income inequality is so subtle, few if any actually see it happening

When George H. W. Bush Sr. was appointment as CIA Director — that was probably where the *Shrub Dynasty* first took root. Then later, as Vice President and ultimately President of the United States for one term, while still acting as the *"Overlord"* of the Shrub Dynasty, he openly introduced to the public the term *"New World Order"* (NWO) in his State of the Union Address on January 29, 1991:

> *"What is at stake is more than one small country, it is a big idea - a new world order ... to achieve the universal aspirations of mankind ... based on shared principles and the rule of law ... The illumination of a thousand points of light .... The winds of change are with us now."*

Did *"We the People"* ever really believe the United States was a small and unimportant country? Did we really believe Americans wanted to forfeit this great country's national treasures? In any event, our politicians and the Shrub Dynasty have perhaps inadvertently cast their lot with this Shadow Government (NWO), even though this was never something *"We the People"* dreamed up. And now this NWO — which comprises the top one percent of the wealthy International Investment Banks and their International Corporations — has a strangle hold over our Democracy. This is not something new, in that this NWO actually was created when this upper crust was allowed to establish their own privately owned Federal Reserve back in 1913. Then in 1934, a total overthrow of the United State's Democracy was actually attempted during FDR's first term, when these very same powerful bankers and corporations that comprised this NWO attempted to unseat FDR in a plot that was publicly exposed by retired Marine Corps Major General Smedley Butler, at the 1934 McCormack- Dickstein Congressional Committee meeting. In Butler's testimony, he told the committee that on July 17, 1932, he was approached by several wealthy businessmen who had asked him to help overthrow this nation's democracy in a military coup. In the Congressional Committee's report, Butler's allegations were validated, but these traitors were never sought-out and punished for their treasonous act. In retrospect, the devastation of the Great Depression had caused many of these very rich families to actually question the foundation of our Democracy, considering Fascism, Socialism, or even Communism as an alternative that would give them greater control over their wealth. But since that 1934 failure, they've only grown stronger, and between 1913 and 2013, this NWO has aggressively been buying off our Congress, while the Republican Party and a few southern Democrats have completely ignored the needs of the working class of this great nation, the backbone of this once successful and respected Democracy of the People. And now, after the people have chosen the Democratic Party to lead our country in the 2013 term, the Republican minority has totally cast its lot with this NWO, preventing any decisions that might help the people regain their financial stability under today's Democratic leadership. Worse yet, President George W. Bush, during his nepotistic appointment as President, set out to accomplish what his father failed to accomplish as President, involving this country in two very questionable and simultaneous costly and unjust religious wars during his tenure, while also accomplishing a budget breaking deficit with his NWO's controversial tax reduction plan for the top one percent of all wage earners at a time when the former Democratic Administration had for the first time in many years finally accomplished a $236 billion surplus in this country's budget.

So, although the twentieth-century was a remarkable and abundant time to live under a worldwide respected Democracy, our children will not be given this same chance. In fact, it currently looks like they are almost doomed to this new Fascist Government that intends to secure total control over their vast fortunes they have stolen from the working class, our children, and the public treasury. Now that this NWO has leveled the

United State's financial ability, they next intend to seek control over other smaller nations as they offer loans to rebuild the seventeen nations they had the United States destroy for them, so these tyrants can next gain control over these smaller countries businesses and their natural resources.

Yes, the United States is well on its way to finally reaching a point of no return after 237 years of Democracy, and therefore the 2016 election will most likely try to select another member of the Shrub Dynasty as the future Dictator of their powerful fascist NWO. And yes, there will be many revolutions that follow, but they will be as short lived as the failed *"Occupy Wall Street"* protest in New York — when the working class openly challenged this powerful one percent.

Looking back, FDR's New Deal and its social welfare program resulted in a 94 percent income tax for those at the top in 1944. But in spite of all this, in 1988 the top CEO was still earning 42 times the average worker, while the top ten percent of the wage earners tax dropped to 70 percent. But in spite of this, there was still a false sense of optimism for the American middle class because of the strong economic growth from World War II, high taxes, and FDR's widespread social welfare programs, all supplemented by the continued move toward the worldwide industrial revolution and globalization. Then during Reagan's Presidency he slashed the highest tax rate from 70 percent to 28 percent and reduced the maximum capital gains tax to 28 percent. He also took steps to control unions, cut social welfare and deregulated the economy as his trickle down economy failed to accomplish what he'd promised. And now, as a result, we have a financial crisis in America. Today, CEO's earn 380 times more than the average worker, while George W. Bush slashed the upper crusts tax even further. And now, with our ridiculous exporting of both jobs and industry abroad, and the reemergence of our dysfunctional but wealthy plutocrats while the upper one percent spirals their earnings to unheard of new levels, we are certainly well on our way to destroying this country's middle class. And while all this has been going on, between 1950 and 1973, per capita income in India and China grew from 68 percent to 280 percent — and while America's economy tripled our GDP during that same period, China's GDP has increased twelve-fold. So as a result, the Chinese are strategically positioning themselves to eventually rule the world in direct opposition to this powerful NWO. And so this powerful NWO will predictably draw us into a third world war with China, or they'll be forced to ally with them under a new Fascist World Government. Jim O'Neil, a Chief of Economics at Goldman Sachs identified Brazil, Russia, India and China as "the BRIC" comprising today's second worldwide gilded age, which is trending toward a Fascist leadership worldwide as it stands directly in opposition to the United States and its two hundred and thirty-seven year old Republic. John Van Reenen, head of the Center for Economic Performance at the London School of Economics said it very well:

> *"Although the overall pie is getting bigger, there are plenty of people who will get a smaller slice."*

Conversely, the famous Capitalist Milton Friedman in his book, *"Capitalism and Freedom,"* on page ix said:

> *"Only a Crises –actual or perceived-produces real change"*

And that's what this NWO and our dysfunctional politicians are intentionally creating — one crisis after another.

So you ask, why should you listen to what I have to say?

Having received a Masters Degree in Hospital Administration under James A. Hamilton, the father of hospital administration at the University of Minnesota, the then ranked number one graduate degree program in Healthcare Administration in the Country. And yes, I was trained by this remarkable healthcare leader whose brain-child was the development of the first healthcare insurance program in the United States. This program was the Blue Cross Blue Shield nonprofit privately owned healthcare insurance program that was not only a huge success but the only single prepayment program available. My residency was also under a *Gold Medal* winner of the American College of Healthcare Executives, William N. Wallace, whose hospital was ranked third in the nation, back when the Joint Commission actually ranked hospitals for their level of quality care they provided for the sick and indigent. I was also fortunate to continue my career at this top rated hospital as an Associate Administrator, and my Medical Staff was composed of leading specialists, many trained at Rochester Mayo with faculty appointments at the University of Minnesota. In those days the computer was only a bunch of punch cards and tape drives, but my boss perceptively asked me to do some research on the application of computers in healthcare — and I immediately recognized a huge potential for the computer to standardize systems in healthcare along with the potential of creating a confidential database for a universal patient medical diagnoses and treatment program that would revolutionize healthcare — and so my job was expanded to find adequate money for my research, since all hospitals were nonprofit and I needed help to finance my research under what was to became my nonprofit *"Health Systems Institute."* Thereafter my research became one of my many jobs in addition to running hospitals. I was also later hired to help financially troubled hospitals and clinics get back on their feet, running several large hospital systems, clinics, and professional organizations while serving as their CEO, and as a board member for two health insurance companies. During all these assignments I also conducted hundreds of educational institutes, and served as the principle investigator, researching the health record database system with four major universities, which would eventually require a comprehensive universal nonprofit single prepayment system to provide cost effective high quality care that was to be led by healthcare professionals, not plutocrats. Back then this country's very successful single privately owned nonprofit healthcare system was ranked first in the world instead of 37th by today's World Healthcare Organization (WHO). Healthcare also had many important community responsibilities such as *Cost Containment* and *Regional Planning*, which I rapidly immersed myself into as a leader. After Medicare was established, I served on a Washington appointed Diagnostic Related Grouping Committee of five members. In that our self serving politicians had previously created the McCarran Ferguson act in 1945, they had in so doing set the scene for making profit from what had previously been a nonprofit human service benefit to our sick and disabled — and this Act actually opened the door to our politicians so they could receive big financial kick-backs from this already costly service to humanity. Then in 1965 the profit insurance industry forced its way into healthcare and the destruction of the number one benefit system for the working class was well on its way. This of course destroyed comprehensive cost effective healthcare planning and my research soon came to an end as competition replaced our high quality community oriented healthcare service in America. Of course the corrupt plutocrats found they could better spiral their income to unheard of new levels and make far more money under a confused decentralized and deregulated healthcare system, in which there was little chance of ever returning to our once very successful professionally run and cost-effective healthcare system.

In discussing my concerns over what was the destruction of our healthcare system with former President Gerald Ford, he whispered to me after our all day meeting:

> *"The Washington politicians now have a strangle hold on healthcare, and the current system will have to collapse before it can get better."*

And you know what? He was right, and Alexis de Tocqueville said it even more clearly:

> *"If one looks closely at what has happened to the world since the beginning of society, it is easy to see that equality is prevalent only at the historical poles of civilization. Savages are equal because they are equally weak and ignorant. Very civilized men can all become equal because they all have at their disposal similar means of attaining comfort and happiness. Between these two extremes is found inequality of condition, wealth, knowledge — the power of the few, the poverty, ignorance and weakness of the rest."*

Since then, I've watched many other types of nonprofit human benefit systems be destroyed by this *"New World Order"* and their disgusting plutocrat's tactics that seek even more wealth at the cost of destroying our working class benefits — and now they're looking at our very successful Social Security and Medicare benefits as they openly steal from our public treasure. Instead of solving our infrastructure problems, our air pollution and the resulting climate changes, or our tragic water and population evils, we are driving this once great nation into this profit seeking NWO's abyss, which now clearly seeks to destroy and level the United States to that of other nations.

Because I was often referred to as the father of the computer based medical record, I was frequently sought out, or was in contact with the very wealthy investor or some prominent politician. Those contacts often exposed me to their best behavior and sometimes their worst. I often flew on their jets, and one time an entrepreneurial corporation flew me to meet with the Canadian Prime Minister Pierre Trudeau and his staff of some twenty-five people, who all ran his country very aggressively — solely to advise them on the successful healthcare system that WHO now recognizes as the second best healthcare system in the world. I also watched Hubert Humphrey accept a suitcase full of tax free cash for turning the right corporation's head at the right time. And I will never forget how the largest privately held corporation in the world offered me millions if I would have taken my company public, and walked off with the money instead of developing my comprehensive and sought after computer based medical record for some 270 hospitals, clinics and nursing homes who were anxiously prepared to support this system, which would have revolutionized healthcare. But I refused them. And because of that refusal, I was ironically destined to eventually fail miserably many years after the politicians passed the McCarran Ferguson act, which opened the door to profit, decentralization and deregulation of healthcare in America. Yes, profit insurance is the culprit that has spiraled our healthcare costs out of control and ushered in a profit seeking pharmaceutical drug industry that has now destroyed any hope of a professionally run healthcare service. And now, almost all of our highly trained physicians have become insurance agents instead of remaining the number one professional occupation in the world.

And now while we're still suffering from the housing bubble bailout crisis, the NWO is already planning to take our attention off them by creating a huge bond bubble crisis that will be far more disastrous and fraudulent than the housing bailout we just experienced.

So this is why I am speaking out on this tragic situation that is about to shut down our entire Democracy.

And so you ask — do we have a choice?

Yes, but it has a very short fuse, and it's going to require our Congress and the people to immediately take action against this treacherous and powerful *"Enemy Within,"* just as they did in WWII. And it's also going to require every American that loves their country to immediately face up to this enormous crisis we're in and ban together, without any more conflicts or political division, if Americans can ever expect to take back our Democracy.

Section II proposes policies that will be essential for the United State's survival, but they will prove valueless if Americans do not expose and confront this enemy soon by taking them on in a third world war that will be more challenging than anything we've ever encountered before — and the entire world is waiting and watching to see if we are really willing to face up to this huge conspiracy within. Therefore I request that you use Appendix XII on page 313 to help prepare your letters, and make your phone calls and contacts with your state and federal politicians, demanding an immediate change in the direction this nation is heading.

BIBLIOGRAPHY

Adelmann, Bo 1986. *The Federal Reserve System.* The New American, October 17, 1986.

Allen, Gary with Abraham, Larry. *None Dare Call it Conspiracy.* Rossmoor, CA: Concord Press, 1972.

Allen, Gary. *The Rockefeller File.,* Seal Beach, CA: Press 1976.

Allen, Gary, October 1972 issue of <u>American Opinion</u> article www.sweetliberty.org/beware_metro.html - 75k - Cached

Andrews, Edmund L., March 29,2007. "Ex-Auditor Says He Was Told to Be Lax on Oil Fees." <u>http://www.nytimes.com/2007/03/29/business/29royalty.html</u>

Baker, Jeremy, n.d. "PBS Documentary: Silverstein, FDNY Razed WTC 7," Infowars.com <u>http://www.infowars.com/print/Sept11/FDNY.htm.</u>

Barter, Sheila, 2001. "How the World Trade Center Fell." <u>BBC News</u>, September 13 (http://news.bbc.co.uk/1/hi/world/americas/1540044.stm).

Beams, Nick. February 21, 2002. "Enron fallout is spreading." www.**wsws.org**/articles/**2002**/feb2002/enro-f21.shtml - 18k - Cached

Beams, Nick. February 28, 2002. "Greenspan predicts US 'recovery' but sounds some warnings." <u>www.wsws.org/articles/2002/feb2002/gpan-f28 prn.shtml - 11k - Cached</u>

Beams, Nick. March 14, 2002. "The World Economic Crisis: 1991- 2001 <u>lecture</u> January 16, 2002 www.wsws.org/articles/2002/mar2002/nb-srn.shtml - 88k - Cached

Beams, Nick. April 5, 2002. "A peculiar economic recovery in the US <u>wsws.org/articles/2002/apr2002/usec-a05.shtml - 18k - Cached</u>

Beams, Nick. April 16, 2002. "How Merril Lynch boosted 'junk'stocks." www.wsws.org/articles/2002/apr2002/merr-a16_prn.shtml - 11k - Cached

Bergen, Peter L. *Holy War, Inc.: inside the secret world of Osama bin Laden.* New York: Free Press, 2001.

Blase, William. "The Council on Foreign Relations (CFR) and the New World Order," The Courier p. 1-16 http://www.conspiracyarchive.com/NWO/Council_Foreign_Relations.htm

Blue Cross and Blue Shield. *Abandoning the Mission: Consumer Reports* Vol. 55 #8" (August 1990): 543.

Bollyn, Christopher, 2001. "Some Survivors Say 'Bombs Exploded Inside WTC,'" American Free Press,October 22. http://www.americanfreepress.net/10_22_01/ Some_Survivors_Say__Bombs_Expl/some_survivors_say__bombs_expl .html.

_____, 2004. "New Seismic Data Refutes Official Explanation," American Free Press, updated April 12.

_____"New York Firefighters' New York Firefighters' Final Words Fuel Burning Questions About 9-11. Evidence that could debunk the official explanation for the collapse of the ...prisonplanet.com/new_york_firefighters_final_words_fuel_burning_que... - 25k - Cached

Botte, John – *Aftermath: Unseen 9/11 Photos by a New York City Cop,* Publisher: New York : Regan Books, 2006 www.harpercollins.com/books/9780060789718/Aftermath/index.aspx - 36k - Cached

Borger et al., op cit; "CMS National Health Statistics Group," NHE summary including share of GDP, op cit. p 1

Brehm, Elisa. April 18, 2002. "Michigan auto supplier robs workers wages, pensions, health benefits." www.wsws.org/articles/2002/apr2002/dct-a18_prn.shtml - 17k - Cached

Brookfield, James. March 20, 2002. "PBS documentary probes initial public offering swindles of 1990s" www.wsws.org/articles/2002/mar2002/pbs-m20_prn.shtml - 15k - Cached

_____ January 31, 2002. State of the Union speech: "Bush declares war on world." www.bushwatch.com/archives-jan06.htm - 225k - Cached

_____ "Building a Better Mirage: NIST's 3-Year $20,000,000 Cover-Up of the Crime of the Century." August 21, 2005. 911 Research, http://911research.wtc7.net/essays/nist/index.html.

Bush, George W., 2001. Address to the General Assembly of the United Nations, November 10. http://www.september11news.com/PresidentBushUN.htm

Cappannari, Andrea. April 25, 2002. "A hearing before the Senate Commerce, Science, and Transportation Committee on April 11, California Public ... crisis." www.wsws.org/articles/2002/apr2002/cali-a25.shtml - 18k - Cached

Cappannari, Andrea. June 9, 2002. "More evidence of price-gouging in California energy market." www.wsws.org/articles/2002/apr2002/cali-a25.shtml - 18k - Cached

_____ "Carlyle's Way - Making a mint inside "the iron triangle" of defense, government and industry." 12/11/01. Red Herring. http://www.redherring.com/PrintArticle.aspx?a=6793&sector=Archive

_____ *Chief Engineer, The*, 2002. "We will Not Forget: A Day of Terror". http://www.chiefengineer.org/article.cfm?seqnum1=1029

Cockburn, Alexander and st. clair, Jeffrey. "Bush and the Neo-Con Pharsees." 12/14/02. Counter Punch. http://www.counterpunch.org/nimmo1216.html

Chomsky, Noam. *9-11*. New York: Seven Stories Press, 2001.

Chossudovsky, Michael. "Financial Scams and the Bush Family." 02/18/02. Western Press. http://www.globalresearch.ca/articles/CHO202C.html.

Collins, Loren," The Truth About Tytler" http://lorencollins.net/tytler.html

_____"Council on Foreign Relations" Website. _ http://www.cfr.org/about/mission.php

Collins, Paul & Philip. *"The Ascendancy of the Scientific Dictatorship: An Examination of Epistemic Autocracy, From the 19th to the 21st Century."* Book Surge,LLC. 2006 www.booksurge.com.

Dall, Curtis B.- FDR *My Exploited Father-In-Law: Washington D.C.*: Action Associates. 1970.

Davidson, Lawrence. *Islamic fundamentalism*. Westport, Conn.: Greenwood Press, 1998.

_____ "Democratic Senator to be Assassinated Soon." 05/25/01. Vox News. www.voxfux.com/archives/senator-assassination.html - 7k - Cached

Dobb's, Lou - CNN Anchor - June 9, 2005, *"Council on Foreign Relations wants borders to incorporate Mexico and Canada.*

Doyle, Ronan, Documentary *"Smoke and Mirrors"* October 5, 2006 www.OilSmokeAndMirrors.com.

Dunbar, David and Reagan, Brad. *Debunking 9/11 Myths* Hearst. August, 06.

Dwyer, Jim and Fessenden, Ford. August 4, 2002. "Lost Voices of Firefighters, Some on 78ᵗʰ Floor." The New York Times.

Dwyer, Jim. August 12,2005. "City to Release Thousands of Oral Histories of 9/11." The New York Times.

Dwyer, Jim. August 13,2005. "Vast Archive Yeilds New View of 9/11." The New York Times.

Dwyer, Jim, and Kevin Flynn, *"102 Minutes: The Untold Story of the Fight to Survive Inside the Twin Towers."* New York: Times Books. 2005.

Eagar, Thomas, 2002. "The Collapse: An Engineer's Perspective," which is part of "Why the Towers Fell," NOVA, April 30 (http://www.pbs.org/wgbh/nova/wtc/collapse.html).

Eagar, Thomas, and Christopher Musso, 2001. "Why Did the World Trade Center Collapse? Science, Engineering, and Speculation," *JOM: Journal of the Minerals, Metals & Materials Society*, 53/12, pp. 8-11.

Elias, Robert. *"Terrorism and American Foreign Policy,"* September 25, 2001 http://www.tanbou.com/2001/fall/USForeignPolicyElias.htm

Epperson, A. Ralph. *"The Unseen Hand."* Tucson, AZ: Publius Press. 1958.

"F.D.R.: His Personal Letters." New York: Duell, Sloan and Pearce. 1950. Families USA,"Study Finds HMO Exces Are In The Money," Hospitals & Health Networks April 20, 1998

Fein, Rashi - Prescription for change. Modern Maturity. August September, 1992.

_____ "US Takes Chance to Target Peacekeeping," Financial Times of London July 2, 2002

FEMA, 2002. *World Trade Center Building Performance Study*, May (http://www.fema.gov/library/wtcstudy.shtm).

Flexner, Abraham - *Medical Education in the United States and Canada* — Published by the Carnegie Foundation, 1907, x, xiii, xiv-xvi

Fleck, John, 2001. "Fire, Not Extra Explosives, Doomed Buildings, Expert Says," *Albuquerque Journal*, September 21
http://www.abqjournal.com/terror/anniversary/pmvan09-21-01.htm.

Floyd, Chris. "Bush Watch." 04/24/05.
http://www.bushwatch.com/floyd.htm

Floyd, Chris. "Game over: "Living With Bush-Cheny Kleptocracy." 05/02/05.
http://www.conspiracyplanet.com/channel.cfm?channelid+39&contenti d=2075&page=2

Fink, Mitchell, and Mathias, Lois. *Never forget: an oral history of September 11, 2001*. New York: ReganBooks/HarperCollins Publishers, 2002.

_____ Fire Engineering - WTC "INVESTIGATION"?: A CALL TO ACTION
www.fireengineering.com/articles/article_display.html?id=130026 - 51k

Fitts, Catherine Austin. "Connecting the HarvardWatch Dots." 04/22/05
http://www.conspiracyplanet.com/channel.cfm?channelid=107

Fitts, Catherine Austin. "And You Thought Government Was Really Doing Something About Enron."
www.fromthewilderness.com/free/ww3/feb11_2002_enron_CAF.html - 64k - Cached

Fraser, T.G. *The Arab-Israeli conflict*. New York: St. Martin's Press. 1995.
_____ MSNBC. October 16, 2005. "Full Text of Iraq Constitution"
http://www.msnbc.msn.com/id/9719734

Gagger, Nicholas. *The Syndicate: The Story of the Coming World Government*. Maple Vail Book Manufacturing Group, PA. 2004.

Gardner, Richard N. "Former deputy assistant Secretary of State testimony." Foreign Affairs - April 1974

Glanz, James & Lipton, Eric. City in the Sky: The Rise and Fall of the World Trade Center. Times Books. 2003.

Glanz, James, and Eric Lipton, 2002. "Towers Withstood Impact, but Fell to Fire, Report Says," *New York Times*, March 29.

Glanz, James. 2001. "Engineers Are Baffled over the Collapse of 7 WTC; Steel Members Have Been Partly Evaporated," *New York Times*, November 29.

Goldsmith, Sir James. "Testimony at Ernest Hollings committee" Washington Times, Dec. 6, 1993.

Goldwater Jr., Senator Barry Morris. *With No Apologies*. New Haven, CT: Yale University Press. 1995.

Gray, Geoffrey. "Bush Sr. Could Profit From War – Legal Group Blasts Papa Shrub on Bin Laden Link." 10/11/01 NEWS. http://www.villagevoice.com/generic/show_print.php?id=29113&page=gray&issue=0141.

Gray, Berry – July 9, 2002, "Bush's past dealings come back to haunt him" www.rense.com/general26/bushspastbusiness.htm WSWS.org 07/09/02

Griffin, David Ray. The 9/11 Commission Report: Omissions and Distortions. Olive Branch Press. 2004.

Griffin, David Ray. *The New Pearl Harbor: Disturbing Questions about the Bush Administration and 9/11*. Interlink Publishing. 2004.

Griffin, David Ray. *Christian Faith and the Truth Behind 9/11*. Westminster John Knox Press. 2006.

Hagger, Nicholas. *The Syndicate: The Story of the Coming World Government."* O Books. 2004.

_____ "Harken Energy Chronology" 10/05/02. Scoop Independent News. http://www.scoop.co.nz/stories/HL0210/S00178.htm

Halberstam, David. *Firehouse*. New York: Hyperion. 2002.

Hoar, William P. *Architects of Conspiracy*. Belmont MA: Western Islands. 1984.

Hodge, Neil. June 5, 2002. "Wall Street broker rebuked for misleading investors."
www.wsws.org/articles/2002/jun2002/merr-j05_prn.shtml - 8k - Cached

Hoffman, Jim, 2003. "The North Tower's Dust Cloud: Analysis of Energy Requirements for the Expansion of the Dust Cloud Following the Collapse of 1 World Trade Center," Version 3, 9-11 Research.wtc7.net, October 16
(http://911research.wtc7.net/papers/dustvolume/volume.html).

Hoover, Herbert, *The Memoirs of Herbert Hoover, The Great Depression 1929-1941*. New York: Macmillan. 1952.

Hopsicker, Daniel and Ruppert, Michael C. "Why Does George W. Bush Fly in Drug Smugglers Barry Seal's Airplane?
www.fromthewilderness.com/free/ciadrugs/W_plane.html - 95k - Cached

Howe, Frederick C. *Confessions of a Monopolist*. Chicago: Public Publishing Co. 1906.

Hufschmid, Eric. *Painful Questions* Tree of Life Pubns. 2002.

Isaacs, Jerry. March 9, 2002. "US flaunts scheme to use weapons inspections as pretext for war vs.

Iraq."www.wsws.org/articles/2002/mar2002/iraq-m09.shtml - 20k - Cached

Isaacs, Jerry. May 10, 2002. "Enron defrauded California out of billions during energy crisis." www.wsws.org/articles/2002/may2002/enro-m10_prn.shtml - 14k - Cached

Isikoff, Michael and Hosenball, Mark. "Another Halliburton Probe." 02/04/04. Newsweek National News. http://www.msnbc.msn.com/id/4163810/

James, Alexander, 2006. "The Hidden History of Money." http://portland.indymedia.org/en/2004/03/282679.shtml - 532k - Cached

Jacquard, Roland. *In the name of Osama bin Laden: global terrorism and the bin Laden brotherhood.* Durham, N.C: Duke University Press. 2002.

_____ "Jeb Bush seized flight school records at 2 AM on September 12." 04/01/04 http://www.democraticunderground.com/discuss/duboard.php?az=show_topic&forum=104&topic_id=1328855

Jones, Shannon. February 14, 2002. "US layoffs continue to mount in new year." www.wsws.org/articles/2002/feb2002/jobs-f14.shtml - 19k - Cached

Jones, Dr. Steven. *"Why Indeed Did the WTC Buildings Completely Collapse?"* Journal of 9/11 Studies. September 2006/Volume 3. http://www.surfline.com/home/index.cfm.

Kay, Joseph -"The morality of plutocracy and the Harken Energy Distraction" SWSW - 12 July 2002

Kay, Joseph – "The Harken Energy" *The* Washington Post 15 July 2002 - lead editorial July 12 Washington Post www.wsws.org/articles/2002/jul2002/wp-j15.shtml - 22k - Cached

Kay, Joseph. August 1, 2002. "How George W. Bush made his millions." www.earthrainbownetwork.com/Archives2002/CorruptionGreed.htm - 37k - Cached

Kay, Joseph. October 19, 2002. "Corporate corruption and academia: The Bush Harvard Enron Connection." www.wsws.org/articles/2002/oct2002/hark-o19.shtml - 24k - Cached

Kay, Joseph. "Profiteering and the war on terrorism" 07/25/02
http://www.wsws.org/articles/2002/jul2002/hall-j25.shtml.

Kean, Thomas H., and Lee H. Hamilton. *"The 9/11 Commission Report: Final Report of the National Commission on Terrorist Attacks upon the United States.* 2004 Authorized Edition, New York: W. W. Norton. "The 9/11 Commission Report." http://www.9-11commission.gov/report/911Report.pdf.

Keightley, Allen. "The Story Leading To 9/11."
http://www.scholarsfor911truth.org/TheStoryLeadingTo9_11.html

Kennedy, John F. - Speech, "The President and the Press," April 27, 1961, the American Newspaper Publishers Association meeting at the Waldorf-Astoria Hotel, New York, NY
http://www.archive.org/details/jfks 19610427

Kennedy, Robert F. Jr. "Was the Election Stolen? Rollingstone.
http://www.rollingstone.com/news/story/104323334/was_the_2004_election_stolen/print.

Kershaw, Peter. *"Economic Solutions."* 1994.

Kidd, Devvy,- Friday, "Treasonous agenda of the Council on Foreign Relations" Posted: June 17, 2005 WorldNetDaily.com
www.worldnetdaily.com/news/printer-friendly.asp?ARTICLE_ID=44841 - 8k - Cached

Kidd, Devvy - "Treasonous agenda of the Trilateral Commission," Posted June 24, 2005, WorldNetDaily.com
www.worldnetdaily.com/news/article.asp?ARTICLE_ID=44965 - 34k - Cached

Kidd, Devvy. *"Why A Bankrupt America?"* Colorado: Project Liberty. 1995.

Kingman Brewster, Jr. - "Reflections on Our National Purpose," the 50th anniversary issue of "Foreign Affairs."

Kinsley, Michael. "Thanks for Nothing-Bush's gift to taxpayers-and Halliburton." 04/17/03. MSNhttp://slate.msn.com/id/2081640/

Krismer, John R. *"Should Corporations Practice Medicine?* AmErica House, Baltimore. 2004

Kristol, William, "Bill Kristol" article - http://www.nndb.com/people/401/000048257/

Lippman, Thomas W. *Understanding Islam: an introduction to the Muslim world.* New York: Meridian. 1995.

Lind, Michael. "How Neoconservatives Cpnquered Washington – and Launched a War." 04/10/03. http://www.antiwar.com/orig/lind1.html.

Lundberg, Ferdinand. *America's 60 Families.* New York: Vanguard. 1938.

Latham, Earl. "John D. Rockefeller: Robber Barron or Industrial Statesman?" ed. 1949, p.104 Wikipedia http://en.wikipedia.org/wiki/John_D._Rockefeller

Lydon, Christopher, July 1977."The Trilateral Commission" July 1977 Atlantic www.4rie.com/rie 5.html - 15k - Cached

Marrs, Jim. *Inside Job: Unmasking the 9-11 Conspiracies.* Origin Press. 2004.

Martin, Patrick. May 15, 2002. "Anthrax attacks: FBI cover-up and New York Times whitewash." wsws.org/articles/2002/jul2002/anth-j20.shtml - 18k - Cached

Martin, Patrick. November 20, 2001. "US planned war in Afghanistan long before September 11." www.wsws.org/articles/2001/nov2001/afgh-n20.shtml - 36k - Cached

McFadden, Louis T. *The Federal Reserve Corporation, remarks in Congress.* Boston: Forum Publication Co. 1934.

Miller, Roger. Bush & Bin Laden – "George W. Bush Had Ties to Billionaire bin Laden Brood." 1988. http://cc.msnscache.com/cache.aspx?q=1732582078834&lang=en-US&FORM=CVRE

Murphy, Dean E. *September 11: an oral history.* New York: Doubleday, 2002. North, David. "After the Slaughter: Political Lessons of the Balkan War." 06/14/99. http://www.wsws.org/articles/1999/jun1999/balk-14.shtml

New York City Police Department. *Above hallowed ground: a photographic record of September 11, 2001.* New York: Viking Studio, 2002.

_____ "Opinion and Judgement of the Nurnberg International Military Tribunal." http://www.derechos.org/nizkor/nurenberg/judgment/caps5.html.

_____ "Palestine Facts Israel 1991 to present Oslo Accords." http://www.palestinefacts.org/pf_1991to_now_oslo_accords.php

Paul, Don & Hoffman, Jim. *Waking Up from Our Nightmare, the 9/11/01 Crimes in New York City.* Irresistible Revolutionary I/R. 2004.

Paul, Don – "Facing our Fascist State" www.wireonfire.com/donpaul/911.html - 14k - Cached

Paul, Ron. http://www.raven1.net/ronpaulowg.htm

Paulsen, Steve. January 14, 2002. "Workers lose jobs, health care and savings at Enron." www.wsws.org/articles/2002/jan2002/enro-j14 prn.shtml - 12k - Cached

Perloff, James. *The Shadows of Power.* Appleton, WI: Western Islands. 1988. http://www.pushhamburger.com/secrecy.htm.

Pincus, Walter. "Ex-CIA official faults use of data on Iraq." 02/09/06. The Washington Post.

_____ "9/11: Debunking the Myths," March, 2005. Popular Mechanics, 2005.
http://www.popularmechanics.com/science/defense/1227842.html?pag
e=1&c=y.

Quigley, Carroll. *Tragedy and Hope*. New York: Macmillan. 1966.

Randall, Kate. "US considers use of torture in interrogation of terrorism suspects." 10/24/01.
http://www.wsws.org/org/articles/2001/oct2001/det-o24.shtml.

Randall, Kate. April 13, 2002. "US jobless claims hit highest level in 19 years."
www.wsws.org/articles/2002/apr2002/jobs-a13.shtml - 19k - Cached

Robertson, Pat. *The New World Order.* Thomas Nelson Inc. Publisher. 1991.

Roosevelt Franklin Delano –
www.whitehouse.gov/history/presidents/fr32.html.

Rosenfeld, Alvin H. "Anti-Americanism and Anti-Semitism: A New Frontier of Bigotry." 06/27/03.
http://www.ajc.org/InTheMedia/PublicationsPrint.asp?did=902

Romans, Christine, CNN correspondent (voice-over): On Capitol Hill, testimony, "North America treat U.S., Mexico and Canada like one big country" ...transcripts.cnn.com/TRANSCRIPTS/0506/09/ldt.01.html - 77k - Cached

Roth, Kenneth –"The Law of War in the War on Terror"
January/February 2004 p. 1-2 Foreign Affairs,
http://www.foreignaffairs.org/20040101facomment83101/kenneth-roth/the-law-of-war-in-the-war-on-terror.html

Ruppert, Michael. "Was Paul Wellstone Murdered?" 11/01/02
Wilderness Publications.
http://www.fromthewilderness.com/free/ww3/index-govt.html.

Scheer, Christopher - "Ten Appalling Lies Were Told About Iraq" http://www.alternet.org/story/16274 Alter Net 06/27/03

_____ 'Secrecy surrounds a Bush brother's role in 9/11 security' infowars.com/.../sept11/marvin_bush_secrecy_surrounds_role_911.htm - 37k - Cached

_____ "Senator Wellstone Assassinated by group linked to Bush Sr." 10/25/02, Vox News. http://www.voxfux.com/archives/00000039.htm

Seymour, Charles. ed., *The Intimate Paper of Colonel House*. Boston: Houghton Mifflin. 1926.

Shaler, Robert C. "Who They Were: Inside the World Trade Center DNA Story" 10/28/05 Free Press

Simpson, Colin. *"The Lusitania,"* Boston: Little, Brown. 1972.

Sklar, Holy, *Trilateralism- edited.* South End Press, 1980._ www.thepeoplesvoice.org/cgi-bin/blogs/voices.php/2006/08/21/p10179 - 50k - Cached

Smith, Dennis. *Report from ground zero.* New York: Viking Penguin. 2002.

Spak, Steve – "Mayday! Mayday! Mayday!" 2004 – Fire Service Publications

State Department Publication # 7277. "Freedom From War: The United States Program for General and Complete Disarmament in a Peaceful World"

Steinberg, Jeffrey. "The Ugly Truth About G.W. Bush." August 20, 2004. Executive Intelligence Review. http://www.larouchepub.com/other/2004/book_reviews/3133bush_on_couch.html.

Stiglitz, Joseph. "Corporation corruption." 07/04/02.
http://www.buzzle.com/editorials/7-4-2002-21744.asp

Sutton, Antony C. *America's Secret Establishment: An Introduction to the Order of Skull & Bones.* Liberty House Press. 1986.

Sutton, Antony C. *Wall Street and FDR..* New Rochelle, New York: Arlington House. 1975.

Szymanski, Greg, July 19, 2005. "NY Fireman Lou Cacchioli Upset that 9/11 Commission 'Tried to Twist My Words,'" Liberty Post.
http://www.arcticbeacon.com/articles/article/1518131/29548.htm.

Tarbell, Ida. *The History of the Standard Oil Company.* McClure, Phillips and Co. 1904.

Taylor, Curtis L., Sean Gardiner, September 12, 2001. "Heightened Security Alert Had Just Been Lifted." *New York Newsday*, September 12 newsday.com/news/nationworld/nation/ny-nyaler122362178sep12,0,12556... - 54k - Cached

Terms and Organizations. Editorial. http://www.sanspap.com/terms.htm

The Constitution in Crisis. The Downing Street Minutes and Deception, Manipulation, Torture Retribution, and Cover ups in the Iraq War – Investigative Status Report of the House Judiciary Committee Democratic Staff.
http://www.afterdowningstreet.org/constitutionincrisis

"The Council on Foreign Relations." Website
http://www.unc.edu/~ltolles/illuminati/cfr.html

_____ "The Downing Street Memo(s), June 8, 2007."
http://www.downing streetmemo.com/

_____ "The political roots of the terror attack on New York and Washington." 09/12/01 editorial board http://www.wsws.org/articles/2001/sep2001/terr-s12.shtml

_____"The New World Order." www.lagunajournal.com/new_world_order.htm - 61k - Cached

_____"The Harken Energy Distraction." July 12,2002, *The Washington Post*

_____"The Trilateral Commission: World Shadow Government" http://afgen.com/trilateral.html

Thompson, Mark and Washington, Michael Duffy. "Pentagon Warlord." 01/19/03. Time. http://www.time.com/time/magazine/printout/0,8816,409507,00.html

"Titan: The Life of John D. Rockefeller, Sr." Warner Books. 1998

_____"To Conquer the World," *http://www.maxexchange.com/ybj/chapter12.htm*

_____"Trilateral Commission (TC)." http://www.4rie.com/rie%205.html

Trimpe, Herb, 2002. "The Chaplain's Tale," *Times-Herald Record* http://archive.recordonline.com/adayinseptember/trimpe.htm

Turnipseed, Tom."Sheriff Bush Wages War Against Evil To Cover Corporate Corruption of Government." 02/06/02. Common Dreams News Center

Tyler, Alexander, "The Fall of a Republic." http://www.mcsm.org/democracy1.html

Unger, Craig. *"House of Bush, House of Saud: The Secret Relationship between the World's Two Most Powerful Dynasties."* New York, New York, U.S.A.: Scribner, 2004.
com/search.php?...&author=Unger+Craig&title=House+of+Bush+House - 69k - Cached

Uyttebrouck, Olivier, September 11, 2001. "Explosives Planted In Towers, N.M. Tech Expert Says," *The Albuquerque Journal*, September 11
http://www.abqjournal.com/aqvan09-11-01.htm

Vann, Bill. June 29, 2002. "Washington's phony pretext for Iraqi Invasion." www.hartford-hwp.com/archives/27c/313.html - 12k - Cached

Vann, Bill. "US preparing full-scale invasion of Iraq." July 10, 2002
www.wsws.org/articles/2002/jul2002/iraq-j10.shtml - 22k - Cached

Vann, Bill. July 4, 2002. "US pushes Europe to the brink on international court." www.wsws.org/articles/2002/jul2002/icc-j04.shtml - 24k - Cached

Walsh, David. January 18, 2002. "Enron and the Bush administration: Kindred spirits in fraud and criminality."
www.wsws.org/articles/2002/jan2002/enro-j18.shtml - 26k - Cached

Walsh, Trudy, GCN Staff. 2002."Handheld app eased recovery tasks."
911research.wtc7.net/cache/wtc/evidence/gcn_handheldapp.html - 59k - Cached

Walt, General Lewis. "The 11th Hour."
http://www.maxexchange.com/ybj/chapter12.htm

Warburg, James. February 17, 1950. "Owen Lattimore Papers (Library of Congress) Testimony before the Senate Foreign Relations Committee." www.loc.gov/rr/mss/text/lattimore.html - 54k - Cached

Ward, Admiral Chester Charles, & Schlafly, Phyllis. *Kissinger on the couch.* Publisher: New Rochelle, N.Y. 1975.

Warrick, Joby. "Lacking biolabs, trailors carried case for war." 04/12/06. The Washington Post

Webster, Nesta Helen. *World revolution: The plot against civilization.* London, Constable and Co. 1921. worldcat.org/wcpa/ow/60d13d59deaf92b2.html - 16k

Webster, Nesta Helen. *Secret Societies and Subversive Movements._* London, Boswell Print. & Pub. 1924. worldcat.org/wcpa/ow/52f8ba5d9fb38b00a19afeb4da09e526.html - 89k

_____ "Why the Bush administration wants war." 09/14/01. WSWS Editorial Board. http://www.wsws.org/articles/2001/sep2001/war-s14.shtml.

Williams, James, 2001. "WTC a Structural Success," *SEAU NEWS: The Newsletter of the Structural Engineers Association of Utah,* October.

Zarembka, Paul. *The Hidden History of 9-11-2001.* Elseviar Ltd. 2006.

Reference - Federal Legislation
Glass-Steagall Act, 1929

Federal Reserve Act, 1913
Article I, Section 8, of the U.S. Constitution. "Granted the Congress the power to coin money and regulate its value."

The Federal Hospitalization Act of 1919

The Federal Hill-Burton Program - Hospital Survey and Construction Act of July 1, 1944

The McCarran-Ferguson Act: Federal legislation (U.S. Code Title 15, Chapter 20) 1945

Veterans Health Services and Research Administration, Secretary of Veterans Affairs §§ 4101–4115 of Title 38 of the United States Code and statutory authority and regulations 1945

Medicare (Title XVIII of the Social Security Act) July 30, 1965
    1972 amendment
    1979, "Carter Caps" Amendment
    1982 Tax Equity and Fiscal Responsibility Act
    1983 amendment altering Medicare payments to hospitals from a cost-based reimbursement system to a prospective payment system based on *Diagnostic Related Groupings of Diseases.* (DRGs)
    1988 Medicare Catastrophic Coverage Act
    1984 Deficit Reduction Act for *Participating Physicians*

Medicaid (Title XIX of the Social Security Act) – July 30, 1965

Health Securities Act, 103d Cong.,1st Sess.151–183. 1993.
General Agreement on Tariffs and Trade (GATT). 1947.

World Trade Organization (WTO). 01/01/95.

North American Free Trade Agreement (NAFTA). 10/92

Central America Free Trade Agreement (CAFTA). 08/02/05.

Free Trade Areas of the Americas (FTAA). 01/01/94
North Atlantic Treaty Organization (NATO). 04/04/49

Public Law 495, Section 112, 82d Congress, (NWO)

Senate Document # 87, Congressman Bernard Kearney

2002 - The Netherlands Invasion Act

Senate Report No. 93-549, the International Organization control over the financial well being - granting the President the full capability to declare *Martial Law* via an Executive Order.

Public Law 95-147; 91 Stat. 1227 - October 28, 1977 allows Multinational and State banks, to administer the International Monetary Fund.

Wolfowitz, Paul - appointment to head World Bank –Bush
http://en.wikipedia.org/wiki/World_Bank

Federal Reserve Banks IRS US Government Treason Rebellion Insurrection www.maxexchange.com/civic/ybj/chapter12.htm - 82k - Cached p.1-10

Federal Reserve – http://www.federal
reserve.gov/pubs/frseries/frseri.html

United States Treasury - http://en.wikipedia.org/wiki/United _States Treasury Department

Investigation Status Report of the House Judiciary Committee

Democratic Staff "The Constitution In Crisis"
"Congressional Record," December 22, 1913, Vol. 51.

Executive Orders:
EO 10995, takes over all communications-Bush

EO 10997, takes over all electric power, petroleum, gas, fuel, and minerals-Bush

EO 10998, takes over all food resources and farms; EO 10999, takes over all means of transportation, highways and seaports-Bush

EO 11000, drafts citizens into work forces under government supervision-Bush

EO 11001, takes over all health, welfare and education functions-Bush

EO 11002 empowers the Postmaster General to register all citizens nationwide-Bush

EO 11003, takes over all airports and aircraft-Bush

EO 11004, takes over housing and finance authorities, designates areas to be abandoned as "unsafe", establishes new locations for populations, relocates communities, builds new housing with public funds-Bush

EO 11005, takes over all railroads, inland waterways and public storage facilities-Bush

EO 11051, designates responsibilities of the Office Emergency Planning, gives authorization to put the above orders into effect in times of increased international tension or economic financial crisis . . . and on June 3, 1994, -Bush

EO 12919, "This order places all federal, state, and local law enforcement directly under the control of the President."- Clinton

Books by John R. Krismer

Our Puppet Government

The New World Oligarchy

The Magic Aquifer

Fair Use Notice

This research manuscript contains copyrighted material the use of which has not always been specifically authorized by the copyright owner. We are making such material available in our efforts to advance understanding of criminal justice, human rights, political, economic, democratic, scientific, and social justice issues, etc. We believe this constitutes a 'fair use' of any such copyrighted material as provided for in section 107 of the US Copyright Law. If you wish to use copyrighted material from this book for purposes of your own that go beyond 'fair use', you must obtain permission from the copyright owner.

www.ingramcontent.com/pod-product-compliance
Lightning Source LLC
Chambersburg PA
CBHW031458270326
41930CB00006B/149